Books by J. Frank Dobie

A VAQUERO OF THE BRUSH COUNTRY

CORONADO'S CHILDREN

ON THE OPEN RANGE

TONGUES OF THE MONTE

THE FLAVOR OF TEXAS

APACHE GOLD AND YAQUI SILVER

JOHN C. DUVAL:
First Texas Man of Letters

THE LONGHORNS

GUIDE TO LIFE AND LITERATURE OF THE SOUTHWEST

A TEXAN IN ENGLAND

THE VOICE OF THE COYOTE

THE BEN LILLY LEGEND

THE MUSTANGS

THE MUSTANGS

THE MUSTANGS

by J. Frank Dobie

ILLUSTRATED BY CHARLES BANKS WILSON

CASTLE BOOKS

The lines from W.H. Hudson's *The Book of a Naturalist* are reprinted by
permission of E.P. Dutton & Co., Inc., and J.M. Dent & Sons, Ltd.
The lines by Rudyard Kipling are reprinted from *Departmental Ditties and Ballads
and Barrack-Room Ballads* by permission of Mrs. George Bambridge,
Doubleday & Company, Inc., The Macmillan Company of Canada,
and Methuen & Co., Ltd.

This edition published by arrangement with
Little, Brown and Company, (Inc.). All rights reserved.

Published by Castle Books
a division of Book Sales, Inc.
114 Northfield Avenue
Edison, New Jersey 08837

Printed in the United States of America

ISBN 0-7858-1131-1

The earth does not think and does not care what people think, but it gives and takes with undeviating justice, and it remembers. To that plot of earth in Live Oak County, Texas, known as the R. J. Dobie ranch, where I was born and reared and where I lived with horses, I dedicate this book —

And to Genardo del Bosque, who during the many years he worked on the ranch used to say, "*Yo tengo raíces aquí*" (I have roots here).

CONTENTS

A PERSONAL INTRODUCTION

LIKE the wild West Wind that Shelley yearned to be, the mustangs, the best ones at least, were "tameless, and swift, and proud." Their essence was the spirit of freedom. Writing about them at a time when so many proclaimers of liberty are strangling it, I have desired a book that from the first sentence to the last would express "a pard-like spirit."

The historian must have the perspective of imagination in order to arrive at truth, but he cannot, like the novelist, discard those facts that "fail to comply with the logic of his character." Only stubborn facts in human history can explain the arrival of mustang horses upon the land where, in association with mustang men, they ran their course of freedom. After all, only segments in their lives were "pard-like." Components of the full round included very earthy materials. To comprehend stallions that bore conquistadores across the Americas, I had to go back to mares beside black tents in Arabian deserts. Before I could release myself with the runners of aboriginal wildness, I had to trace the Spanish horse through the Age of Horse Culture that he brought not only to Western tribes but to white men who took their ranges. My chief pleasure has been in telling tales, legendary as well as factual, of mustangs and of rides on horses of the mustang breed — but historical business had to come before pleasure.

No naturalist ever went out to study the habits of wild horses as many naturalists have studied possums, muskrats, rabbits, sparrows, mice, ants, fever ticks, cockroaches, fruit flies, and other lesser creatures. The best I have been able to do on the biology

[xi]

and habits of the most picturesque wild species of the land is not enough. Much else on the side of fact that I wanted to know I could not learn.

I do not mean that my ambition was ever to write "pure history." Pure history is a naked collection of documented facts; if the facts are patterned into pictures or directed into conclusions, purity is defiled. Yet I am more appreciative of pure historians than I once was. Most of them are teachers, and while they may not open windows they do not shrink intellects, like political school superintendents and academic flunkies of material power. They seek truth and discipline minds, and the pure histories they write are profitable to consulters. Nevertheless, excellence in historical writing comes only when interpretative power, just evaluation, controlled imagination and craftsmanship are added to mastery of facts.

I am not at all satisfied with my craftsmanship. "The artistic representation of history," Aristotle said, "is a more serious pursuit than the exact writing of history, for the art of letters goes to the heart of things." Perhaps no writer could get to the heart of life by sticking to horses. I do not know. Few writers more than approach it through any subject. Industry can amass facts — and few will charge me with not having been industrious on a subject for which I began consciously fortifying myself nearly thirty years ago. Industry is necessary for art also, but the absolute requisite for getting to "the heart of things" lies beyond knowledge and art, though it employs both. My consciousness of lack in that requisite is acute.

If I have idealized the horse, I have not overestimated his importance in social history: the climax of horse riding in America was the climax of free enterprise of the frontier kind. A man could mount and ride until he found what he chose to appropriate out of nature's bounty. He could drive a herd over free grass to fresh, unclaimed pastures a thousand miles away from those he and his neighbors had denuded. In whatever direction he traveled, grass and water and meat were free. Horses to travel on, for those who could catch them, were as free as venison. Meanwhile, population and machinery were increasing according to the law of geometrical progression, and the day came when the traveler could not ride and camp wheresoever he pleased. He found himself fenced out from water and grass and fenced in by lanes. Neither the machine in which he now traveled nor the owners of land along the ribbon-narrow highways permitted him to turn aside and linger with placid cows under trees by clear water. No vociferation of "DON'T FENCE ME IN" could alter the fact that machinery, population and attendant complexities had fenced in, as they increasingly fence in, the singers. The rule is simple: the more machinery man gets, the more machined he is. When the traveler got off a horse and into a machine, the tempo of his mind as well as of his locomotion was changed. All my nature is against machinery and for the horse — but I refuse to join the chorus paid by the National Association of Manufacturers to sing psalms over a dead horse.

Horses remain necessary on ranches of cows and automobiles and on ranches of dudes and automobiles. Many people who can afford them ride horses for pleasure. Girls who clerk in department stores and men who screw taps on bolts in automobile factories contribute to the prosperity of horse racing. Horse breeders and users scattered all over the country passionately cherish their horses. To a few minds horses still give something of a cast, but I should have to ride a long distance to find the interpenetration between man and horse that makes the tempo and serene simplicity of horseback thinking. As a determinant in social economy, the horse is utterly of the past.

Centuries before the word *cowboy*, in the American sense, came into existence, there were treatises in all polite languages of Europe on equitation. The original gauchos, vaqueros, horseback Indians and cowboys of the Americas of wild horses never heard of the rules. They learned to ride by riding just as their horses learned to travel by traveling. They were as devoid of riding formulas as a Turkish martinet found the Sham-mar Bedouins to be of other things. "The men have no religion," he reported, "the women no drawers, and the horses no bridles." Books on equestrianship and magazines on horses now proliferate over North America as they have never proliferated elsewhere in history, but they no more indicate horseback thinking than college degrees in Business Administration indicate cultivated minds.

Even to this latish date a saddle seems to me a more natural seat than a parlor chair. I was beginning to learn to ride before I finished learning to walk. During the first World War while I was training in Field Artillery at Leon Springs, near San Antonio, our battery received fresh from West Point a dapper little captain named Anderson. A few days after his arrival it received a contingent of horses. He led us on our first ride. He was as officious as Dogberry, jockeying up and down the line, giving each individual words of wisdom. When he came to me, he said, "Just have confidence in your seat. When we trot, remember that. Have confidence in your seat and you will not fall." There was no more likelihood of my falling from the plug I rode than there will be of my ascending in the style ascribed by papal decree to the Virgin Mary. However, "Yes, Sir," was all I said.

Before dismissing the battery that evening, the captain announced that if during off hours any of us came to his office and found him unoccupied he would welcome consultation. Among all the anxious candidates for commissions I was foremost only in diffidence. After supper I neared the captain's office and saw him within not very busy, I judged. I knocked, saluted, and upon invitation sat down.

I wanted to explain to him that although I felt myself a minus in military affairs, I hoped he would not set it down against me that I lacked "confidence in my seat." The only reason I had chosen Field Artillery, I told him, was that I wanted to ride. With his little black mustache twitching, he replied, "I suppose you are a product of one of these Texas ranches." I admitted that I was. He concluded the consultation by saying, "I had rather have a Field Artillery recruit who had never seen a horse than one spoiled by ranch riding."

"*Qué secreto tiene aquel rocinante?*" Elojio had never read of Don Quixote, but the name of his steed is in vaquero language a synonym for horse. That is fame. Elojio was my *mozo* on a pack trip. I was traveling not to arrive but to savor and learn. We had many profitable talks by campfires. I remember a crane-colored horse with a fringe of black on each ear about which he told. "No man or woman has ever understood me as that grullo did," he said. He had a tale about a mulberry-colored horse that drank mescal with his owner. He had operated on the Rio Grande with a smuggler who rode a red roan that could smell Texas Rangers five leagues away and would give warning. Now we had just unpacked our mules on the Cañon de Árboles, beside water, wood, and grass and with an outlook on a low mesa about half a mile off.

"What secret does that rocinante have?" The horse in question was a runty stallion gazing at us from the mesa in wonderful animation and trying to get our odor against a soft breeze, every now and then emitting a snort as rousing as the "you-got-to-get-up" bugle call. About a dozen mares and colts were pointing their ears in the direction his were pointed.

Elojio's question was not altogether rhetorical. He knew that at the moment the stallion had no secret beyond what his senses gave him and that what had aroused his distrusting curiosity was man. Just the same, he knew, as I know, that some secrets of equine senses have not been found out by man. I think that wild horses have more secrets than gentle ones.

I came after the day of the mustang had passed, and I myself early passed from the occupation to which I was born, though I have often returned to it in body and shall never cease returning to it in mind. I remember wild Spanish horses running over a level in Nuevo León, the light of the morning sun on their streaking bodies. Once in Wyoming I saw mustangs of a heavier type silhouetted, in the alert posture of the hunted, on a mesa. As a child I saw a little brown Spanish gelding with a bullet hole at the root of his mane. Alone he had eluded ropers and runners in a brushy pasture and been brought to his knees by a careful shot that only stunned him. A lithe Mexican was riding him; he was dripping sweat and his sides were heaving. It was on a Sunday morning, and men and boys who had gathered for a monthly church service surrounded him and gazed. The look of a caged eagle was still in his eyes. In youth I ran untamed mares, all bays and sorrels, in a big pasture and knew that no form of pursuit could be more animated.

> These beauteous forms,
> Through a long absence, have not been to me
> As is a landscape to a blind man's eye.

When I remember, though only through report, the seas of pristine grass that my forefathers rode out upon while the flowing vitality and grace of wild horses were still inherent properties of the earth, I know — at least during some whiles of happiness — that "a thing of beauty will never pass into nothingness."

Legions of footnotes in the back of this book attest my indebtedness to many scholars, to many writers, especially travelers, who were not scholars, and to various men who have never written. In the fall of 1948 I received a grant from the Henry E. Huntington Library in San Marino, California, providing for six months of research in that extraordinary institution. While I was getting closer to the Spanish horse through his Spanish introducers and Indian dispersers, the entire staff of the Huntington Library helped me with skills and good hearts that I shall never forget. To certain individuals in other libraries I wish to express thanks for aid: Mrs. Eleanor Bancroft of the Bancroft Library, University of California, Berkeley; Mrs. Ella L. Robinson of the Southwest Museum, Los Angeles; Mr. Nyle Miller in charge of the newspaper files of the Kansas State Historical Society Library at Topeka and also Misses Helen McFarland and Lorene Anderson of the Archives in that Library; Professor L. F. Sheffy and Mr. Boone McClure of the Panhandle-Plains Historical Society records at Canyon, Texas; Professor E. E. Dale, curator of the collection on Western history in the Library of the University of Oklahoma; Miss Winnie Allen and Miss Helen Mar Hunnicutt in the Archives of the Library of the University of Texas, and Miss Nettie Lee Benson in charge of the Latin-American collection at the University of Texas.

José Cisneros of El Paso, Henry Nash Smith of the University of Minnesota, Henrietta Randall of San Antonio, and Malcolm McLean of Austin discovered certain materials to me that I should otherwise have missed. Dr. Carlos Castañeda of the University of Texas has been my arbiter on Spanish terms.

I name three men who helped me beyond facts to understand range horses: Bob Lemmons, long dead, the Negro mustanger who is in this book; Asa Jones, rancher at Alpine, Texas, who "learned me his lore" while we traveled far and lingered long together; L. W. Van Vleet of Denver, generous host on his Arabian horse ranch in Colorado.

Mable Davis Raup has been patient as well as efficient in copying over and over my manuscripts.

Bertha McKee Dobie, my wife, has applied her logic and learning to almost every word and sentence in the chapters that follow.

THE MUSTANGS

"He doth nothing but talk of his horse."
—*The Merchant of Venice.*

THE PROGENITOR OF THE MUSTANG

I

THERE WERE no horses in the Western Hemisphere when it was discovered, nor had there ever been any of the historic type, though fossil discoveries over North America have enabled scientists to trace here the evolution of the prehistoric horse.[1] The wild horses * that became common to both North and South America were from stock introduced by the Spaniards. Horses brought over by the English, French and Dutch

* They were not wild in the sense of being aboriginal, like the tarpans of the Asiatic steppes, with an unbroken line of wild ancestors. In precise language, they should be called *feral*, but usage justifies *wild*, as it has substituted *buffalo* for *bison*.

made history and some of their descendants ran wild, especially in Virginia and the Carolinas and on adjacent islands, but the mustangs of the West at the zenith of their numbers were barely tinctured with this blood.

Long before the 16th century, Spanish horses were world famous. From the time of William the Conqueror, England had been importing them occasionally, earlier for coach heaviness and then for racing lightness.[2] At the time America was discovered, there was a marked shortage of horses in Spain, but on his second voyage, 1493, Columbus began the transporting of seed stock to Santo Domingo. Here and on other islands, ranches both royal and privately owned were soon prolific in horses. From the islands they were taken to Mexico, Florida and South America.[3] Following the Conquest, the Council of the Indies ordered ships sailing from Spain to take plants, seeds and "selected livestock" to Mexico. Some wealthy *hacendados* in time imported Arabian horses to breed up their caballadas.[4]

Transportation was an ordeal favoring survival of only the hardiest. It has been estimated that a third of all Spanish stock embarked for America died on the voyages. Ships becalmed in a certain area of the Atlantic frequently ran so short of drinking water that horses were cast overboard. Hence — probably — the name Horse Latitudes. Many horses died from constant exposure on deck and from being slung fast in one position for months.[5]

The American progeny sustained the ancestral reputation. William Cavendish, Duke of Newcastle, an urbane and much-traveled man, who wrote one of the earliest works of modern validity on horses and who considered Spanish horses "strangely wise, beyond any man's imagination," reported Sir Walter Raleigh as having found "in the West Indies the finest shaped horses and Barbs he ever saw."[6] Shortly after the Spaniards became established in Peru, one of their chroniclers noted that "so far as build, stamina and other good qualities are concerned, the

[4]

horses here need not yield to those of Andalusia, whence they have descended." During the next three centuries other travelers confirmed such opinions. Reporting observations made in North America about 1823, Paul Wilhelm, Duke of Württemberg, asserted: "There are better horses now in Mexico than in Spain."[7] Horse breeding — and many other enterprises — in Spain had deteriorated with the revival, prolonged indefinitely, in the mid-16th century of the Inquisition against liberated minds.

The reputation of Spanish-American horses lasted long and was often higher over on the other side of the mountain than where the horses actually grazed. In 1778 and 1779, inflammable Patrick Henry burned as governor of Virginia to acquire Spanish stock from the west as he had burned for liberty and was to burn against the Constitution. Colonel George Rogers Clark had been sent by the State of Virginia into the Northwest Territory. While he was in the Illinois country west of the Wabash, riding a fine Spanish stallion from Santa Fe, he received letter after letter pressing Patrick Henry's eagerness.[8]

Without valuing "the cost of the horses or the expense of sending them in," Patrick Henry would have "Two Horses" and "Eight Mars" of "the true Spanish Blood." Clark must not "loose a moment in agreeing for them, for Vast numbers of people are about to go out after them from here and will soon pick them all up and raise the price very high." He preferred "Blood bays as large as possible, fine Delicate Heads, long Necks, Ears small and prick'd and near at Ends, Deep Shoulders & Chest, large Arm, well legg'd, Upright pasterns, Clear of Long Hair, Bodys good, Loins Round and Very Wide, Out Hock'd, Haunches straight and go Wide behind. [If the horse] Stans on small Blazes, with either Hind foot white, so much the better. . . . But there is something so striking and inexpressibly beautiful in a Fine Horse that it is impossible to describe [what I want]." Patrick Henry sent money, he sent directions for getting the horses to Virginia, he repeated his admonitions to "be quick."

The horses might be secured from either Indian tribes or Spanish settlements.

After months had passed, Clark mildly wrote that "you have conceived a greater opinion of the Horses in this country than I have." True, he had an excellent stallion from New Mexico "three hundred leagues" — a thousand miles — to the west and south, but could not at the time send him across the drowned lands of the Wabash. The Pawnees six hundred miles away had superior horses. Maybe later he could get some of them. As for the Illinois mares, he had seen some good ones, but "hard usage" from their "barbarous Horse Masters" had ruined them.

Spanish horses transplanted to America were unmarked by the uniformity that white-faced cattle from "sweet Hereford-shire" now show on estancias, haciendas, ranches and stations over the continents. For multiplied centuries Spanish horses had been undergoing modification. Two hundred years before Christ, Hannibal had brought the hot blood of the East, in the form of North African horses, to mix with the cold blood of the dun and striped horses of Norse ancestry in Spain. The effect that six centuries of Roman domination had on the horses is a subject only for speculation. Northern horses brought in by the Goths must have revived the ancient Norse strain. Then, about 710, Moslems crossed the Strait of Gibraltar and, largely through superiority of light cavalry, conquered the Spaniards. They stayed for seven centuries.

Before crossing to Spain they had refreshed the Barb stock of North Africa with Arabian blood. Presumably they brought with them pure Arabians as well as Barbs. The best Spanish horses, the Andalusians, were developed where Arabian-Barb blood dominated. Andalusia was the chief source of horse exportation to the New World.[9]

Historians have talked about the Barb as if the name were a

definition. The Barb was more a type than a breed, with widely varying characteristics, developed in the Barbary states of northern Africa — Algeria, Tunisia, Morocco, Tripoli, Fez. The typical Barbary horse seems to have been somewhat larger than the Arabian, coarser in conformation, but swift and exceedingly hardy and enduring. Originally, the Barb was an offshoot from the Arabian. Wise and scholarly Tweedie calls the Barb "the African Arab." [10] At the time, the Elizabethan Age, when demand for Arabian horses began to grow strong in England, direct importation from Arabia was difficult, southern Europe and northern Africa being more available sources. Thus in England an Arabian was frequently classified as a "Barbarie."

Beyond all question, the best Barbs and the best Spanish horses — terms often not exclusive of each other — of the 16th century were strong in Arabian characteristics. Contemporary paintings — like modernistic art, too stylized for anatomical proof — do not show them with such low-swung tails, sloping rumps and convex heads — characteristics alien to Arabian conformation — as some commentators have deduced. Thornton Chard has reproduced some paintings of the 16th and 17th centuries that represent emphatically the small muzzles, pointed ears, broad foreheads and wide-set eyes of the Arabian head. Variations in the Spanish horse have resulted in contradictory descriptions. Richard Berenger of the 18th century, learned without being pedantic, saw the Barb with "tail placed high" (Arabian). Following him by more than a hundred years, Captain Hayes, a true scholar who had lived with horses in both the Orient and the Occident, described the Spanish horses during the period of the conquests as having "Roman noses, arched necks, goose rumps, long manes and tails and extravagant action." In short, the Spanish horse was a mestizo.[11]

While Spain was still exporting seed stock to America, Jean Jaquet wrote, in 1614: "Spanish horses are of two sorts. Jenets,

[7]

beautiful, gentle, noble, not tall but stout and well made, holding their heads and necks very high. One could hardly paint finer horses. They are fast without being as fast as the Moors, though they are bigger and stronger limbed and come from Oriental stallions. The other Spanish horses, 'Villanis,' [lowbred] are smaller, less noble and not so pleasing as the jenets." The chief preserver and historian of the Spanish horses of South America distinguishes two types of heads among them: the rectilinear (Arabian) and the convex (Barb).[12] Comparison of the modern *criollo* horses of South America with the Spanish horses common in Texas and Mexico a half century ago leads to the conclusion that a larger proportion of Arabian blood was planted in North America than to the south.

Though we read of Turkish horses, Persian horses, Moorish horses, and so forth, the supreme horses of all the countries of northern Africa and western Asia were for many centuries the Arabian studs kept by powerful rulers. Tribes in Morocco, noted for its Barbs, maintained Arabian horses that were *asîl*, purebred. Horses thrive on the water, grass, air, minerals of one region and decline on those elements in another, but region does not fix breed. There are more true Arabians in America today than there are among the tribes of Arabia, at last being overtaken by the Machine Age. One might ride now through all the Barbary states without finding a horse representing the Barbs that crossed to Spain in the 8th century. Few horsemen searching through contemporary Spain would find duplicates of the animals that stocked the West Indies and then the Americas so long ago — though the black Andalusian stallion on which George Borrow carried Bibles over Spain in 1837 must have fulfilled the type. The Spaniards never fixed and maintained a breed of horses as they did a breed of fighting bulls.

The one horse of history whose features today exhibit in every line and limb those of its ancestors a thousand years back is the Arabian horse, with iron muscles, bones of ivory density, steel hoofs, a tail that is the flag of its patrician heritage, a neck as lovely in arch as any curve that Phidias ever dreamed, refined head, gazelle-like concavity between forehead and delicate nostrils, eyes luminous with intelligence, gentleness and spirit, and, burning steadily in every fiber, the flame of vitality. This "hot-blooded" Arabian has been the taproot of all good riding horses of modern times. "Fire and quality belong to the sun." Hot blood and cold blood mix and change through variations like moisture passing from cloud to rain and back to vapor. So fixed has been the Arabian in long-inherited characteristics and so potent in transmitting them that the English Thoroughbred and his American derivative, the Lippizan of Hungary, the Orloff of Russia, the Morgan, and the Palomino of Hollywood, more glorious in parade than the assembled ten thousand white steeds of Genghis Khan, along with every other outstanding light horse on the globe, all incorporate Arabian blood. The steel, the spirit and the bottom of the best mustangs traced back to him. Through Thoroughbred stallions and Spanish mares, the Quarter Horse of America, now in the ascendant, derived Arabian virtues. The word *Thoroughbred* itself is but a translation of the Arabic *Kehilan* — spelled several ways — meaning "pure bred all through." Among the Bedouins there have always been more horses called *Kadishes* (mongrels) than *Kehilans*. In an ancient proverb of Bagdad, "For every noble horse that neighs, a hundred asses set up their discords."

My deductions on the Arabian and the Arabian-Barb are based primarily upon Lady Wentworth's *Thoroughbred Racing Stock and Its Ancestors* (1938) and *The Authentic Arabian Horse and His Descendants* (1945), both ponderous tomes with hundreds of costly illustrations drawn from the remotest times to the present — and both already rare. Out of thousands of horse books, most of them superficial duplicates of each other, these stand forth in their brilliant combination of research, wit and honesty; at the same time, they are marred by incoherence, prejudice and occasional falsity as to fact.

No horse history yet written by an American can be called literature, though William Robinson Brown's *The Horse of the Desert* approaches it. The only horse pertaining to America with a history ample enough to warrant noble treatment has been the Spanish horse of the West. In *The Horses of the Conquest* Scottish R. B. Cunninghame Graham has come nearer to literature on the subject than anyone else. He wrote what he knew but disregarded what he might have learned. He indulges so much in haughtiness — the expression of littleness rather than of magnanimity — that it becomes cant.

W. H. Hudson called Graham *singularísimo*. Lady Wentworth is singularly singular also. Her father and mother traveled over Arabia in the 1870's and purchased the foundation for the great Crabbet Stud of Arabians. He was Wilfrid Scawen Blunt, poet, artist, revolutionist, diplomat, aristocrat in tastes, democrat in principles, intimate of literati, statesmen, Asiatic liberals and women of beauty and brilliance. He believed in the pope's power to work miracles and distrusted empire builders. Devoid of pretense, he delighted in manipulations behind the scenes. A sense of justice burned in him. He had common sense in most matters and was a fantastic original in all. His wife Lady Anne, with more talent perhaps, was a granddaughter of Lord Byron and a descendant of the Darcy who imported the Darcy Arabian — not "Barb" — that, along with the Godolphin Arabian, the Byerley Turk (an Arabian), and other sires moulded the Thoroughbred. Both the Blunts wrote on Arabia and Arabian horses. Lady Anne, besides being linguist and scholar, had that rare knowledge that comes from within. The story of the conjugal career of these two surpasses in tragedy and *divertissements* the complexities of most novels. A good deal of the story is told in *The Authentic Arabian Horse*. Lady Wentworth inherited the best parts of her progenitors as well as the Crabbet Stud.

The prejudice in America, shared to a less degree in England, against Arabian horses is explainable by psychology more than by equine realities. It is based on an indifference to the beautiful and an at-easeness with the ugly. It expresses a distrust of the truth, as phrased by Thucydides, that "we lovers of the beautiful cultivate the mind without loss of manliness." A horse that is poetically beautiful, as only to the highest degree the perfect Arabian is, makes many Americans resist him as something fanciful and, therefore, impracticable. People naturally develop their horses — as they do their gods — in their own image. One of the most preposterous pieces of American folklore is that Arabian horses are calico-colored. Ascribe it to Barnum. Their colors are unvaryingly solid: dark bay, chestnut, gray in various shades, nutmeg roan, white with a black skin, an occasional black, but never a *grullo* (a blue) or a paint of any combination. Divergencies from solid colors, infinite in composition, showed up among the Barbs. As Darwin taught, crossbreeds revert. The farther away the Spanish horses got from the strength of the Arabian, and the farther away the wild horses got from the strength of their source, the more reversion there was.

The easiest tag for the lax-minded has always been color, and from the remotest times to the present, superstitious beliefs pertaining to horse colors have been as common as those pertaining to man colors. Truth is compacted into an old saying: "A good horse can never be of a bad color, no matter what his coat." Those who judge by colors are "Philosophical Mountebanks," wrote Cavendish in the 17th century. Nevertheless, certain colors are persistent concomitants of true breeds. One difficulty of ascertaining what were the colors of Spanish horses four and five centuries ago is that changes in the meanings of some color terms now set scholars at wide variance in interpreting them.* *Bayo*, meaning bay in Spain, came in Mexico to signify dun. Advocates of the *criollo* horse — pure descendants of Spanish stock — in South America hold that *tostado*, a color that Azara noted about 1800 among the great plenitude of mustangs on the pampas, is to be interpreted as dun, though "lively light brown" is the old dictionary translation.[13]

Furthermore, while mention of horses among contemporary chroniclers of the conquistadores is constant, descriptions of colors and other points are comparatively sparse. In all that members of the Coronado expedition into the Southwest (1540) say about their thousand and more horses, of certain ones ridden to *la cola del mundo* — the tail end of the world, of some killed by Indians and of others that perished, they specify only one black, one chestnut, and one dappled gray. The hardest ride made on an original Spanish horse on the North American continent, so far as detailed records go, was by a young man named Gonzalo Silvestre with De Soto in Florida. His horse had a bottom not to be fathomed, and, wrote Garcilaso de la Vega, he was "good beyond words because he was a pitch-hued chestnut, his left foot white-stockinged, the blaze on his face coming so low down on his nose that he appeared to drink it." Another youth who rode with Silvestre had a "fox-colored chestnut with black points and tail." †

Afterwards in Peru, this Gonzalo Silvestre rode another horse just as good, but description of him is lacking. A loyalist on the minority side, Silvestre rode him two hundred leagues, fighting pursuers almost daily. Then his horse received three blows from a mace, two cutting through his muzzle to the teeth, the third

---

* See in the University of Oklahoma Press edition (1949) of Cunninghame Graham's *The Horses of the Conquest*, Robert Moorman Denhardt's table, page 57, of comparative translations of color terms used by Bernal Díaz in describing the horses landed with Cortés.

† The translation is Cunninghame Graham's. Robert Moorman Denhardt interprets the Spanish as meaning buckskin or coyote dun. John and Jeannette Varner have "toasted bay."

breaking the bony circle above his eye, but leaving the eye uninjured. Immediately after these blows, pikemen gave the horse two more wounds in the face and pierced both forearms through the flesh. Gonzalo floundered across a swamp, cut off alone. He considered his horse wounded to death and himself as good as captured — but "there is always time to die." Upon gaining solid ground, he spurred, and the horse "bounded away like a goat, snorting and tossing bloody foam from his nostrils." No horse of the enemy had the power to follow. After galloping about ten miles, until darkness fell, Gonzalo halted. Without food for himself, he unbridled his horse to pick what he could. In the bitter cold, the horse "ate with so much fury that he pulled up the grass roots and ate them, earth and all, and Gonzalo was comforted by seeing his horse eat." [14] A tired horse or man who eats in that fashion is quickly restored. I knew an old rancher who would never hire a man until he had seen "how he eats."

The two horses that Pizarro rode into Peru were both dark brown. The one full detailment, as to color but not as to conformation, found among the chroniclers is Bernal Díaz del Castillo's often-quoted description of the sixteen horses that landed in Mexico with Cortés. Along with eight bays and sorrels, two browns, three grays and one black, were two horses variously described in English translation as dappled, dark bay, piebald, spotted, paint. Of the two off-colored horses, one, says Díaz, "turned out to be worthless" but the other "had a good mouth." The early Spaniards preferred solid colors, not excluding the dun. The bay — some say chestnut — was "the natural and perfect color of the horse." According to Mohammedan myth, the first horse that God created — created as a matter of course out of the wind — was a bay, or perhaps a chestnut, with a star in its forehead, the sign of glory and good fortune.

Absurd and ridiculous would be any person who tried to find nonexistent similarities between some hammer-headed, ram-nosed, ewe-necked, goat-withered, cat-hammed, sore-backed, hard-mouthed, mean-natured, broom-tailed bronco of the West at the close of the 19th century and an Arabian of *Kehilan* perfection. Just as absurd would it be to regard that bronco as representative of the Andalusian Barbs that Cortés and his handful of men rode to conquer the kingdom of Montezuma. One quality out of the original that never withered was hardihood.

The Arab bred for endurance always — endurance that is the test of generosity. One Arabian, carrying one third his own weight, went 310 miles in forty-nine hours. Another stood on his feet one hundred days aboard ship, without once lying down, and shortly thereafter won a race. Living intimately with and devotedly breeding his horses through the centuries, the Arab cultivated in them qualities of nobility and gentleness that even the best of the mustangs did not have. To the Arab, moral and physical qualities are inseparable in a horse. Long intimacy with the animal has permitted him to discern qualities of intelligence and spirit that no man who regards a horse as merely a tool of sport or work can comprehend. "There is no secret so close as that between a rider and his horse." If the horse is stupid, however, perhaps the Russian saying is true: "The more stupid the peasant, the better does the horse understand him." The Arab traces ancestry through the mare, generally rides the mare, and makes the mare a part of his household. His mares are more trustworthy as camp animals than stallions and more enduring on raids.

No rawhided gaucho, vaquero or cowboy ever rode a mare named Wadduda, which means Love and Affection. Wadduda had been kept imprisoned in the town of Aleppo for a long time. As Homer Davenport tells in *My Quest for the Arabian Horse*, he rode her forth on his expedition among the tribes of the desert. It was a journalist's expedition and not that of a Doughty, a Blunt, or a Tweedie. For hours the mare was nervous and Davenport was conscious of not having made friends with her. "She wanted something; I could not make out what."

Fretfully, she pushed ahead of the caravan. Then at sunset they came to the desert. "Wadduda stopped as if she were paying tribute to the closing day. Presently she started galloping with a delightful spring. It was the return to her home. Now she stopped short, apparently to scent the rapidly cooling atmosphere. Now she pranced, picking her way through the camel thistles, her eyes blazing with the expression of intense satisfaction. Again she bolted and was scanning the horizon. I touched her with my heels but she did not move. For a long time we waited together in the gathering dusk, the call of the desert strong within us." Yet this horse of the desert "so loves trees, verdure, shade and running water that he will neigh for joy on seeing them." [15]

Many travelers have found it easy to sentimentalize over the steed of the desert and the affection between Bedouin and mare. Charles M. Doughty was not a horseman and was without sentimentality. His two-tomed *Travels in Arabia Deserta* is one of the great travel works of all times; no other is so penetratingly realistic and detailed on the minds and manners of a people. On topography, surface geology, climate, philology, archaeology it is exact. Properly, it has maybe fifty times as much on camels as on horses. Doughty's only illusion lay in archaisms of the English language. Take this picture:

"Mahanna's old mare had lately foaled. The mare is that which the nomad sheykh holds most precious among his cattle. When the foal was fallen from this sack of bones, they tied up her dry dugs (as it is done with the milch camels); and the healthy foal was bound in the sheykh's tent, to be reared of their sour milk and mereesy [dried buttermilk]: the decrepit dam they abandoned to die, and cut her off from water. As I lay awake I saw her return by night and smell miserably to the water-skins in the tent, she gnawed hay out of the camels' pack-saddles for hunger. I asked the Arabs, 'Wherefore not end her lingering pain with a gun-shot?' I thought them cruel, but they thought my words such, and outlandish! . . . The dogs of our household looked back every idle hour into the desert, to see where the mare would lie down to die; the third midday she was fallen and could not rise. At the break of day the rákhams were come, with the brown ágab, to devour the putrifying carcase. . . .

"His mare is not a little chargeable to a sheykh in the desert, who must burden oftentimes another camel with her provision of water. Twice she will drink, at the hottest of the summer season, even thrice in a daylight; and a camel-load of girbies [water-bags] may hardly water her over two days." Yet on hard rides this mare sometimes goes two and three days without water, still enduring — like the gazelle, drinking of the wind. There is "a foster camel to every nomad mare, since they taste no corn, and the harsh desert stalks could not else sustain her. It is unknown in the desert so much as to rub them. The Beduin milks first for the mare and then (often in the same vessel) for the nomad household. She stands straining upon her tether, looking toward the pleasant sound of milking: the bowl frothing from the udder is carried to her in the herdsman's hand and she sups through her teeth the sweet warm milk, at a long draught." The human body, says Doughty, "fed with milk in the sunny drought, is slender, full of pith, of perfect endurance." The milk-fed mare has the same qualities.

If ever there was a rawhided man, the Arab is he, his heart "cased with buffalo hocks" and as hard, in the Western view, as the flints of his wandering-land. His wasted mare, his sick stallion, his weakly foal if they cannot endure to the next water are left to perish. His own destiny is to die. The fittest only survive. Horsemen from the Occident looking at shaggy-haired, runted-from-birth, belly-pinched, yet fittest Arabian horses have been fooled into not recognizing their *Kehilan* essence. Abstemiousness is one of their most marked characteristics. Their essence survived on the arid borders of Texas where the saying was common: "A white man will ride the mustang until he is played out; a Mexican will take him and ride him another day until he thinks he is played out; then a Comanche will mount him and ride him to where he is going." Call the Spanish horse Barb. He brought from the deserts of the East that flame blended of body and spirit that made him endure.

The Bedouin tradition that their horses descended from wild runners on their own deserts, less barren and arid tens of centuries ago than now, seems plausible to some,[16] but learned Doughty holds that the vast tableland of Arabia has been rainless since Cretaceous times. Nobody can be positive whence Arabian horses descended. Their origin, like other origins, lies in the land of speculation. The aboriginal was smaller than the *Kehilan*. Perhaps he was the Biblical "horse of the desert that stumbleth not."

Arabia and the Arabs made the Arabian horse. In times antedating chronicles the Arab was breeding his mare for the Parthian warfare of the desert. This warfare required swift dodging, craft in twisting, as well as endurance. The Arab's only school was, in Gibbon's phrase, "a clear firmament and a naked plain." His science in breeding was boiled down into the practice of mating for generation after generation one animal of proven excellence with another of like excellence. Better barrenness than degeneration. In the old tradition a tribesman would ride his mare a month's journey to conjoin her with a horse of fame. The Americas and the heterogeneous mixture of men who used and abused the mixed-blooded descendants of the Arabian on these continents made what the Spanish horse became.

Among all the wild and far riders of plains and pampas, there was no type exampled by Jabal. A Bedouin by that name possessed a mare of great celebrity. Hassan Pasha, governor of Damascus, heard of her and made liberal offers to buy her. The higher his offers rose, the more emphatically did Jabal refuse them.

At length, Gafar, of a tribe hostile to Jabal's, heard of Hassan's desire and came to him and asked, "What will you give the man who makes you master of the mare?"

"I will fill his horse's nose bag with gold," replied Hassan.

Report of this reward went abroad. Jabal became more watchful of his mare than ever. Every night he fastened one end of an iron chain around the fetlock of a front foot, passed the other end under his black tent, drove the picket pin to which it was attached into the ground, and over it spread the felt on which he and his wife slept.

One midnight Gafar crept into the tent and stealthily eased himself between man and woman, pushing each out so gently that each, sleeping on, felt that the other was wanting more room. Gafar pulled up the picket pin. After he had removed the chain and had the mare free and was ready to mount, he called loudly into Jabal's tent, "I am Gafar. I have stolen your noble mare. I give you warning." This warning, in accordance with Bedouin custom, would make his deed more glorious.

Jabal rushed out, alarmed his tribesmen, and, mounted on his brother's mare, led them after the thief. This mare was a sister to his own. She ran faster than any mare ridden by his tribesmen. She gained on Gafar, but when he drew near, Jabal suddenly yelled, "Pinch her right ear and give her a touch of the left heel." The Bedouin trains his mount by special signals.

Gafar pinched and touched and the mare shot forward.

"Oh, father of a jackass," his companions cried, "thou hast enabled the thief to rob thee of thy jewel."

"I would rather lose her than sully her reputation," he replied. "Would you have me suffer its being said among the tribes that any other mare proved fleeter than mine? It still can be said that she has never met with her match."

Was it love of himself or love of his mare that motivated Jabal? Whichever the motive, it developed the breed. Stories linger in Nejd, the Arabian highland, of unhorsed tribesmen calling out

with dying breath the pedigree of a mare in order to make the captor prize her properly.

Despite the cult of cowboy and gaucho, the Western Hemisphere has known no such continuing rapport, prolonged like the sculpturing of wind-driven sand against granite, between man and horse, with marked results on both species, as has existed between the Arab and his Arabian. The Horse Indians were taken from their horses just as they were becoming well accommodated to them, before they came to depend upon raising rather than raiding them. The second generation of cowboys became a part of the Machine Age, in which even the most intense users of horses live apart from them. For mustang horse and mustang man came too soon that time when it might be said:

How are they blotted from the things that be!

II

THE GUARDED ATOM BOMB OF THE SPANIARDS

THE SPANIARDS came with horses, not only for war, but for exploration, for christianization of the natives, for colonization. Gold might be the "great pacifier" and "solvent of hardness" and gifts might "break rocks," but, as Bernal Díaz of the Conquest wrote, the gifts were mere gauds, and in the unrelenting fight of one against thousands, the horses were "our fortress" and "our only hope of survival." "The horses and mares were our salvation," Cortés reported to Emperor Charles V. "My country was won *á la gineta*" (on horseback, riding Moorish fashion), cried Garcilaso de la Vega of Peru. "Next to God, we owed our victory to the horses," wrote a chronicler of the Coronado expedition, though *salvation* would have been more precise than "victory."

Caballo is masculine for horse. At the time of the Conquest and for long afterwards the word implied an *entero* — an entire horse, unemasculated. The spaying of *yeguas* (mares) was an unknown practice. All the original Spanish stock could breed. Of the sixteen memorialized animals, along with a colt born aboard ship, first landed by Cortés on the North American continent, at Vera Cruz in 1519, eleven were stallions and five were mares. More horse stock came shortly thereafter.

In contrast to Arabian warriors, *caballeros* preferred riding stallions to mares as more powerful and proud. In battle some of their war stallions bit and kicked "the barbarous Indians." [1] After horses became plentiful on the continent, no *hidalgo* (son of somebody) would deign to ride a mare.* Spanish men boasted of their *huevos* (testicles), source of virility — excelled in by jackasses, as John Randolph of Roanoke taunted. The ideal Spanish horse had *huevos* also. Those stallions that neighed the loudest, particularly in the heat of desire, were considered "the most noble and powerful." [2] Their manes were never roached nor their tails docked. Yet many a saddle stallion hardly knew — in Biblical phrase — a mare, but lived as "chaste and peaceful" as Don Quixote's Rocinante.† They were much harder to keep together than geldings with a bell mare. Any mares among them aroused jealousy and a desire to separate; yet most expeditions probably used both mares and stallions. On one among Texas

* One thing the Spaniards did not take from the Moslems was mare-riding. The preference for stallions in Western civilization went far back. The Greeks used stallions, trained to be savage against the enemy in battle. The Venerable Bede, who about 730 finished his Latin history of England, recorded that in 630 the bishops, who before that time traveled afoot, were mounted, but rode only mares as a mark of humility.

† Major John N. Merrill, U. S. Army Cavalry, retired, told me that while serving with the Persian cavalry in World War I, he had about a thousand Arabian horses, all stallions, under his command. Never having been used for breeding, they were, he said, not vicious.

[22]

Indians in 1779, the difficulty of herding the mixed mounts was set down as a military handicap.[3]

The time at which Spaniards of the Western Hemisphere began castrating non-breeding stallions — and bulls likewise — seems to be undeterminable. About the close of the 18th century, Félix de Azara found stock raisers on the pampas castrating *potros* (unbroken males) at the age of two years and riding only geldings. By 1830, probably earlier, the Californians were gelding their saddle horses.[4] Some rancheros gelded their choice *potros* for riding and left the indifferent for breeding. Few were careful to castrate all but the breeders. Many a small Mexican ranchero following the *costumbres* of his forefathers still lets his horses go uncut and works bulls for oxen. In unchanging Spain, until the middle of the last century at least, stallions were seldom gelded. During colonial times, the sexual potency of all horses and cattle on the ranges was an enormous factor in stocking the Spanish Americas — without selection, for there is no breeder like a scrub among either men or beasts.

Spanish horses found vast American ranges corresponding in climate and soil to the arid lands of Spain, northern Africa and Arabia in which they originated. And these ranges were as virgin in fertility to them as to the first European farmers. Is it fresh vitamins, richer nourishment, something in the very air — what impetus is it — that not infrequently makes a species introduced to a new region thrive beyond its own precedent and even out-thrive native species? English rabbits and American prickly pear introduced into Australia, English sparrows into the United States, American squirrels into England, mongooses of India into Hawaii, European thistles into South America have all spread as spectacularly as a prairie fire before a dry norther. Spanish horses and cattle found new predators in America, but not potent enough to retard extraordinary multiplication.

One of the first acts of any successful Spanish general was to establish a hacienda for raising livestock. In this custom, as in many other practices, the Spanish-American countries of today demonstrate what was going on in the 16th century. A modern soldier-politician of Mexico who advances to a generalship, though he be as poor as Job's turkey before advancement, is quickly possessed of a hacienda. Cortés, Alvarado and other conquistadores were raising horses before the Indians of southern Mexico quit resisting. Antonio de Mendoza, the first viceroy of New Spain, had eleven or more haciendas out in different directions from Mexico City; presumably horses were raised on all of them; one, very extensive, was called a horse ranch. During his years in office, 1535-1550, the ranching frontiers of Mexico extended rapidly and the private enterprise of grabbing public lands boomed.[5] Oaxaca, Chiapas, Honduras and Nicaragua became extensive horse-breeding centers. On Cuba and other islands meanwhile, feudal lords were raising fancy palominos and pintos and riding a new kind of saddle, jewel-studded and covered with silver inlaid with gold.[6]

During the Conquest of Mexico, horses brought fantastic sums. In South America, farther away from the breeding grounds of the West Indies, initial prices were still higher. Yet only twenty years after Cortés landed, Coronado had no difficulty in assembling 1500 head of horses and mules * for his great expedition into New Mexico. At far-away outposts as well as around their capital bases, the Spaniards continued to raise horses until on

---

* The records do not agree. "Coronado's Muster Roll," discovered and edited by Arthur S. Aiton, *American Historical Review*, Vol. 44 (1938-1939), 556-570, lists 558 horses. "We get a more complete picture of the nature of Coronado's force by piecing together the scattered records that have survived. We learn from Castañeda, for example, that there were 1000 horses and 600 pack animals. Mota Padilla gave the figure as 1000 horses, not including mules and pack animals. Coronado himself testified in 1547, in the Mendoza residencia, that there were 1500 animals, horses, mules and [other horse] stock, by actual count. As this is the most direct and authoritative statement on the subject, we may conclude that it is pretty accurate." — George P. Hammond and Agapito Rey, *Narratives of the Coronado Expedition, 1540-1542*, University of New Mexico Press, Albuquerque, 1940, in *Coronado Historical Series*, II, 7.

some ranges the common run had no monetary value whatsoever and whole herds had to be destroyed in order to leave grass for the remainder.

Almost the first ordinance passed by the conquerors of New Spain prohibited any Indian from riding a horse.* It was kept on the books long after peons were riding as vaqueros. Ranching on the open range necessitated mounting the serf, the cow-worker, or *vaca*-worker — the vaquero from whom the cowboy of North America took not only the occupation but the techniques and diction of his occupation. *Peon* means literally pedestrian, man-on-foot, the antipodes of *caballero*, man-on-horseback. The vaqueroized peon had a different status from the peon slaving in mines or as household menial. Sometimes he took horses and rode away from ranch or mission back to freedom.

The Spaniards set out to guard the horse as their secret atomic bomb. It was not the fairness of their complexions — the "Fair God" hoax — that most impressed the Aztecs; it was their horses. At first the combination of mount and man was regarded as "a monster that could uncouple itself into two parts." The master race encouraged the Indians to believe that the monsters devoured human flesh. When fiercely resisting Tlascalans killed Pedro de Morón's mare, they cut off her head and sent it around to towns to show that the monsters were also mortal. The Spanish said, "Lies told to the heathen are not recorded." As long as they could find tyros, they tried to keep up the myth. As late as 1582, Antonio Espejo upon meeting a horde of natives in the New Mexico country gave them "some presents of little value, assuring them that we would not harm them but that our horses might kill them. The horses were very ferocious, we told them, and the

* In the Mixton War of central Mexico, 1541, Viceroy Mendoza put allied Aztec chieftains on horses to lead their tribesmen. This seems to have been the first official handing over of horses to natives. According to J. Lloyd Mecham (*Francisco de Ibarra and Nueva Vizcaya*, Durham, North Carolina, 1927, 210) the law became inoperative after twenty years, but it was still enforced in some regions as late as 1611. See *Instrucción y Orden de Gobierno* for Jan. 11, 1611, Chap. 15.

Indians must construct a stockade to hold them." The Indians constructed it.[7]

On the Coronado expedition into New Mexico, Spaniards saw Indians smearing their bodies with the sweat of horses, so as to transfer to themselves the magic of the "Big Dog." [8] The magic soon evaporated. Not one of Coronado's thousand and more Indian servitors and allies was mounted. Some who had fallen behind on the march and were without food or so much as a knife came upon a worn-out horse. They tied all four of its feet to a tree, heaped up wood around it, started a fire and "burned the horse alive, eating it singed and half-roasted." One night not long after the expedition went into winter quarters on the Rio Grande, Indians overpowered the horse guard and drove off their horses. Following their trail, the camp-master found the carcasses of two or three arrow-killed horses, on a little farther at least twenty-five other carcasses, and then heard "a great hulla-baloo" coming from a palisaded enclosure. The sweat-anointers were running the horses around "as in a bullring" and shooting arrows into them. Some, yelling defiance, "waved as banners" tails cut from slain horses.[9]

Upon the arrival of horses, the Indian comprehended very quickly two facts: that he, being a man like the Spaniard, could also ride and that horse meat was good to eat. A few tribes only ate, notably the "Horse Thief" Indians of California, who stole horses solely for their meat. Some Texas Indians developed an especial appetite for colt flesh. The Sioux, Blackfeet, Cheyennes and other northern tribes seldom ate horse flesh except in extremity. Like white plainsmen and mountaineers, any starving Indian would turn on the beast that carried him.

Apaches were the chief eaters. "When they can get flesh of horse, mule or burro," wrote a chronicler of the 18th century who had often suffered from their raids in Sonora, "they shun the flesh of all other animals. . . . After capturing horse stock, they keep only the choicest for riding, eating the others. Returning to their native grounds from a successful raid, they send up smoke signals to invite neighbors to feast. . . . Their favorite morsel is the thick and fleshy upper part of the neck, and for this reason dead horses with only the neck consumed are sometimes found on the ranges. They prefer the meat half-roasted and have excellent teeth for chewing it. The diet is supposed to give them a very unpleasant odor, and the inhabitants of Sonora maintain that when they ride within the neighborhood of hidden Apaches their horses sense this odor and will not go forward except under compulsion." [10]

Neither Indians nor white men of North America relied on horse flesh to the extent that their opposites in South America did. The Querandis and other Indians of the pampas lived on mare's meat while they raided, shampooed their hair in mare's blood while they rested, and mixed mare's blood with gin when they celebrated. They burned the bones and grease of wild horses for fuel. Horses were as cheap as wishes: beggars rode. In 1833 Charles Darwin was delayed at a river crossing by "immense troops" of mares following Argentine soldiers in pursuit of Indians. "Mare's flesh," Darwin wrote, "is the only food which the soldiers have on an expedition. This gives them great facility of movement, for the distance to which horses can be driven over these plains is quite surprising. I have been assured that an unloaded horse can travel a hundred miles a day for many days successively." Rosas, the celebrated gaucho queller of the pampas Indians, had been elected to leadership by excelling in the following feat: He placed himself on a crossbar over a gate to a corral full of wild horses; when the gate was opened and they rushed forth, he fell astride of one outstanding for strength and wildness and, without bridle or saddle, not only stayed on it but brought it back to the corral.[11] Later he interdicted this sport.

No tribe in Mexico became mounted as the great tribes of the plains and pampas became. The fiercely resisting Yaquis of

Sonora, admirable in their love of liberty and homeland, made superb riders but could not maintain numbers of horses in their mountain fastnesses. Resistance to Europeans was by no means confined to mounted tribes, but horseback Indians never became "poor churchyard things," like certain foot tribes, obeying and adoring padres. No tribe *reducido* — "reduced," as the christianized were frankly called — ever became riders of freedom. In the end, only arms and might reduced the mounted tribes, breaking them, as many a wild mustang was violently broken in both body and spirit before he acknowledged serfdom. I know not what process would have incorporated the Sioux, the Cheyennes, the Crows, the Nez Percés, the Blackfeet, the Comanches, the Pawnees and other horse tribes into the American melting pot, but their noble physiques, their noble pride, their admirable love of liberty and their superior mentality would have made — and might yet make — a far more valuable ingredient to the American mixture than hordes of *reducidos* from across the ocean have made.

The progressive acquisition of the Spanish horse among North American Indians west of the Mississippi has been well charted, though it is impossible to say in just what year, at just what place, this tribe and that obtained its first horse. The spread of the horse was by long, thin currents that formed pools growing wider and wider and deeper and deeper, rather than by all-covering inundation. Whoever desires details may get them, fully annotated, from the scholars herewith noted.[12]

Rumor delights in maligning good men while they are still alive and in romanticizing bad ones after they are dead. The tenacity with which the loose-minded, the ignorant, the malicious, the zealous and the opinionated cling to rumor frequently drags it into histories and gives it the status of fact. Beliefs long popular that the wild-running mustangs of the plains sprang from seed lost by the Coronado and De Soto expeditions and that the Plains Indians snared their first horses from mustang herds are based on mere rumors. Evidence to the contrary is positive.

Of all the notabilities of the True Faith who explored into the unknown vastnesses of America — to inform the natives of their fealty to Emperor and Pope, to clarify their minds on the identity of the Holy Ghost, to sack their gold and silver, if they had any, and to make them dig for more if veins could be located — Hernando de Soto had the best horses and suffered the worst disasters. His part in raping Peru and murdering Atahualpa had brought him fortune and imperial favor before he again sailed, at the age of thirty-seven, from Spain. A royal contract made him governor of Cuba, authorized him to "conquer, pacify and populate" Florida, and forbade any lawyer to enter the Floridian paradise. Among the 600 or so followers, many of wealth and rank, on his ten prodigally supplied ships hardly one had a gray hair.

He tarried in Cuba nearly a year, establishing his governorship, accumulating a great store of supplies, buying the best of the "excellent" horses with which the island was stocked, and receiving others as presents from patriots who wanted to be remembered from Utopia. The pick of his mount, "a most brave and handsome animal," dapples shining through the gray of his coat, was named Aceytuno — or perhaps Acetunero — after the *caballero* who presented it.

The chroniclers of the expedition contradict each other consistently on figures, thus, as caustic Cunninghame Graham remarks, "investing history with greater dignity." The numbers I give seem to me the most trustworthy. When the expedition sailed from Havana in May, 1539, it certainly carried 233 horses, probably 250, and a few mules. A contingent of sows and boars multiplied bountifully and probably ancestored the razorbacks that centuries later were still adding to the picturesqueness of the South. Also, there were dogs trained in bringing down Indians. On the voyage of 19 days to Tampa Bay 20 horses died.

Eleven years preceding, Pánfilo de Narváez had landed in Florida with 42 horses alive out of 80 with which he had embarked. Not long after De Soto went ashore, an Indian showed him the skulls of horses that Narváez survivors had butchered upon leaving the land of famine and death. They had sailed away with the skins of horse legs for water buckets and ropes woven from horse mane and tail to rig their sails of shirts and horse hides. All but one of the 42 Narváez horses had been slain in battle or slaughtered by their masters. What happened to the solitary remnant is not recorded.[18] Meantime the *ignis fatuus* tossed into the air by that Narváez survivor named Cabeza de Vaca was leading Coronado on a quest as futile as De Soto's.

The very first horse landed by De Soto's men received an arrow in its vitals. The natives were remembering what other Christians had taught them. Horses mired and sank from sight in the marshes. The Christians slugged on north and west into Georgia, Alabama and the Carolinas, burning habitations, destroying crops, feasting on dogs, starving, capturing men to carry one kind of burden and women another, proclaiming peace and demanding submission, killing and being killed. The Governor-Adelantado was "much given to the sport of slaying Indians." The Indians "looked upon the horses with as much terror as if they had been tigers" and "were more pleased to kill one horse than four cavaliers."

In one battle fought in the region where Mobile now stands they killed at least 12 horses and wounded six times that many. Despite salve from the leaf fat of dead Indians, many wounded Spaniards died and, presumably, some of the wounded horses died also. The conquerors habitually jerked the meat of slain horses, saving their hogs for hard times. The strength that corn, plundered between famines, gave their horses was a marvel to them. As time went on, some men who had lost their mounts offered thousands of pesos — to be paid when gold was found and divided — for the horses of their more fortunate companions.

A strayed horse was a lost fortune, but it was recoverable and it was invariably recovered.

At the end of the year 1540 De Soto took up winter quarters in a large Chickasaw Indian town, where he banqueted the subdued chief on one of his greyhound-shaped hogs, which throve better in the forests and swamps than either men or horses. One northery night the chief reciprocated by having his warriors fire the thatched houses which the peace-proclaimers had commandeered. Besides destroying all the clothes, equipment and stores, including gunpowder, of the expedition, the fire burned 20 haltered horses to death. Between 30 and 40 others were killed by arrows. One shot was so mighty that De Soto had it notarized: the arrow went clean through the largest and fattest horse in camp and stuck in the ground beyond.

The seekers sought on. De Soto would never turn back. *Más allá* and *más allá*, always on and on. One Pedro de Atienza fell sick and died on his horse, legs clinched to its sides and hands on the reins. Other men died calling for salt. Horses were so famished that many could not carry burdens.

After two years of wandering, the half-naked men and emaciated horses came out of the forest upon the bank of the Great River. The discovery brought to De Soto no fine frenzy like that of Balboa staring "upon a peak in Darien." The men hewed logs for barges and bolted them together with iron hammered out of their gear. After they had crossed the Great River, riders jumped their horses off the barges into shallow water and chased away Indians gathered to attack.

De Soto went on to where fields were drouth-withered. He gratified friendly natives by praying down a rain. Now he turned southward. From comfortable winter quarters he led a foray for slaves among Indians notably "handsome and well disposed." A cavalier named Diego de Guzmán, who had left Cuba with costly apparel and three horses, captured the chief's daughter. "She was extremely beautiful and she was only eighteen years old." He was a gambler. One night in a card game he lost his clothes, his arms, "a fine coal-black horse," the last of his three, and then the girl. He delivered all the losings but the girl, whom he promised to send to the lodging of the winner within five days. He stole away with her to her people. No Christian ever saw him again. He took no horse. In reply to a letter urging him to rejoin his brother cavaliers, he signed his name across the paper with a piece of charcoal and sent it back.

Now the Spaniards were among Indians who hunted "cows" to the west and had hides and horns of these animals. Horsemen made breastplates of the hides for the horses, but ambushed Indians still arrowed into their vitals.

Three full years of conquering passed, and Hernando de Soto knew that he was dying. He tried to frighten back enemies by telling them that he was "the child of the sun." "If so," a cacique replied, "cause the sun to dry up the river." He died beside the Great River that will ever be associated with his name, and his men sank the corpse by night in water nineteen fathoms deep. Along with two male and three female slaves, he left many swine and three horses.

By now only 40 horses remained to the conquerors. Some of them were useful only for display, like wooden cannon. The three hundred surviving men rode and walked westward to the edge of the buffalo range, but came back to the Great River. In the soggy lowlands horsemen spent nights in the saddle, like Don Quixote, rather than lie in mud and water. Horses as well as men died of sickness.

Amid flooding waters, the Spaniards constructed "brigantines" to carry them down the Mississippi to the Gulf and to Mexico. They made jerky of several horses and of what hogs they had not given, for breeding, to friendly Indians. On July 2, 1543, after more than four years of seeking for treasure, they put on board what horses remained alive, twenty-two head. One was "of a comic shape," but he was hardy.

There are two accounts of what became of these horses. According to Garcilaso the Inca, Indians swarming about in canoes killed all but eight. On the twelfth day after embarkation these were landed to graze while their masters ransacked Indian houses for food. A surprise attack forced them to the boats with such haste that the horses were left behind. While putting off into the current, they saw Indians "hurl arrows at the horses with great fiesta and rejoicing until all had fallen." According to the Gentleman of Elvas, the Spaniards became so weary of defending the horses and managing the craft holding them that they took them ashore, killed all but four or five, mere skeletons, and jerked the meat. Then, pulling away from shore, they heard the horses neighing and saw them jumping about, frightening Indians who had come out of the growth with bows and arrows.

How far this final sight of the last of De Soto's horses was above the mouth of the Mississippi, "anyone can give the number of leagues he may wish," the Inca Garcilaso says. It was in a vast expanse of water-soaked, mosquito-tortured, grassless tangle of trees, brush and vines. Even if four or five horses were left alive, they either perished shortly or were killed by the relentless Indians. Furthermore, they were all stallions. No wild horses have ever been reported in that region.[14]

Out of such facts, the "pretty legend" * has an escaped De Soto mare sniff her way west from somewhere along the Mississippi until, far out on the plains, an eastward-sniffing stallion escaped from Coronado's caballada scents her. Oh, joy! and there the multiplication of mustangs begins. If another fable had placed

* "Six great horses of Spain, set free after his death by De Soto's men, ran west and restored to America the wild race there lost some thousands of years ago. — A legend." — Prefatory note to his poem "The Distant Runners," by Mark Van Doren.

In "The Barb of Spain," by H. H. Knibbs, a lone stallion survivor of Coronado's expedition goes forth with "questing neigh" until "a fleet young Spanish jade" breaks free from another expedition, somewhere — and then the first mustangs were born.

[34]

Adam in Asia and Eve in Africa, the chances of mating would have been about as high.

We have already seen how Indians disposed of those Coronado horses on which they could lay hands. They killed horses in battles; they schemed to starve the Spaniards out on the Great Plains so that they could destroy their horses. The Coronado muster roll lists only two *yeguas* (mares) along with 556 *caballos*. Among the thousand or so head of additional horse stock, including mules and other pack animals, additional mares may have been included; if so, the proportion was certainly small. When the expedition turned back, a man who remained with a friar rode a mare — in accordance with his unsoldierly choice. He showed up in Mexico afoot four or five years later; presumably the mare had perished.[15]

Out on the Great Plains, with "nothing to see but cattle and sky," buffaloes gored to death the horses of several hunters. Scouts frequently became lost, but only one failed to return to camp. Only three *caballos*, so far as the chronicles tell, escaped. Running after stampeding buffaloes, these threw their riders at a gulch and, saddled and bridled, ran on out of sight.* On the weary back track to Mexico, many of Coronado's horses perished from either starvation or sickness, and others were killed by Indians. The Indians of the West had yet to comprehend horses as something apart from new enemies, something that they might use.[16]

---

* Few Spaniards became so expert at killing buffaloes from horseback as the Indians who took their horses and then prevented their hunting on the plains. In 1599, a large exploring party sent out from Juan de Oñate's settlement in New Mexico sighted thousands of buffaloes near the edge of the plains, built a pen next timber, and undertook to drive buffaloes into it. At first the herd went as desired, but soon stampeded back upon the drivers. "These animals are so savage and furious," a report of the expedition runs, "that they killed three of our horses and wounded forty. Their horns are very sharp and fairly long and bend upwards. They attack from the side, putting the head down so that whatever they hook they tear badly."

Trained by Indians, Spanish horses showed as much buffalo sense as, under vaqueros and cowboys, they showed cow sense.

The first and most important center of distribution for Spanish horses in what is now the United States was the settlement begun by Oñate on the upper Rio Grande in 1598, Santa Fe becoming the capital of New Mexico about ten years later. A man with Oñate's caravan moving northward from Mexico saw the wagons leading the way, "oxen, then the goats, sheep, lambs, mares, mules, and last a great herd of horses" following in "the wheel tracks." [17] There were about 100 mares and colts in addition to 700 horses and mules.[18]

Immediately after the Spaniards established themselves, successive expeditions went out to explore the country east and west. They rode far out on the plains, "provided with mares and other supplies." They reported in writing on geography, on the plant and animal life of the country, and on Indian ways of living, especially the use of dogs as burden bearers. The Indians were all hunting buffaloes afoot. There were no horses among them or at large to report upon.[19]

Not long after domestic livestock began turning the grass-covered mesas around Santa Fe into a desert, the Apaches started raiding. They ate the first horses they took as well as cattle and minor animals. Here was a commissary much handier than the buffaloes on the plains away to the east; the Spanish stock could be driven to their camps, whereas buffalo meat, in dried form, had to be packed afoot with only dogs to help drag it.

News of a bonanza spreads rapidly. The name Apache is said to be a Pueblo Indian word signifying *enemy*, and early Spaniards classified the Navajo and other hostile tribes as Apaches.* No one hive of bees can keep to themselves the honey of a flowered prairie. Navajos and Utes came to the honied Spanish horses. The semi-converted Pueblo Indians, of whom the wild tribes were hereditary enemies, did what they could — for a while —

* The Benavides *Memorial*, which is full of gross exaggerations, says that in the early part of the 17th century the pueblos on the Rio Grande were "surrounded on all sides" by Apaches, "the largest tribe in the world," outnumbering "all the nations of New Spain." — Ayer translation, 16, 43.

to guard Spanish stock from raiders, but were not effectual. Yet by 1630 the stock had materially increased.

The horse population of the Spanish settlements went up and down; among Indians it went steadily upward. The concerted Pueblo uprising of 1680 forced Spanish abandonment of all New Mexico. Leaving most of their stock behind, the refugees settled at and below El Paso on the Rio Grande. Here the Apaches raided as effectively as they had raided around Santa Fe. Now they, the Comanches and other tribes, were looting far down in Chihuahua and Sonora. Indians of northern Mexico aided them in the dispersal of Spanish horses. These Mexico Indians, in the words of the best historian of the Coahuila region, "preferred death to enslavement, in contrast with the patient submissiveness observed by the Indians of central and southern Mexico" and became superb riders. Although the sedentary Pueblo Indians early learned to use horses, they never lived by them. They valued them primarily for passing on to Plains Indians in exchange for jerked buffalo meat and robes.[20]

There are records of replacement horses coming up to New Mexico from the south by the thousand both before and after the Pueblo uprising. As late as 1775 "the enemy had destroyed the mares" of the colonists to such an extent that the central government ordered 1500 head of horse stock sent to them for riding and breeding.[21] Army officers at the outposts did not mind losing horses to the Indians even if their soldiers were left afoot and inactive for six months at a time. They had their *mordido* — their "bite" — out of replacement purchases.[22]

If the Apaches were the first *indios broncos* to acquire horses in what is now the United States, it took the *broncos* on the plains, Indians more docile southeast of the plains, and tribes in the Rockies to the northwest only a limited time to share in the acquisition. Horses were the most wanted things that the Spaniards of the outposts had for trade and bribe as well as for stealing. Their policy from the beginning was to play tribe against tribe. There was never any real peace with the Plains tribes, only truces, during which the Spanish regularly traded off horses, along with tobacco, for buffalo robes. Indians on the Pecos were paying horses for women by 1680.[23]

Before the Spaniards had more than glanced into Texas, much less made any move towards establishing an outpost in the territory, La Salle, wandering afoot and lost in the eastern part of the state, in 1686, bartered with Indians for five horses and brought them back laden with beans and corn to his fort on Lavaca Bay. He tried to get more, but they were scarce. After he was murdered, his men, probably in the vicinity of the Trinity River, met three mounted Indians, one on a "fine grey mare," went with them to their village, and there saw various Spanish artifacts and learned that some of the tribe had been among the Spaniards in New Mexico. They traded an ax for a "very fine" stallion. The Indians said they knew where to barter for more horses.[24] Henri de Tonty in search of La Salle three years later found numerous horses among the Caddoan Indians of east Texas and Louisiana. Some of the horses wore Spanish brands and bore Spanish-style equipment. For seven hatchets and a string of glass beads, Tonty got four. These Indians had been warring with the Spaniards to the west and with the Osages to the north.[25]

As soon as the Spanish in Mexico learned that Frenchmen were in Texas, they rushed thither. An expedition of 1690 traveled north and east of the Rio Grande without seeing a horse until they were four days beyond the Colorado River. Then they encountered "a very tall Indian youth on an excellent bay stallion." He was hunting buffalo.[26]

In 1719 a Frenchman named Du Tisné counted 300 horses among Pawnees in the Arkansas River country. Many warriors were still unmounted and no owner wanted to part with an animal, but the French finally offered enough wares to get two horses and a mule. All three wore Spanish brands. The Pawnees were armoring the breasts of their war horses with leather, Spanish style. The Osages were becoming horsed with stolen Pawnee stock. Just one hundred years after Du Tisné made his observations, Stephen H. Long on a military reconnaissance reported the Pawnees, numbering about 2000 warriors, as having "6000 or 8000" horses.[27]

Tribal traditions on origins usually have little validity, but I incline to credit one told me by an educated half-breed Crow. The Crows, he said, acquired their first horses from the Pawnees. When a band of young men who had been on an excursion brought the animals into camp, their chief, filled with wonderment, laid the long black braids of his own hair in his hand and leaned over to compare it with a horse's tail of the same color. The horse snorted and kicked him in the belly. Then he rode and felt the life of the horse pass into himself. As soon as he dismounted, he announced that the name of his clan was changed to Kick-in-the-Belly. That is the name of the clan to which the half-breed who told the story belongs. The 10,000 horses and mules that a fur trader estimated on grass out from the main Crow camp in 1831 were, he said, "chiefly stolen from the Spaniards." The proportion of stolen animals was probably exaggerated, though not the grand total.[28]

To illustrate further the gradualness of horse acquisition, in 1724, M. de Bourgmont of New Orleans found some three hundred warriors and their families of what he called the "Canzas" tribe on the lower Missouri River moving camp with all their possessions loaded on the backs of women and dog travois. They had no horses. On southwest he found the Padoucas, another name for the Comanches, packing goods on horses, some of which had been traded to them by the Spaniards for buffalo "mantles." They were not lancing and shooting buffaloes from horseback. A band of mounted warriors in crescent formation would take after a bunch of buffaloes and chase it until, with tongues lolling out, the animals could hardly walk; then the warriors would dismount and shoot arrows into them. They were going to war on horseback, armoring their horses with dressed leather. At night they secured their mounts by staking a forefoot to a bush or a peg driven into the ground.[29]

In 1738, La Vérendrye, a French-Canadian trader, found the Mandan Indians of the Dakota territory horseless. Three years later his son found Indians on the upper Missouri possessed of such "great numbers of horses, donkeys and mules" that he named them *Gens des Chevaux* — People of the Horses.[30] If they had burros, they disposed of them. No Plains Indians wanted burros, though they liked mules and had great numbers of them. They disdained the sheep that made the semi-sedentary Navajos self-sustaining, the goat that fed Mexican Indians, and the cattle now making the Apaches prosperous. Only the horse they chose from among all animals of European introduction. It made them masters of the illimitable herds of buffalo that gave them food, shelter, bedding, raiment, tools, saddles, lariats, twine and the core of their religion.

Towards the middle of the 18th century — two hundred years after Coronado's expedition — horses were appearing in the Saskatchewan country of Canada, and they were Spanish horses. About the same time, east and north of the Canadian plains, that remarkable aggregation of untribed Indians and half-breed Frenchmen called Bois Brûlés, or Burnt Woods, became suppliers of Spanish horses and pemmican to the trapper-traders on Hudson's Bay and along the Red River of the North.[31]

From the winter-locked waters of the upper Saskatchewan to the lone grove of palms at the mouth of the Rio Grande on the Gulf of Mexico, the tribes came to their zenith in ownership and use of horses just as westward-moving white men were about to unhorse them forever. Nobody will ever know how many horses they had. In the Peace River country in 1811, Alexander Henry made these observations: "Some of the Blackfeet own 40 or 50 horses [apiece]. But the Piegans have by far the greatest numbers; I have heard of one man who has 300. Those animals are got from their enemies southward — the Snakes, Flatheads, and other nations, who have vast herds. A common horse can be bought here for a carrot of tobacco, which weighs about three pounds and costs in Canada four shillings." [32] The Cayuse Indians in Idaho owned so many horses that their name became the name not only of Indian horses in general but for cow horses over the Northwest — *cayuse*.[33] The great camp of 10,000 Sioux and Cheyenne Indians, including women and children, along the Little Big Horn in June, 1876, the time of Custer's Last Stand, had, according to varying authorities, from 20,000 to 40,000 horses.

The horses of the Californians multiplied astoundingly; the Californians themselves developed a way of life based on horses that distinguished them from all other Spanish groups in North America. But, in the large, California had negligible effect upon the horse life of the Plains. By the time of the first California settlement, 1769, Indians both above and below the Missouri River were horsed. Even after horses became superabundant in California, mountains and deserts barred their spread eastward, and the 19th century was well advanced before California horses reached New Mexico — the initial base of supply for the horse tribes. Spanish settlement of Texas added greatly to the supply, but Indians were riding Spanish horses under loblolly pines a thousand miles eastward from Santa Fe before an outpost in the province of Texas had been planned or a Spaniard had ridden up from Mexico to scout out the land.

III

INDIAN HORSES AND HORSEMANSHIP

THAT PERIOD of time from along in the 17th century when Indians of the West acquired Spanish horses until the English-speaking Americans, by 1880, had taken their horses and ranges from them and confined them to reservations is designated as the Age of Horse Culture. The buffalo-hunting Indians were already nomads; horses made them more nomadic, extending both reach and grasp. Horses transported the Cheyennes from crop-bound camps to a boundlessness limited only by the winds of winter, the drift of buffaloes, the fruiting of berries, fresh grass, which was nearly everywhere in season, and cottonwood when the grass was ice-locked. Pressed by the Cheyennes, the Kiowas deserted the Black Hills for the "Land of Ever Summer" next Spanish grazing grounds. Horses turned war into a game and food-getting into the most animated form of the chase. Their effect upon the Plains Indian was not less than that of automobile and airplane upon his conquerors.[1]

The horse was the first form of property that could make a warrior rich. The horse was something to own and trade, to cherish and to take from other cherishers. Its ostentation value was enormous. No horses were tribally owned. Yet the horse hardly modified at all the Indian's cooperative economy. His psychology of ownership was quite different from that of a white man who, owning three score stores in a chain, expends his dying energies to add one link more. A tribesman's first loyalty was to his people, not to his family estate. Upon death most of his property was dispersed. The Indian's horse did not own the owner.

No man by taking thought can add to his stature, but by taking a horse he can. Heroizing Andrew Jackson as a fighter against unhorsed Indians east of the Mississippi became obsolete even before boys ceased to read the romances of James Fenimore Cooper. The whole tradition of Indians fighting afoot has faded from the popular mind. On the other hand, the tradition of fighting the wild-riding Indians of the West remains on screen and in pulp fiction almost as alive as it was when Buffalo Bill's arena presented it in pageant form. There are no Easterns. A Western without horses would be as intolerable as one with a cowboy wearing oxfords instead of boots. To "ride like a wild Indian" has been the aim of thousands of actors and millions of boys.

The horse dilated the imagination of the Indian as it has dilated the imaginations of millions viewing him horsed. It elevated him in pride and put motion into his spirits commensurate with that of his mount galloping over grass through which he had once crawled up to his game. It put him on a par with the Tartars, the Parthians, the gauchos, the cowboys of the open range and all the other free riders of remembrance whose very names stir the gasolined and the seated towards a life of movement, freedom and spaces.

[43]

Perhaps the most magnificent exhibition of Indian equestrianship described by white witnesses was at the making of the Medicine Lodge Treaty in Kansas, in October, 1867. Plans had been made to have the Cheyenne, Arapaho, Kiowa and Comanche tribes meet representatives of the United States government on Medicine Lodge Creek. General W. S. Harney led five hundred dragoons, a great wagon train freighting gifts and supplies, a United States senator, Indian commissioners, several newspaper correspondents, and other functionaries. In order to make an impression, Harney formed his whole command into an enormous S and there on the prairie awaited the Indians. Two thousand strong, the mounted warriors, led by Black Kettle, White Antelope, Lone Wolf, Kicking Bird, Satanta and chieftains less notable, appeared over a grass-covered slope about two miles away. They were formed in a great V, the point of it directed towards the middle of the S. They rode slowly, in silence, their horses groomed and painted, they themselves in war paint and feathers. About a mile away, without a pause or a signal visible to the white spectators, the two thousand riders dashed from V formation into a huge circle. This circle became a revolving wheel, spokeless and hubless, the rim made by five lines of riders. As it rotated, faster and faster, it moved forward until within about a hundred yards of the waiting formation. Then it ceased to revolve, leaving a gap in the forward rim. Now the chiefs gathered to the center of the circle, and a warrior rode through the gap to the flag and ushered the general and commissioners to the chiefs.[2]

In the dawning of a June day of 1874 — "the time when horses get fat," as the Cheyenne calendar marks the month — buffalo hunters camped at Adobe Walls on the Canadian River in the Texas Panhandle saw approaching them "a black body of moving objects spread out like a fan." They heard "one single, solid yell — a war whoop that seemed to shake the very air of the morning." It set the white men's tied horses lunging in fright. "There was

never a more splendidly barbaric sight," Billy Dixon said long afterwards. Towards a thousand Cheyenne, Comanche and Kiowa warriors, "mounted upon their finest horses, armed with guns and lances, and carrying heavy shields of thick buffalo hides were coming like the wind. Over all were splashed the rich colors of red, vermilion and ochre, on the bodies of the men, on the bodies of the running horses. Scalps dangled from bridles, gorgeous war-bonnets fluttered their plumes, bright feathers dangled from the tails and manes of the horses, and the bronzed, half-naked bodies of the riders glittered with ornaments of silver and brass. Behind the wild-riding horsemen the plain shone dazzlingly clear to the horizon of the rising sun. They seemed to emerge from the glow." [3]

Tribesmen drilled in mock battles, marching and counter-marching, charging and retreating. At night the war horse stood staked to a peg at the lodge door, or, in Bedouin manner, to the wrist of his sleeping master within. Even so, enemies often took the best-guarded horses. On a military expedition, the warrior rode a common horse, leading the war horse for mounting just before going into battle.

Prized beyond sale price was the war horse. He was raced often, trained to turn quickly by pressure of legs and feet, leaving the rider's hands free to shoot or lance. He was taught to receive his rider on the run and to run steadily while the rider hung to one side, shooting from under the neck.* On display occasions, powerful young warriors made their steeds squeal, rear and prance by pressing legs against their sides. The Sioux war horse was trained to leap over the body of a fallen enemy; the leap counted coup just as if the rider had struck the body. Geronimo claimed that if he had to dismount in a tight place and then reached safety, his blaze-faced, white-stockinged dun horse would follow at call.[4]

A good war horse was regarded as a tribal benefactor. A hundred years ago, as the Sioux still tell, Used-as-Their-Shield had a red and white horse named Never-Whipped. He had been raised from colthood on "holy medicine," and he was "treated with the kindness and respect due a relative." He was trained to let a wounded man hold to his tail for support. He was tireless. In preparation for battle a medicine bag was hung around his neck, streaks of lightning were painted on his legs and flanks, and his feet were rubbed with a magic herb to add to his swiftness. In 1854 a large party of Crows attacked Used-as-Their-Shield's camp with such fury that for a time it seemed the women

* Catlin found Comanches supporting themselves in this recumbent position by hooking an elbow into a sling made of hair rope that, braided into the horse's mane at the withers, hung against his breast. The rider kept a heel dug into the horse's back.

Darwin details the technique of similar riding by an Argentine Indian: "On an old white horse, the cacique sprang, taking with him his little son. The horse had neither saddle nor bridle. To avoid the shots, the Indian rode in the peculiar manner of his nation; namely, with an arm round the horse's neck, and one leg only on its back. Thus hanging on one side, he was seen patting the horse's head and talking to him. The pursuers urged every effort in the chase; the Commandant three times changed his horse, but all in vain. The old Indian father and his son escaped."

[46]

and children would be captured. Mounted on his war horse, the chief "ran under the sun," back and forth in front of the enemy, so rapidly that they seemed to see an eagle riding a deer; they did not see a man on a horse. They were paralyzed with astonishment, and the Sioux people escaped with their goods. Used-as-Their-Shield painted on his shield a picture of an eagle riding a deer.

The war horse was often a buffalo horse also. The price demanded by the Gros Ventres for a superior buffalo-runner was a white buffalo hide — an object of veneration almost priceless. A horse had to be fast to overtake stampeding buffaloes. He had to be alert and quick in turning. With reins dropped on his neck, he came up on the right side to within fifteen or twenty feet of the buffalo selected by his rider. If the rider missed a shot and had to reload, an operation requiring both hands, the trained horse kept on after the same buffalo. A young man who accompanied Audubon up the Missouri in 1843 saw "a beautiful Blackfoot pied mare" carry, with hardly a touch to the reins, her rider on a three-mile chase after a dodging wolf. At the end, "the motion of her nostrils was scarcely quicker than when she started." [5] Yet in the melee of buffalo-running the best trained horses were sometimes gored.*

No hound could be more eager than a buffalo horse. At

* "Mounted on his magnificent charger, black as a raven and adorned with gay barbaric trappings, Lean Wolf would stand motionless as a statue before the gates of Fort Atkinson. . . . In spite of all the skill of both horse and rider, the former is sometimes severely, if not fatally, injured. Lean Wolf lost his splendid black steed in this way. He had wounded a cow, and closing up had given her another arrow, when at the moment of the charge the horse plunged up to his shoulders in a snow-drift and was utterly powerless to escape. Lean Wolf was thrown, and the buffalo's horn made a terrible gash in the horse's flank. With a convulsive bound he sprang up and dashed wildly over the prairie, treading on and tearing out his entrails, and after running a short distance fell dead. . . . On the very next hunt, the buffalo crowded upon another rider so closely that he had no room to manoeuvre. The sharp horn of a cow ripped the horse's belly, causing the entrails to protrude. The horse was thrown, the entrails replaced, and the rent sewn with a sinew. . . . After the wound healed the horse ran as well as before." — Henry A. Boller, *Among the Indians . . . 1858–1866*, Philadelphia, 1868, 65, 234–235.

sight of "a gangue of buffalow," Indian horses being driven by Sergeant Pryor of the Lewis and Clark expedition would "immediately pursue them and run around them. All those that had speed sufficient would head the buffalow and those of less speed would pursue as fast as they could." In order to get through the country, Sergeant Pryor had to ride ahead, scaring away the buffaloes, leaving two men to bring on the horses.[6]

After horses became numerous among the Plains tribes, any woman who had to walk while moving camp was regarded as unfortunate. The women became as mobile as the men, and their riding, "with a leg upon each side of the horse," was by no means limited to camp-moving. Captain Randolph B. Marcy watched two young Comanche women set out at full speed with lassos in hand after a bunch of antelopes and each rope one at the first throw. Some of the most vivid paintings (1837) by Alfred Jacob Miller show females chasing buffaloes, racing a horse herd, roping wild horses.[7]

The boys who day-herded Indian ponies began riding in infancy. They played that rounded-up beetles were wild horses. The rope was their toy along with bow and arrow. Going into the waters of the Missouri with their horses, Hidatsa (Gros Ventre) boys would jump from back to back and stroke the skittish colts, unable to get away, gentling them. Men and boys alike delighted in swimming on horseback. A boy herder would say to his charges, "You are my gods. I take good care of you." [8] In the time of Lewis and Clark, Hidatsa families kept horses, at night during the winter, in their lodges; later they stabled them in sheds built against their winter lodges. Here the women, occasionally helped by men, fed hay and cottonwood bark and branches to the animals. Some horses chewed up branches as thick through as a man's arm. But usually only selected horses were hand-fed; the others had to rustle for themselves. The Assiniboins, and presumably other tribes, turned horses loose among cottonwoods to winter unguarded. They would not drift far

[48]

from their fodder,[9] but whenever snow melted enough to allow travel they were in danger of thieving enemies.

In pawing through ice and snow to the cured buffalo grass, the horses of the north justified the Arabian name for hoof: *hâ-fir*, or *digger*. "After our hunters have ridden their horses all day and brought them to camp at night sweaty, tired and hungry, they turn them loose to dig their supper in cold ranging down to 30 degrees below zero. Standing belly deep in snow crusted over ice-hard, the horses beat down the crust with forefeet and feed on the dry, withered grass at the bottom. They often pass the winter without a drop of water except from the icicles and snow eaten with their dry food. Yet these vigorous and hardy animals are always in good condition." Thus recorded Alexander Ross, who during the first decades of the 19th century rode with trapping and exploring expeditions on Spanish-Indian horses over British Columbia and the northwestern part of the United States.[10]

"In order to have thare Horseis Long Winded," Peter Pond wrote about 1745, the Dakota Sioux "Slit thair Noses up to the Grissel of thare head which Make them Breath verey freely. I Have Sean them run with those of Naturall Nostrals and Cum in Apearantley Not the Least Out of Breath." [11] Nostril-slitting was widespread. Another method for achieving long-windedness was to blow the pulverized root or leaves of certain plants up a horse's nostrils.

Warriors slit and trimmed the ear-tips of favorite horses, for style and as an aid to identification by feel in darkness. They never became sufficiently refined to dock a horse's tail. They plaited bright ribbons and feathers into the flowing tails and hung scalps from the long manes, sometimes with little bells that made music wherever the prancers pranced. They hung necklaces of bear claws on their steeds and painted them as well as themselves. Human hands painted on hips indicated scalps taken by the rider; painted horse tracks signified notable horse-lifting. Young men especially devoted to themselves chewed leaves of aromatic plants and perfumed their mounts by blowing and spitting the particles into mane and tail.[12]

Indian saddles were either skin pads stuffed with hair or poorly-fitted and poorly-lined wooden frames imitative of Spanish saddles, notoriously cruel on horse backs. The backs of Indian horses were generally raw, but perhaps no rawer than those of Mexican and South American horses. Riding on the raw backs of Argentine horses, in 1833, was to Charles Darwin "dreadful and inhuman." Texas cowboys used to say that a sore-backed horse was "branded with the map of Mexico." Setfasts on the backs of their own broncs accounted for much pitching. The idea of both Indian and cowboy was that a sore does not hurt after it has "warmed up."

A traveler among the Snake Indians about 1800 saw their horses upon being unsaddled "bite and tear raw flesh until the blood flows, and then kick and roll for some time, whilst their whole bodies quiver and appear in great agony." Yet the next day the owners would ride them with "indifferent composure." The wounds, Captain Meriwether Lewis observed, seldom became too "horrid" to deter a rider. The Indian might tie a rag or a piece of skin over the sore of a loose horse as a defense against magpies * or daub it with mud to ward off blowflies. After running buffaloes all day, a Sioux warrior would keep his horse from

* "The magpie, the most beautiful bird of the country, is here the plague of the savages' horses. These barbarians are so clumsy and so careless with their wooden saddles that often the horse's skin and flesh from the neck to the rump are torn away. The voracious bird at the sight of this raw and living flesh buries its claws in it and tears the poor sentient animal. The horse kicks, prances, runs about with all its might, but in vain. The bird, fixed on the sores, loosens its hold only when the horse throws himself upon his back to roll. Yet scarcely does he rise up once more than the enemy seizes again its opportunity. It is observable that among a large number of galled horses, the magpie always chooses the one that it has once tasted, so that the beast succumbs, if it be not rescued. Some owners, more through interest than through pity, cover the sores with a piece of leather or with a buffalo paunch sprinkled with ashes." — *Tabeau's Narrative of Loisel's Expedition to the Upper Missouri* (written 1803–1805), edited by Annie Heloise Abel, translated from the French by Rose Abel Wright, University of Oklahoma Press, Norman, 1939, 88–90.

water until the next morning, prolonging unmercifully the cooling-off process. William R. Leigh once saw a Navajo pony gasping for breath on account of a tightly knotted rope about its neck that had been wet by rain and then shrunk in sunshine. "A bunch of Navajos were looking on laughing." When the white man pulled his knife and cut the rope, he was "regarded as a killjoy." [13]

But whatever a human being takes pride in, he cares for. Many Indians treated their horses kindly. In mountain country they shod them with rawhide. When Captain R. B. Marcy offered a handsome price to a Comanche for his buffalo- and war-horse, the owner, after explaining how he could not part with an animal so necessary to the welfare of his people, added, "Moreover, I love him very much." Regardful friendship existed between a good Indian horseman and his horse, just as between good horsemen of other peoples and their horses. [14]

The horses that vitalized Western tribes were not scrubs, though scrubs were among them. Their number was at its peak about the time of the westward movement to Oregon and California; quality about this time was declining. Good horses were more plentiful among the northern tribes than among the southern. This was not primarily due to the breeding that a few northern tribes practiced. Northern ranges were and are more conducive to growth in livestock. Trail drivers who annually drove herds of cattle from lower Texas to Wyoming and Montana and left their remudas on the new ranges, used to comment on the second growth that a year or two in the north gave eight- and ten-year-old horses. A Longhorn steer on his native range was little heavier at the age of seven than at five, but after he had "double-wintered" on the upper drainage of the Missouri he was filled out, stood higher and weighed more. I have seen wrinkle-horned, scrubby cows that had been shipped from the soggy grass of Florida to dry ranges of southwest Texas go through the same transformation.

Captain Meriwether Lewis of Virginia and Captain William Clark of Virginia and Kentucky knew horses from the ground up. On their expedition to learn the land and life of the Louisiana Territory, just acquired by Thomas Jefferson's purchase — the greatest bargain in all history — they took no horses. In May, 1804, they started up the Missouri River in boats, expecting to reach the Pacific by portages across the Continental Divide to streams flowing Pacificward. This plan they had to give up; moreover, they required horses for exploring country out from rivers.

The first horses they encountered belonged to the Mandans, "invariably severe riders," who sometimes chased buffaloes day after day without "suffering their horses during this time to taste food; yet this valuable anamall under all those disadvantages is seldom seen meager or unfit for service." During the winter the Americans offered bran mash to some of the horses; they refused it, preferring cottonwood bark. The life of abstention in camps of Arabian nomads was fulfilled in camps of American nomads.

West of the Continental Divide, approaching what is now the Idaho line, the expedition saw horse tracks and then found the Snake (Shoshone) Indians with many horses. These Indians were great distributors of horses. From their uniformly "fine" animals — many of which "would make a figure" in Virginia — Lewis and Clark procured thirty or more stallions and one gelding, "nearly all Sore Backs," several bearing Spanish brands. Brought into one group, the stallions fought and cut each other severely and were hard to herd by day and keep secured at night. The Americans hobbled their front feet and side-hobbled them, staked them by ropes and tied "spancels" (clogs) to their ankles. A few succeeded in breaking away. When rocks made their feet tender, they shod them, Indian style, with "Mockersons" of green buffalo hide. In the mosquito season the horses were driven frantic by the biting, and at night fires were kept going for the protective smoke. When game failed, as it often did in the mountains, the explorers ate their horses "with [as] good Stomachs as iver we did fat beef in the States." *

On the untimbered reaches of the Columbia River basin, Lewis and Clark found the Indians, especially Flatheads and Nez Percés, possessed of "emence numbers" of horses as well as "large and fine" mules. Spanish brands on most of the mules and on some of the horses showed their origin. Some individual warriors owned from 20 to 100 horses each. In general the horses appeared to be "of an excellent race, lofty, eligantly formed, active and durable. Many of them look like the fine English coarsers and would make a figure in any country." Hardly a horse "could be deemed poor and many were as fat as seals."

The explorers heard of wild horses running on the Columbian plains. The only free-ranging horses they had encountered east of the Rocky Mountains were occasional strays showing saddle marks. Such horse-breeding as they observed was from the "most indifferent" animals. Yet the surgery of an Indian whom Captain Meriwether Lewis engaged to perform "quieting operations" on several stallions was in his judgment superior to the American (English) method. It was the Spanish method. The Indians would not trade mares or geldings for stallions, though offered two for one.[15]

All the northern tribes seem to have had some geldings, but most of their mounts were "stone horses." Describing, at the close of the 18th century, the "bold and intrepid" horses of the Sas-

* Indians of the Northwest hardly ate as many horses per population as the Mountain Men and some of the military expeditions. Alexander Ross wrote in *The Fur Hunters of the Far West:* "In a camp teeming with buffalo, fowl, fish and venison, I have seen the whites longing for horseflesh and even purchasing a horse from Indians in order to feast upon it." A cavalryman with General George Crook in pursuit of Sioux and Cheyenne Indians in 1876 on "the horse-meat march" wrote: "The infantry boasted that if we only marched far enough they would eat all the cavalry horses. . . . To us who have to depend on them so much, it seems like murder to kill horses. . . . We lived for five days on captured Indian ponies. And let me tell you that fat colts are ever so much better eating than beef." — *General George Crook, His Autobiography*, edited by Martin F. Schmitt, University of Oklahoma Press, Norman, 1946, 206, 209.

katchewan, Duncan M'Gillivray, sharing native opinion, said: "The operation of gelding is seldom performed by the Indians, as it generally diminishes the strength and vigor of the Horse; he is therefore full of fire and can with ease outrun most of the large animals on which we depend for subsistence." [16] Geldings, it was believed, gave out more quickly than stallions, especially in mud or snow.

Mountains fenced the range of the Nez Percés — whose noses were never pierced — against raids by the ceaselessly shifting Plains tribes and enabled them to control their stock. Before they were dispossessed they had learned to brand their horses and let them run free. With the Wallawalla, Cayuse, Flathead, Palouse and lesser tribes protected by the Cascades, they raised thousands of horses. Annually they rode east over the mountains for buffalo meat and hides, often losing their horses to the Blackfeet and other enemies.

As long as any Indians of the West are remembered, the Nez Percés will be remembered for two facts, inseparable from each other: their horses and Chief Joseph. After treaties with his people had been violated by the United States government — in the usual way when U. S. citizens wanted somebody else's land — and after miners and settlers had harried them for years, in 1877 Chief Joseph led the remnant of his tribe, with about 3000 horses, over a 1600-mile flight from an Oregon reservation into Montana, fighting 13 engagements on the route, losing 900 horses in one. When he surrendered just below the Canadian line, 40 of his surviving 78 warriors were wounded and his own children were scattered and starving. He was an ampler man and a better general than the pompous Nelson Miles who, after capturing him, dispersed the 1100 remaining Nez Percé horses and exiled their owners to malarial lands in Oklahoma.

Their outstanding strain of horses, known now as Appaloosas, took their name from the Palouse River of western Idaho and eastern Washington, which was within their original range. The name has been spelled and pronounced Palousy, Apalousa, Apalucy, Appaluchi, etc. If horses were dogs, the Appaloosa would be called Dalmatian. It is sometimes called polka dot, leopard, domino. It is a color phase of the Barb. Some of the Nez Percé horses, Lewis and Clark wrote, "are pied with large spots of white irregularly scattered and intermixed with black, brown, bey or some other dark colour, but much the larger portion are of an uniform colour with stars, snips and white feet, or in this rispect marked like our best blooded horses in Virginia, which they resemble as well in fleetness and bottom as in form and colours."

Perhaps the Nez Percés were at the time practicing selective breeding to a greater extent than Lewis and Clark apprehended. If not, they soon were. The horses stood from 14 to 15½ hands high. Their hardiness was a tradition among all tribes of the Far West. "The fantail Appaloosa" became a phrase all over the range country. Frederic Remington and Charles M. Russell memorialized them in paintings. Now an association of Appaloosa horsebreeders is perpetuating the strain. Splotched horses occurred wherever Spanish horses ran. Whether the Nez Percés began raising them from a considerable collection of individuals or from only a pair or two is not known.[17]

With good rifles, living exclusively on meat, whether buffalo, panther or rattlesnake, the Mountain Men rode "strong horses of Indian blood and training" and asked for no better as they asked for no odds. They traded for many from the Snakes, bought them from other tribes, often took them without trading. In 1832, Nathaniel Wythe and his partner Milton Sublett bought twenty-five "very fine and high spirited" horses — a kind the Snakes owned "in great numbers." Jim Bridger's noted gray race horse was of Comanche origin. Kit Carson's most noted mount was named Apache. At Bent's Fort on the Arkansas the trappers could swap beaver for horses brought directly from California. Old Bill Williams, who expected to turn into an elk when he died, who considered it "against natur to leave bufler meat and feed on hog" and who had a horror of settling down where "white gals look too much like picturs," rode a "grizzled, crop-eared, raw-boned, Nez Percé pony of dogged temper and iron hardiness" to whom he often whined out his thoughts. The gaunt presence of many a Mountain Man's bony horse with tucked-up flank and ewed neck but with cheerful eye and hearty appetite expressing a game spirit, validated the saying: "It's better to count ribs than tracks."

When Alexander Henry came upon the Cheyennes, in 1806, south of the Missouri River during a gala occasion, he saw their horses as "mostly beautiful, spirited animals; some were masked in a very singular manner, to imitate the head of a buffalo, red deer, or cabbrie, with horns, the mouth and nostrils — even the eyes — trimmed with red cloth. They were by far the best built and most active horses I had seen in this country — superior in every respect to those we see northward. The first great war chief was mounted on a handsome black stallion." [18]

The Pawnees probably had better horses than any other tribe on the eastern flanks of the Great Plains. Going west in 1806 to explore the New Mexico country, Zebulon Pike and his little party were sighted by 300 Pawnee warriors riding "naked." "Yelling in a most diabolical manner," they made a wild rush towards the strangers, surrounding them on all sides. They were entirely friendly. Their gesture, a common one among all the Plains Indians, was but an expression of the power and anima-tion conveyed to riders by good horses. The Pawnees, Pike found, owned "vast quantities of excellent horses, which they are daily increasing by attention to their breeding mares, which they never [ride]; and in addition they frequently purchase from the Spaniards." [19] Ashley's noted trapping expedition which set out for the Rockies from St. Louis in 1823 went furnished with 300 horses purchased from the Pawnees.

One night in the year 1835 while the English sportsman-naturalist Charles Augustus Murray was experiencing the hospitality of the main Pawnee camp, "several thousands" of their horses stampeded in from the prairie, "trampling over skins, dried meat and some of the smaller tents." All the next day was taken up with "driving back, securing and appropriating the horses to their respective masters." At this time Murray's host had only five or six horses "of the meanest description," as the Sioux had recently robbed him of many good horses. Another chief had "at least thirty, among which were some wild, some Spanish, and three of American breed." The date here is important as showing the mixture of stock going on.[20]

Zebulon Pike had considered the Pawnee horses "far superior" to those of the Osages. In 1829 an American horseman who visited the Osages on the Verdigris River (Oklahoma) was so taken with some of their horses that he wrote the *American Turf Register* a letter advising breeders of turf horses to strengthen their endurance and weight-carrying ability by use of Osage blood. He had been particularly impressed by an unridable white mare caught from a band of mustangs. She had "a neck like a stallion, was finely formed in every respect, with a long body and remarkably fine limbs." There were a "most beautiful" iron gray stallion, captured from the Pawnees, and another stallion of mahogany bay with "a most superior walk." But the cynosure was a family of three or four cream-colored horses with black manes and tails, a dark stripe running along the back, legs dark from the knees down, about fifteen hands high, of compact, stout frames, owned by Chief Claremore. He was raising these horses.[21] They were the coyote duns, *puros españoles*.

The earliest artists to paint the West were George Catlin and Alfred Jacob Miller, in the 1830's. Both pictured Indian horses and mustangs; both were frequently careless with anatomy, but in their most careful pictures both detailed the compact body, graceful carriage, high-carried tail and refined head, with tapering muzzle and concave face, of the Arabian type. These features are particularly striking in many paintings by Miller, in contrast to the heavy heads and dropped tails of his cart horses and mules. I regard him as a more veracious documentarian than Catlin. He tried to paint what he saw. Rudolph Kurz, who traveled and painted about 1850, shows some Indian horses as sheep-headed but more of Arabian conformation.[22]

Let no one be cocksure about the looks of Indian horses of the early 19th century. The Navajos have a legend about one of turquoise color and "a joyous neigh" ridden by the sun-god. The far-removed ancestors of the little "copper bellies" now existing on Navajo barrens must have been larger and better proportioned. Fabre demonstrated that even insect species are dwarfed by undernourishment.

Performance counts, and Indian horses often deceived their looks. Among those he saw on the upper Missouri, a European cavalryman found "only now and then noble animals of beautiful form," but, he added, "it is unbelievable how much the Indians can accomplish with their horses, what burdens they are able to carry, and what great distances they can cover in a short time."[23]

There may be a "divine average," but definition of it runs inevitably into individual specification. Perhaps Colonel Richard I. Dodge came as near to a just generalization as any definer. He saw the Indian pony as scarcely fourteen hands high, rather light in build, with good legs, short strong back, full barrel, sharp nervous ears, bright, intelligent eyes. Never stabled, washed, curried, shod, doctored or fed, he starved through winter, but when grass came he filled out and, with ears up and eyes lighted, was ready for any ride. Adversity brought out his values.[24] "Praise the tall, but saddle the small," a Mexican saying went.

"Teach him to deny himself," Abraham Lincoln said to a woman holding up her man-child. "The greatest enemies of the horse are repose and fat," an Arab saying goes. The lean and hungry look is no more against action in horse than in man. Living in starkness, the Indian pony, authentic mustang, remained true to his desert heritage. "Horses, mares, colts, all alike are starved during great part of the year, no corn being ever given, and only camel's milk when other food fails," wrote Wilfrid Scawen Blunt of the Arabians. "They are often without water for several days together, and in the most piercing nights of winter they stand uncovered, and with no more shelter than can be got on the lee side of the tents. Their coats become long and shaggy, and they are left uncombed and unbrushed till the new coat comes in spring. At these times they are ragged-looking scarecrows, half-starved, and as rough as ponies."

While Colonel Dodge was at Fort Chadbourne on the Texas frontier, some of the officers bantered a band of Comanches for a horse race. The chief appeared indifferent, but a match was finally arranged for 400 yards. When a 170-pound buck appeared on a long-haired, churn-legged "miserable sheep of a pony," the Americans were disgusted. They were intending to run their cherished Thoroughbred Kentucky mare, but now brought out their third-best horse. The Comanches wagered buffalo robes and other plunder against flour, sugar, coffee. The rider of the "Sheep" flourished a ridiculously heavy club. In the race he swung it ostentatiously — and won.

The army officers wanted another race, and now brought out their second-best racer. The husky brave with the husky club rode his "Sheep" the second race and won. Thoroughly aroused now, the Americans brought up the Kentucky mare. Bets were doubled. The Comanche rider threw away his club and gave a yell. The "Sheep" shot into the lead from the start and held it. About fifty yards from the goal, the Comanche reversed himself on his horse so as to face the American trailing him and with "hideous grimaces" beckoned him to catch up.[25]

As the 19th century advanced, the horses of the Plains Indians ceased to be straight-out Spanish in blood, as did also many bands of wild horses — the wild and free horses towards which this book is rationally advancing. Over the Trail of Tears from their ancient homes east of the Mississippi River to the Indian Territory, the extirpated Cherokees, Chickasaws, Creeks, Seminoles and Choctaws brought their ponies * (1835–1840). Taking horses where they could find them, the Indians on the eastern fringes of the Plains modified their stock with that obtained from the English-speaking Americans. The Americans were riding and driving their horses west and ever west. These horses were patriotically called "American." They were not a breed; they were no more fixed in type than American dogs; they were bigger than the Spanish-Indian-Western horse. To the majority of American patriots, bigness long before this had become a synonym for superiority.

Coming west by south from Canada, were other modifiers. Louis XIV had begun sending mares and stallions to New France in 1665, and this stock had crossed with Spanish stock brought northward by Indians. In 1831 the Hudson's Bay Company shipped a red-roan stallion named Fireaway from England to the country of the Red River of the North and selected two groups of twenty-five mares each for starting an improvement in buffalo-runner stock. The influence was marked, but it came comparatively late.[26] To try to distinguish all the strains in the blood streams of nations, whether of men or horses, is like trying to trace to their geographical origins the component drops in a bucket of the ocean's water.

During the era of frontier wars, critics constantly asked, "Why cannot our cavalry on picked, grain-fed horses overhaul Indians on their scrub ponies?" Texas rangers on cow ponies of Spanish blood overtook them where grain-fed cavalry horses fell behind.

* As Thornton Chard has shown (see Note 12, Chapter II), none of the Spanish horses landed in Florida and Georgia during the 16th century survived. The one-time noted Chickasaw and Cherokee horses came from west of the Mississippi.

In a phrase applied to some men, these ponies, whether ridden by Indian, cowboy or ranger, would do to ride the river with. They would stay — stay till hell froze over and a little while on the ice. That is not a necessary quality for horses in the glorious Santa Barbara parade starring Hollywood and the sheriff's office. It has become only a modified requirement on ranches where remudas of automobiles make more tracks than cow horses. Yet this quality is good to remember out of times when it was the absolute for men who lived not only on but by their horses.

IV

THE COMANCHE MOON

SPANISH HORSES had by the opening of the 18th century drawn the Comanches far south of their accustomed range between the Platte and the Yellowstone. If in the beginning they traded a few "buffalo mantles" for horses, they soon began taking them with less cost and more excitement. Riding from the Rocky Mountains in Colorado to Natchitoches in Louisiana and from the Platte to Durango, they regarded themselves as a nation like Mexico and the United States, and the Spaniards so regarded them. In an official report in 1770, de Mézières, the competent Frenchman who served the Spaniards as Indian agent over the Louisiana Territory, said: "They compare their number to that of the stars. They are so skilled in horsemanship that they have no equal, so daring that they never ask for or grant truces." [1]

They despised as slaves all *indios reducidos* and even those who traded with the Spaniards. For them sufficed

> the simple plan,
> That they should take, who have the power,
> And they should keep who can.

In 1779 Governor Anza of New Mexico made an expedition against the Comanches and in one engagement captured "more than five hundred horses." The Comanches retaliated and, according to Zebulon Pike, drove away 2000 New Mexican horses. If now and then the Comanche nation lost a battle, a band or a *rancheria* to the Spanish enemy, it had replacements, transportation and arms; it held invasion-swallowing space. Individuals picked up individual horses, but the tribal glory was in driving off entire herds.[2]

The only reason, the Comanches boasted, that they allowed Spaniards to remain in New Mexico, Texas and northern Mexico was to raise horses for them. Pawnees and other strongly mounted tribes called them "*the* Horse Indians," and not infrequently they verified the compliment. The Osages claimed to have carried off 500 "hunting ponies" from a Comanche camp in a single night.[3] According to de Mézières, the Comanches in his time "devoted themselves to raising horses." [4] Most of their "raising" was in the form of lifting; application to breeding among them could not have been other than haphazard.

During most of the 17th and on past the middle of the 19th centuries, the Comanches, with the Lipans and other lesser tribes, stole horses by the droves from every outpost planted by the Spaniards from the Louisiana line to the upper Rio Grande, "leaving only the worst, the leanest and the most unserviceable" for their providers. As long as the French were in Louisiana, the horse-lifters directly and through intermediaries traded horses to them for muskets, powder, lead, knives, hatchets, kettles, cloth, glass beads, etc. The French found the low, moist lands of Louisiana inhospitable to horse-raising [5] — like other subtropical lands, Queensland in contrast to more arid parts of Australia, for example. Indian and Caucasian smugglers traded Spanish horses to British-Americans as well as to the French.[6] At one time the Spanish government considered paying the Comanches a kind of Danegelt as protection against raids, but never got beyond doling out tobacco and *eslabones* — pieces of steel for striking fire out of flint. By forbidding all trade with the French, the Spanish government stringhaltered its colonists and promoted wholesale horse-stealing.

The official records of San Antonio de Bexar during a thirty-day period in the year 1774 illustrate the brazen horse-thieving of the "Nations of the North" — mainly the Comanches. On January 11, a citizen who had ridden west a few miles was robbed of his horses. On January 13, word reached San Antonio that a party traveling south to Mexico had been killed on the Nueces River and their horses taken. On January 14, men out killing cattle for beef were set on and forced to abandon their horses. On the same day a band of Indians drove away two stallion-guarded bands of mares owned by a ranchero of La Bahía (Goliad) down the San Antonio River. Two days later, Indians took a *mulada* — drove of mules — from the same neighborhood. On February 5, Indians stampeded the presidio's horse herd and got away with 300 head out of 400. A detachment of troops pursued until the inferior horses left to them were ridden down. Turning back for San Antonio, they left their tired remuda — the remounts — to be trailed in slowly by a corporal's guard. The Indians took these horses. The raiders did not leave the country; they entered the presidio daily "as friends." The military were afraid to punish them.[7]

About 1767 a world traveler who signed his name Monsieur de Pagés rode into San Antonio just as raiders drove off 400 horses. "The alarm being given, the garrison beat to arms and, mounting their horses, pursued to the distance of a hundred leagues."

[65]

> The King of France went up the hill
> With twenty thousand men;
> The King of France came down the hill,
> And ne'er went up again.

At the Guadalupe River on their way down the hill, the garrison troops were ambushed and lost "150 horses." A few days later a detachment of tribesmen "insulted them again and the governor began to see the necessity of putting the fort in a better state of defense. . . . The whole affair ended in a pitiful little skirmish." [8]

In the year 1813, about 1500 Comanches presented themselves before the vice-governor demanding *un regalo* — a gift. He told them to go on down the river to Goliad, where Governor Manuel Salcedo was opposing Magee's army of filibusters out of Louisiana. The Comanches rode on, found the governor, and asked him for *un regalo*. He replied that all he had to give was powder and lead and that he would furnish them to fight against the American filibusters. The Comanches said they did "not care to be killed." Here was their ultimatum: unless *un regalo* came forth, they would destroy all the ranches on the San Antonio River and drive away all the horses. They seemed, however, in no hurry for a reply and settled down in their camps. Governor Salcedo dispatched a courier to San Antonio ordering all horses driven into stockades and guards posted. "About 7000 horses were gathered nightly into San Antonio, sixty men herding them by day." This is too many horses, but exaggeration is an unvarying means for being interesting. At the end of "fifteen days" — which is the Mexican addition of the days comprising two weeks — the Comanches "took the horses all away." Two years later the military in San Antonio did not have a single horse. Five years later there were so few horses to be obtained from the San Antonio stock-raisers that the Comanches entered into "a kind of peace" and sold them "some of their own horses." [9]

As any examiner of the Bexar Archives may see, even when the Spanish garrisons had a supply of horses, they were often so weak from being close-herded on over-grazed land and from being penned up constantly that they were incapable of effective service. The Indians moved camp often to fresh grass, but the garrisons were fixed. Some day some historian of Spanish America may graduate from the recording of facts to fulfill Emerson's definition of Scholar as "Man Thinking." If so, he will explain the melting away of the enfervored vigor of the Cortés-Pizarro conquerors into ineffectual defense and parochial intolerance. The instrument of decay was an iron band around every orthodox Spaniard's brain that shut in superstition and shut out the growth that freedom of thought and desire for freedom for others give.

Before the Mexican War took the United States across the Plains there was little conflict between Americans and Comanches. Indeed, the American government was at times ammunitioning Comanches against Spaniards and Mexicans. Thus in 1847, the Osage agency traded powder, lead, firearms and other goods to the Comanches for 1500 mules.[10] Long before this the Comanches had become hostile towards the encroaching *Tejanos,* whom they differentiated from other Americans — a differentiation still pleasing to Texans. A few old ones can remember when the full moon of each month was called the "Comanche moon," and there was a song:

> Oh pray for the ranger, you kind-hearted stranger.
> He has roamed the prairies for many a year;
> He has kept the Comanches from off your ranches,
> And guarded your homes o'er the far frontier.

Meantime, the Comanches were reaching the climax of their raids into the border states of Mexico and on down into Durango, Zacatecas and San Luis Potosí. They lifted young women and children, who often developed into loyal members of the tribe, as well as horses and mules. The governor of Chihuahua, acting on a policy adopted by other Mexican states, contracted with a reckless band of American borderers to pay bounties on Comanche and Apache scalps — and the scalpers turned in hair of Mexican citizens along with that of hostiles. Lack of money in the treasury more than moral indignation broke the contract. In the calendar of the Comanches, September was the "Mexican moon"; in the calendar of the Mexicans, it was the "Comanche moon." Every fall, for a third of a century, beginning about 1830, the Comanches rode down established trails to despoil ranges and huddle inhabitants into ruin and terror hundreds of miles below the Rio Bravo.[11]

Across the Llano Estacado of Texas, over the arid sub-plains of the Pecos, by Comanche Springs, where Fort Stockton was established to halt the Cossacks of the Plains, through the mesa-topped hills on south, then through the roughs to the Rio Grande and on into the land of Comanche milk and honey, the main war trail made "a great chalk line. It was worn deep by the hoofs of countless travelers and was whitened by the bones of abandoned animals." In September troops of from half a dozen to a hundred Comanches, warrior women among warrior men, joined by Kiowas, Plains Apaches, Utahs from the Rocky Mountains, out-laws from other tribes and renegades from Mexico, strung over it, riding for their carnival south of the Rio Grande. At this natural boundary, the scourgers fingered out, some to follow up the fertile valley of the Conchos to the mining camps and *rancherías* about Chihuahua City, some for expectant but impotent hacien-das on down in Durango, others for other lodes in Coahuila and beyond. Along in November and December the Great Trail again came to life with herds of cattle, horses and mules from the Mexican supply grounds, with captives laced to their mounts, with hordes of herdsmen and with outriders firing the prairie grass to balk pursuers. Then carrion crows marked the trail from the sky, while dust and smoke signaled it from below. "There was no way to hide or cover it." [12] The purpose of it and the result of it was Spanish horses.

Among travelers with portraying pen, the incomparable

George Frederick Ruxton rode his horse Panchito, followed by two pack mules, into the wide zone of destruction late in 1846. He was an Englishman twenty-five years old, fluent in Spanish and decided in character. The Comanches, he wrote, "generally invade the country in three divisions, of from two to five hundred warriors in each. Every year their incursions extend farther into the interior, as the frontier haciendas become depopulated by their ravages and the villages deserted and laid waste. . . . They are now [September] overrunning the whole department of Durango and Chihuahua, have cut off all communication, and defeated in two pitched battles the regular troops sent against them. Upwards of ten thousand head of horses and mules have already been carried off, and scarcely has a hacienda or rancho on the frontier been unvisited, and everywhere the people have been killed or captured. The roads are impassable, all traffic stopped, the ranchos barricaded, and the inhabitants afraid to venture out of their doors. The posts and expresses travel at night, avoiding the roads, and intelligence is brought in daily of massacre and harrying." [13]

Coming to the noted Hacienda de la Zarca in northern Durango in 1846, James Josiah Webb, Santa Fe trader, found all the people "in great dread of the morrow." The Comanches had been sighted. The people said that it was their custom to surround the hacienda, make prisoners of females and "order the men to bring up the herd of horses." After selecting the best, if they had any tired or poor animals they would leave them, "making the sign that they must be well cared for and be rested and fat" when the Comanches made their next visit. According to talk, this hacienda had been so rich that one time the owner sent as a present to the Spanish government "a thousand gray horses of one year's foal." In other reports the horses were "milk-white." * Never mind the

---

* "It is upon record that a rich widow lady mounted her son's regiment upon six hundred pure white horses." — Captain Flack, *The Texas Ranger*, London, 1866, 61–62. George W. Kendall and John R. Bartlett got the *white* horses from La Zarca into their narratives also.

color. La Zarca became a place of "impoverishment and demoralization." In 1852, John R. Bartlett, U. S. Boundary Commissioner, passed La Zarca soon after 150 Comanches had killed 40 or more defenders and swept away a large number of cattle and mules.[14]

Yet, long before they reached the apex of raiding into Mexico, the Comanches had settled down to comparative peace with the New Mexicans and were supplying them with mules rapined from the mother republic. Bands of New Mexicans, called *Comancheros*, rode out on the Plains annually to barter arms, ammunition, blankets, corn and trumperies for mules. In mood equally pacific, occasional parties of Comanches entered New Mexican settlements to trade.[15]

West of the Rocky Mountains and the Comanche range, "the great stealing road of the Apaches" into Sonora was hard-beaten by the hoofs of captured livestock.[16] Like the Comanches, the Apaches saw in international lines no barrier to horse-lifting.*

American observers among the Comanches during the first half of the 19th century reported concentrations of their horses and mules numbering up to 3000 and even 5000 head, Spanish brands always prominent. Successful warriors owned from 50 to 200 head each. In the 1820's while Thomas James of Illinois was swapping British strouding, calico, flints, knives, tobacco, looking-glasses and the like for Comanche horses, refusing many inferior ones but getting some worth "at least $100 each in St. Louis," a chieftain boasted to him that on the headwaters of Red River his people had 16,000 head, "better than any he had bought." This may have been more than a boast. In 1867 an Indian agent named Labadi reported 15,000 horses and 300 or 400 mules concentrated about Comanche camps on the Texas plains.[17]

* After the Mexican War the government of Mexico held the United States responsible for raids out of its territory and made many claims for damages, offsetting American claims against Mexico. Literature on the subject is extensive. One item with picturesque details is *Reclamaciones de Indemnización por Depredaciones de los Indios*: Dictamen del Sr. D. Francisco Gómez Palacio, Mexico, D. F., 1872.

The quality, of course, was mixed. A chief presented Thomas James with his own war horse, a black stallion named Checoba, "worthy to have borne a Richard Coeur de Lion into battle, the finest limbed, the best proportioned, the swiftest and the most beautiful horse" the Illinois trader had ever seen. A rattlesnake bit this horse, injuring him permanently, while James was losing 100 of his 323 picked Indian horses and mules in a stampede; flies in the Cross Timbers and then disease took most of the remainder. Surveying, in 1834, a herd of "at least three thousand" Comanche horses and mules grazing on a prairie, George Catlin looked in vain for "the splendid Arabians" that frequent reports had led him to expect. He estimated the mules to number perhaps a thousand head and considered them "much more valuable than the medley of horses of all colors and shapes, generally small, but tough and serviceable, with some tolerable nags amongst them." In 1847, Ferdinand Roemer, a German geologist, saw some "very fine mules" among about a thousand Comanche horses on the San Saba River in Texas, but the horses appeared to him mostly "unsightly and small, light in color, their heads and tails painted a carmine red." He naturally had heavy German horses as his ideal.[18]

However their horses may have looked, and they certainly looked like the run of Mexican horses, the Comanches were to ride high for a little while longer. But, "as the sword outwears its sheath," the vigor of all powers declines and the stimuli of new continents, fresh philosophies and revolutionary inventions lose their glandular spur. The Comanches and other tribes of the Plains did not have the horse long enough for the nerve it added to their energies to become enervation. They were cut down at their riding best while the fit of vitality was still hot within them.

V

INDIAN HORSE–STEALING
AND MUSTANGING

AS WE HAVE SEEN, the Indians of the West got their first horses from the Spaniards and not from wild stock. There were no wild horses on the plains when they began riding. Wild horses did not become numerous until after they were well mounted. The Indians themselves added enormously to this stock of wild horses and were altogether responsible for their occurrence in some northern regions.

No form of property has ever been more fluid than the horses of the Western Indians. When they were not trading horses they were raiding them. Day and night all horses had to be guarded against thieves. Next to counting coup, success in stealing horses

— not scrubs but prized and guarded horses — was at the top of warrior virtues. It was a kind of game, in which skill brought far more glory and satisfaction to the players than mere possession could bring. To them it was as exhilarating as the discovery of gold to prospectors and of oil to wildcatters.

In 1856, a party of Crow warriors captured a paint horse from another tribe. He was soon regarded as the most beautiful and the fleetest horse among the thousands owned by the Crows. He was the pride of the whole nation, and was guarded accordingly. As his fame spread, many enemies tried without success to reach him.

In 1858, Little Dog of the Piegans boasted to a council of war that before two moons had passed he would own the pinto. He set out alone and located the Crow camp on the Musselshell River. After trying for several nights to steal the horse, he took to watching the Crow camp for a daylight opportunity. Whenever the owner of the paint rode about, his pride and that of his horse were shared by all beholders. One morning the camp began moving. The rider of the paint took the lead, along with other dashing riders. They were moving in the direction of Little Dog's stand. He ran ahead, under cover, and hid in a coulee where the advance guard would pass.

Luck surprised him. The rider on the pinto had dashed away from his companions and came right by him. One shot brought him to the ground, and one leap fixed Little Dog in the emptied saddle. With scores of Crows shooting at him and trying to overtake him, he raced ahead. The pinto left everything far behind. As soon as he was ridden into the Piegan camp, he became that tribe's most cherished object of protection. The Crows tried time and again to recover him and took many Piegan horses. Little Dog kept the pinto for years. Such a horse could not be bought, only taken.[1]

White people never understood that Indians who raided their

horses usually had no design on scalps. Granville Stuart, at one time the most influential rancher in Montana, and, while married to a Snake woman, the most civilized reader and lender of books who has yet impressed himself upon Montana history, wrote: "These Blackfeet Indians were not blood-thirsty at this time [1858], for they could have ambushed and killed us almost any day or night. But to be an expert and successful horse thief gave the Indian great prestige, and he was emphatically 'It' among the damsels of his tribe. Except in actual war, it was considered a greater achievement to get the horses without bloodshed and without being seen than it was to murder the owner in order to secure his horse." [2] Among those Cheyennes who went on the warpath solely to capture horses and who boasted of never having killed a man was Big Foot — a name common to many tribes. On one raid, he singled out a fine war horse, roped his rider, jerked him to the ground, and left him there unhurt while he rode off with the mount. [3]

The game, not the gain, made Indian men risk and often pay their lives for horses. In the early days of Arizona the company operating the once noted Heintzelman mine fortified the Arivaca Ranch as headquarters. Here the work mules were kept by night in a corral made by a thick, high adobe wall. Beside the gate was a small adobe house in which the vaqueros slept, the door always open so that any movement outside would, presumably, be heard by the men. Watchdogs were kept shut within the corral. The bars of the gate were lashed into their slots with a rawhide reata, and, in addition, were secured by a heavy iron chain that clinked sharply when moved. In quarters near by, white men slept with rifles and six-shooters by their sides.

One night four or five Apaches came. No human being heard them, and the dogs raised no alarm. As signs told next day, the Apaches first tried to saw a gap in the adobe wall with their hair ropes, but the adobe was very resistant. They then stole to the

[75]

gate, cut the reata, unfastened the chain, handling it noiselessly link by link in their serapes as they moved it, and let the bars down. The first sound the vaquero guards heard was made by thirty-nine good mules and several fine horses rushing away. Five armed men followed the thieves but ran into ambushers who killed one and wounded another.

On down in Sonora about the same time, a wealthy ranchero built his great corral of stone ten feet high. Instead of the usual bars, he had a massive iron-bound gate that was locked every night with a massive iron lock. No Apache thieves were going to break through in darkness and steal his horses away. They did not break through, but one night a half dozen scaled the wall and dropped over into the corral, picked their mounts and waited in shadowed places for daylight. After it came, vaqueros as usual unlocked the great gate and swung it open to let the horses out to graze. In a second the waiting Apaches were mounted and with yells of triumph stampeded the horses for the mountains.[4]

To steal horses, warriors might ride for days, but when within reach of the booty they habitually went afoot, leaving their mounts under the care of one or more of their own party. Sometimes a young brave, carrying only a rawhide thong and a little dried meat or pemmican would set out afoot alone to be gone several moons. In 1837, fourteen Cheyenne warriors walked from their camp on the South Platte to the horse herd of a big Comanche-Kiowa encampment on the headwaters of Red River. They captured many horses in the night but the next day were overtaken and all killed. Like the successful thief among the Arabs, an Indian raider wanted credit from whomsoever he despoiled. A certain Blackfoot hung his worn-out moccasins where they would be seen by the owner of the horses he had taken. The sign said plainly: "I have walked until my last moccasin is worn out. Now I am riding. You can wear out your moccasins in search for more horses."[5]

Before horses became a main object in life, the Cheyennes had been friendly with the Kiowas and Comanches. Then the Cheyennes and associated Arapahoes raided them, only in turn to be raided by the Pawnees and others. In 1840, the Cheyennes made a treaty of peace with the Comanches and Kiowas, each side presenting the other with gifts, Chief Satank of the Kiowas, it is said, giving 250 horses to the Cheyennes. A Cheyenne expedition of 1828, twelve years preceding this treaty, illumines the horse world.

The leaders were Yellow Wolf, "a very wise man," Little Wolf, and Old Man. With them were eighteen warriors. They had ridden from the South Platte to the upper Arkansas River to capture wild horses. Walking Coyote, a Pawnee captive who was Yellow Wolf's adopted son, added thirty-five head to a large catch. While the warriors were driving them homeward by night in the Wild Horse Creek country of eastern Colorado, Yellow Wolf and Little Wolf, riding in the lead, smelled burning buffalo chips.

They halted. Just beyond, as they knew, was Black Lake, the alkaline water of which buffaloes and horses but not people drank. A spring on beyond the lake afforded good water. Around these waterings the trails of buffaloes and wild horses were deep. Yellow Wolf told two scouts to reconnoiter the spring.

They rode until the smell of burning buffalo chips became strong. Then they stopped and one held the horses while the other slipped forward afoot. He came close enough to the camp to hear talk. It was in the Comanche tongue. There were many little fires; the prairie around was "black with horses."

When he heard the scouts' report, Yellow Wolf said, "We must turn here and drive our horses around and get on the opposite side of the Comanches." They drove very slowly and quietly until they were well north of the big camp. Now Yellow Wolf detailed certain young men to hold the horses until they should hear firing and yelling; then they must hurry the horses onward.

He and the others went closer to the camp to await daylight. To Walking Coyote he said: "You have a fast horse. While we run off the horses, you must stay behind and hold back the Comanches following us." The waiting Cheyennes watched from a place where the enemy could not see them. As day dawned, they saw horses everywhere. They saw the herders leave them and ride to camp, thinking that now all was safe. Many of the best horses were picketed in camp. Walking Coyote singled out a big bay on the edge.

The Cheyennes made their first rush in silence, but after they got around the horses, they yelled and shot. The horses stampeded; the Comanche warriors added to the stampede by yelling and shooting, but were too far away and excited to hit their targets. Many of the picketed horses broke loose to run after the others. Walking Coyote raced into camp, jumped off his horse, cut the rope holding the big bay, mounted again and, leading his prize, caught up with Yellow Wolf, to whom he handed the rope. Then he and other men with rifles dropped behind to meet the oncoming Comanches. Runaway horses were still joining the Cheyenne herd, and riders behind it had to keep dodging flying picket pins on the loose ends of ropes. Two Comanches were killed and the others turned back. Seeing so many horses in the herd ahead, they estimated their enemies to be in much greater force than they were.

Among the captured horses were many belonging to fellow tribesmen of the captors, for the Comanches had raided them the year preceding. These were restored to their owners, but the other Comanche horses and the mustangs were divided among the raiders, who soon traded, gambled and gave away many to friends.[6]

An entry, dated December 20, 1827, in the journal of Peter

Skene Ogden of the Hudson's Bay Company tells much of the dispersal of horses, left to run wild, in a country hundreds of miles away from any Spanish source. Seven trappers had bought "49 horses from the Nez Percés at an extravagant rate averaging $50 each. They lost 19 crossing the plains from Day's Defile, were obliged to eat 6, and then had 10 stolen by the Snakes." [7]

Sometimes Indians turned exhausted or tender-footed horses loose on the range, expecting to get them back after they had recovered. Members of another tribe might forestall them, or the freed animals might take up with wild horses. [8] Horses with slit ears and mules were often seen among the mustangs. The epidemic of smallpox that swept through the tribes of the Missouri country in 1837, reducing the Mandans, for example, from 1600 to 150, released thousands of horses to run wild. Stampedes, battles, and storms lost horses to the Indians as well as to the Spaniards.

The flux of horses, the confusion and losses to the wild through continual Indian activities, is particularized with Defoe-like realism in Jacob Fowler's *Journal*. In September, 1821, he and nineteen other men set out on a trading and trapping expedition from Fort Smith on the Arkansas to follow up to its source and beyond in Mexican territory. Before long they were abandoning played-out horses. They occasionally sighted wild horses and bought a few tamed ones from the Osages.

On the 19th of November, about 25 miles east of the then uninhabited site of Pueblo, Colorado, where they were to winter, a band of Kiowas dashed up to them at full speed, flourishing their weapons "as though they Ware Chargeing uppon an Ene-mey" — and took them under protection. The region was a great wintering ground for buffaloes and Indians. Within ten days the Fowler party was in the midst of Kiowa, Comanche, Arapaho, Paducah, Cheyenne and Snake lodges and "about 20,000 horses." The Kiowas and Comanches had the most — "great numbers of very fine Horses — Equal to any I have Ever Knone." The Comanches had a Spanish prisoner fresh from San Antonio, Texas, also "28 horses taken from the Crows" on the Platte. Arapahoes had just had a fight with a band of Crows in the vicinity. Three Fowler men out hunting meat ran into these Crows with about 200 horses "captured from some other nation." The Crows took what powder and lead the Americans had and were presenting them with "nine fine horses in exchange" when a band of Arapahoes appeared. After a short contest that injured nobody apparently, the Crows made off in one direction with what horses they could hold, the Arapahoes made off in another with the remainder, and the Americans bolted for camp, leaving their nine fine animals on the prairie. Only a few Snakes were at the rendezvous of horse-hungerers. They had ridden hundreds of miles from their own wide ranges, but were accustomed to going much farther south in much larger numbers. Five years later, Peter Skene Ogden estimated that a thousand Snakes were going "annually to the Spanish settlements to trade and steal horses." [9]

During six nights before the great aggregation of tribes dispersed, between 400 and 500 horses were stolen out of the 20,000. They were stolen at night from areas surrounded by lodges. Nobody seemed to know by whom. The coming and going of thieves and counter-thieves was constant. A little later on the trappers saw several mares and horses that had escaped from Indian owners. [10]

The Crows raised horses, roped mustangs, rode magnificently, and had more horses than any other tribe on the Missouri, probably from 9000 to 10,000 head, about three head for every man, woman and child of the tribe. The ghost-written autobiography of Jim Beckwourth, mulatto chief of the Crows and authentic liar of magnificent proportions, is little more than a chronicle of successive horse raids. According to him, raiders he led against a great Comanche camp south of the Arkansas River swept 5000 horses away from a prairie prolific with other thousands. Back on the Yellowstone with the booty, they found that fellow tribesmen had lifted 2700 horses from the Kootenays. Soon the Crows lost 1200 horses to raiding Blackfeet, but promptly took 2000 from them. Next the Blackfeet took 3000; the Crows recovered 2500 and picked up 3500 from other sources. Jim Beckwourth should have kept a ledger.[11]

No herd of horses running into the thousands can be held or driven on open range without losses to the wild. The more the Indians dealt in horses and the more they acquired, the more they lost. Scattered over half a continent, the escaped ones increasingly multiplied.

What tribesman first captured a wild horse and rode him can never be known. Presumably those Indians more closely associated with the Spaniards first learned to lasso on the run; yet the earliest accounts of Indian roping are from the north. Lewis and Clark in 1805 found the Shoshones "expert at casting the cord around the neck of a running horse." Before this the Nez Percés were lassoing in vaquero manner the "exceedingly swift, well-proportioned and handsome" wild horses of the Columbia basin, and the Flatheads were expert at "leashing." Pictograph records of the Dakota Sioux show the lasso as their symbol for wild horses after 1812.[12]

The 19th century was far advanced, however, before lassoing became a common skill over the plains. Evolution of that skill among the Cheyennes must have been typical. The first Cheyenne mustanger kept his loop open by tying it with light, easily broken strings to a ring made by a willow switch; holding this ring in his hand, he had to ride up even with a running horse in order to place the loop over its head. One early-day Cheyenne mustanger could adjust a hackamore on a wild horse while racing alongside it. In time, the mustanger's reach was extended, giving him an advantage over a dodging animal, by hanging the loop from one end of a long pole. Snaring a wild horse at such close range enabled the snarer to tighten the lariat over the windpipe, against the jaws, and easily choke down the victim; he usually dismounted with lariat in his hands or wrapped around his body to bring his catch to the ground, and he usually had help from another Indian.[13]

In 1832, in Oklahoma, Washington Irving watched a half-breed of Osage and French blood snare a mustang with a loop attached to the forked end of a willow wand eight or ten feet long. After a hard chase he had to get almost head to head with the wild horse before he could draw the noose, but he had a long lariat on which to play the captive. Frontiersmen with the Washington Irving party were also using poles in their attempts to catch wild horses. A decade later, the Osages were making organized hunts with noose on forked stick. Yet in these years lassoing was common among other Indians of the Southwest.[14] At the same time mustangers, presumably both Indians and white men, on the prairies out from the Brazos River in Texas — far east of the Spanish settlements — were using the long pole with noose attached as well as swinging the "lazo." [15]

Professional mustangers among frontiersmen, as we shall see, seldom depended upon roping for their catches; the strongest and fastest mustangs escaped even the best ropers on the best of horses. Indian snarers could come alongside only old, slow, weak animals, mares heavy with foal, colts. "I saw to my perfect satisfaction," Catlin wrote after watching a lively chase, "that the finest of these droves of wild horses can never be obtained in this way, for upon being pursued they take the lead and in a few minutes are a half mile or more ahead of the bulk of their drove." However, the Horse Indians had the immense advantage of numbers. Scores and even hundreds converged from all sides upon a band or several bands of wild horses and kept them running back and forth and around within the human wall until their fleetness was spent. Yet even here, the quickest, most daring and alert mustangs might dodge away between riders.[16] If it were possible, the "surround" was made against a bluff or in a canyon.

After winter shortage of grass had weakened the wild horses, especially northward, a warrior whose racer had been nourished on cottonwood bark and maybe some hay might overtake superior mustangs. Relaying each other in the snow, the chasers could bring almost any mustang to bay. They were brothers to all wild things, knew their nature, their habits, the courses they would run, and every fold in the land. They trapped wild horses in canyons and passes. Out on the plains, away from natural culs-de-sac, the Kiowas, having learned from the Spaniards, built pens in wooded areas, with brush wings flanging out in V-shape and hazed wild horses from the prairie into the trap. The Cheyennes, among others, used gentle mares as lures for young stallions roaming mareless. After the never reliable trick of creasing — stunning with a bullet — was introduced by some white man, now and then an Indian expert at imitating wild-animal calls would hide himself near his saddleless horse and neigh a mustang up within rifle shot.[17]

One day in 1823, highly excited Comanche warriors were mounting and dashing away from camp as if to battle an approaching enemy. Chief One-Eyed guided his horse-buyer friend Thomas James to a hilltop overlooking a vast plain. There they watched a "multitude" of spread-out riders head bands of wild horses towards a deep ravine where something less than a hundred other men waited with coiled reatas. When the terrified wild horses reached the ambush, there was an "apparently inextricable confusion" of horses and horsemen, but almost every roper tied his animal. Most of them lassoed the neck, but some brought animals to the ground by roping the forefeet. Only one mustang broke away, "a fine black stud that flew like the wind."

Yelling Comanches pursued him, and in about two hours one led him back "tamed and gentle."

He walked close to his captor, who offered to sell him, but Thomas James "feared his wild looks and dilated eye." Then the Comanche gave the white man the lead-rope, whereupon "the noble animal" came near him "as to a new friend and master." Within twenty-four hours after a hundred or so wild horses had been captured "amid the wildest excitement and enjoyment," most of them appeared to be as "subject to their masters as farm horses." [18]

The first step in taming a wild horse was to choke it down. No more distressful sound can be heard than the frenzied breathing of a horse choking to death. As soon as it was down, its head was grabbed, its feet were tied, and the choking lariat was slacked. Then when the animal gained its feet, trembling and covered with lather, the captor approached it gently, rubbed its nose, passed a hand over its eyes, stroked its ears and forehead, and breathed into its nostrils. However harsh an Indian might be towards a captured mustang, if he knew and valued horses he was "extremely cautious not to break its spirit." [19] Breathing into the nostrils of a wild animal is an ancient and widespread practice. There may be something to it. No wild animal feels acquainted with anything strange until he has smelled it.*

As soon as a wild horse was captured, the captor would throw a buffalo robe over its back, tie a thong around its lower jaw — the Indian bridle — and ride off on it. Some Indians hackamored the captive and tied it to the tail of a gentle mare so as to accustom it gradually to confinement and the presence of human

* I have seen vaqueros breathe into the nostrils not only of broncos but of wild cows and calves while they were held down. According to George Catlin, Indians tamed buffalo calves by this operation. "In concurrence with a known custom of the country," he says, "I have often held my hands over the eyes of the calf and breathed a few strong breaths into its nostrils," after which "the little prisoner" would follow his horse for miles to camp. Many a cowboy has breathed into the nostrils of a fractious horse to tone him down.

[84]

beings. The Osages kept their captives closely tied for about a week, bleeding them daily.[20]

While John Treat Irving was agent to the Pawnees in the 1830's, a young Indian led up a tractable "jet-black mare." He was followed by another Indian leading a haltered horse recently caught from the prairie and as yet unmounted. He was only two years old, snow white, splotched with brown.

"His tail stood out, his ears were pricked up, his eyes starting, his nostrils expanded, and every hair of his mane seemed erect with terror. He dashed around at full length of the tug that held him. Then pausing and shaking his long mane over his head, he fixed his almost bursting eyes upon his captor. A moment later he raised his head in a long gaze upon the hills of his prairie home and then made a desperate leap towards them, dragging on the ground the Indian who held him. Others rushed to grab the rope, but rearing and pawing he kept them from a near approach. At length a young Indian threw off his robe and crept up behind him. With a sudden leap he landed upon his back and seized the tug. The wild horse uttered a shrill, frantic scream and bounded into the air like a cat. He plunged and reared, but his rider kept his seat, unmoved. He curbed him in and lashed him with his whip until he crouched like a dog. His spirit was crushed, and the last spark of freedom was extinguished. Shortly after, one of the hunters tied a pack upon his back, and they led him off with the rest." [21]

While Charles Augustus Murray was hunting with the Pawnees, he watched a young dandy trying to bridle "a fine horse" only half broken. The horse kept backing away. "With the foolish violence common among Indians on such occasions," the young dandy hauled hard straight out from the horse, a procedure that could result only in increased resistance. Presently, in a fit of rage, the Pawnee "drew his scalp knife, sprang at the horse like a tiger, and buried the knife in his eye."

[86]

To an old chief who was standing by and watching without a word, the white man said, "That is not good." Gravely he answered, "No." Trying to disguise his manifest shame, the young man walked haughtily to a spot about twenty yards away and "throwing his scarlet blanket over his shoulder, drew himself up to his full height, and there stood a motionless statue. The camp moved on. He remained standing in the same attitude. The poor horse, his head now hanging and his ears flapping, was led off by one of the boys." [22]

Generalizations on Indian treatment of wild horses are apt to be misleading. Certainly, however, the Horse Indians were in sympathies too close to animals to be exclusively brutal. Taming horses by the "blanket act," with a minimum of physical force, may have been commoner than is suspected. Among the Blackfeet of Canada four men would hold a wild horse by a reata while the tamer approached it slowly, grunting out from deep down in his chest the *hoh, hoh, hoh* "horse talk" and making many queer motions. The horse would become so attentive to this man that he ceased to plunge. Coming nearer, slowly, slowly, the man would calm him with monotonous *shuhs* and pass a blanket back and forth in front of his face. At length he was near enough to rub the horse's nose and let him get the full human smell. Then he haltered him with a narrow rawhide thong that when tightened pained the nerves around the muzzle and behind the ears. With halter strap in hand, he needed no further aid in controlling the horse.

Next he began the process of working fingers and hand over every square inch of the horse's body, beginning with face and neck and including the flanks and inner legs, *shuh-shuhing* all the while. After he had stroked a segment of the body, the tamer struck it with his blanket. Finally he struck the horse's back with the blanket a number of times. Then he laid it gently on the horse's back, allowing him to feel the weight in relaxation. If the

horse bucked it off, the tamer would jerk at the halter and re-
place the blanket. Before mounting, he placed his elbows over
the blanketed back and lifted himself slowly several times, ac-
customing the horse to his weight. After he mounted, he sat still
for a while, stroking him, before urging him to move. The wildest horse subjected to this process became docile, it is said, seldom bucking at all. Yet no mustang could be expected to react
to gentleness without some rough jerking.[23]

One way to make the wildest horse feel subject to his master
is to take him off alone, away from companions and accustomed
range. George Catlin bought "a noble claybank of the Comanche wild breed" that he named Charley. On a tour with cavalrymen while most of their horses were "drooping and giving out,"
Charley flourished in flesh and spirits.

Then for twenty-five days Catlin and Charley traveled alone.
With some of his verbosity excised, this is Catlin's story. "When
the sun was half an hour high, I usually halted at some little
stream where grass was good and wood and water for coffee
were handy. The first act of camping was to unsaddle Charley
and picket him. He always fed busily. After supper, I moved
him up close to my pallet, driving the picket pin into the ground
near my head so that I could lay hand on the rope if he became
alarmed at something.

"One evening while we were both having supper, he slipped
the rope, tied too loosely, over his head. He kept on grazing, but
seemed to find the grass choicer off a little distance. About dusk
I took the rope and tried to catch him. He had no desire to be
hampered in his freedom and kept evading me until dark.

"In the middle of the night, only half awake, I became conscious of a form standing over me. At first I took it to be an
Indian about to perform the scalping operation. The feeling of
horror fully awoke me and then I saw Charley, his forefeet at
the edge of my bearskin bed, his head hanging directly over me,

while he stood fast asleep. Whether he had come close to me from affection or from fear or from a mixture of both feelings, I do not know. I slept very soundly until sunrise.

"Charley was off a considerable distance grazing. After breakfasting, I confidently took the rope to catch him. He seemed to enjoy tantalizing me by turning around and around, always just out of reach. Remembering his attachment for me shown during the night, I decided to try an experiment. I packed up my things, slung the saddle over my back, and, trailing my rifle, started off. After going a few hundred yards, I looked back and saw Charley standing with head and tail very high, gazing first at me and then at the campfire, still sending up a little smoke. I walked on. Looking again, I saw him walking hurriedly to the camp site. There he began to neigh violently and soon broke for me, running at full speed. He passed me a few paces, wheeled and stood facing me, trembling like an aspen leaf.

"I called him by name and walked up to him with bridle in hand. He lowered his head to receive it. He actually stooped to receive the saddle. As we travelled on, he seemed to be as contented with our reunion as I was. I did not give him another chance to slip away from the picket rope." [24]

Horses and more horses from the Spaniards and Mexicans, and then later many from Anglo-Americans. Horses and more horses from wild bands on the prairies. Horses and horses from tribal mares. Horses by the tens of thousands, traversing continental expanses. What became of all the Indians' horses? The quality deteriorated as the Indians lost ground, power, self-confidence, freedom. Confined to reservations, without buffaloes to run or war to ride to, they had only minor uses for horses.

One of the show places of the plains used to be the great collection of whitened bones on Tule Canyon, in the Texas Panhandle, where, in 1874, General MacKenzie's troops slaughtered more than 1000 horses captured from the Comanches and

Kiowas. Two years later, U. S. soldiers took around 3000 horses from the Sioux and Cheyennes and lost nearly all of them in a drive for St. Paul during a winter blizzard. When, after four years of exile in Canada, Sitting Bull of the Sioux finally, in 1881, surrendered at Fort Buford, North Dakota, his war ponies were sold at auction and bought for a song by post traders. The mares went to that fantastic character, the Marquis de Mores of Medora. Then the Little Missouri Horse Company topped these mares and bred them to a Kentucky Thoroughbred stallion. Among them were grullos and buckskins with black stripe down the back. Some showed scars from the bullets of Custer's troopers. In the terrible winter of '86–'87, which killed a great majority of cattle on all northern ranges, these little Sioux mares survived. Their clean-boned, strong, fast, long-winded offspring are still a tradition among Dakota ranch people.[25]

I am far from being cocksure, but it seems to me that few North American Indians had that affinity for their horses attributed to Indians of the pampas. I will quote from W. H. Hudson's beautiful essay on "Horse and Man," in *The Naturalist in La Plata,* written at a date as remote now, though only a lifetime ago, as that on which Queen Elizabeth for the last time looked into the eyes of Essex. Perhaps Hudson was spraying the mist of romance.

"With the gauchos the union between man and horse is not of so intimate a nature as with the Indians of the pampas. Horses are too cheap, where a man without shoes to his feet may possess a herd of them, for the closest kind of friendship to ripen. The Indian has also less individuality of character. The immutable nature of the conditions he is placed in, and his savage life, which is a perpetual chase, bring him nearer to the level of the beast he rides. And probably the acquired sagacity of the horse in the long co-partnership of centuries has become hereditary, and of the nature of an instinct. The Indian horse is more docile, he understands his master better; the slightest touch of the hand on his neck, which seems to have developed a marvelous sensitiveness, is sufficient to guide him. The gaucho labors to give his horse 'a silken mouth,' as he aptly calls it; the Indian's horse has it from birth. Occasionally the gaucho sleeps in the saddle; the Indian can die on his horse. During frontier warfare one hears at times of a dead warrior being found and removed with difficulty from the horse that carried him out of the fight, and about whose neck his rigid fingers were clasped in death."

VI

SO LONG as a young unbranded animal on the open range
associated with its branded mother, it belonged by law and
common consent to the owner of the brand. After it, still unbranded, was cut off from its mother, no individual could show
title to it. It belonged to whoever could capture it. Many years
before the name of Sam Maverick became a common noun des-
ignating any such ownerless animal of the bovine species, the
word *mustang* was current on the frontiers.

It is an English corruption of *mesteño* or *mesteña* (feminine),
a word already legalized in Spain when Copernicus asserted the
diurnal rotation of the earth. In 1273 the Spanish government
authorized the Mesta as an organization of sheep owners. On the

long "walks" between summer and winter ranges, many sheep were lost. They were called *mesteños* (belonging to the Mesta). They were also called *mostrencos* (from *mostrar*, to show, exhibit). The estrayed animal had to be *mostrado* (shown) in public to give the owner a chance to claim it. *Bienes mostrencos* were, in legal terminology, goods lacking a known owner. The organization of sheep owners, the Mesta, claimed all animals of unproved ownership, but the crown, and then the always clutching church, seized the *mostrencos*. *Mestengo*, a later form of *mostrenco*, is as a word nearer to *mustang* than *mesteño*, and some etymologists have regarded it as the origin. However, English-speakers of the Southwest were hardly aware of its existence.[1]

As wild horses became a salient feature of the landscape in New Spain, the Spaniards characterized them by a variety of names. In historic times Spain had known no mustang horses. Feminine *mesteña* gradually supplanted masculine *mesteño*. *Caballada mesteña* and *mesteñada* (mustang horse stock) were frequent terms, along with *bestias mesteñas* (mustang beasts, or animals). *Caballos silvestres* and *caballos salvajes* conveyed the idea of feral animals belonging to the wilderness. *Cimarrón*, originally a runaway slave, a *marrón*, is still used in Mexico to denote any ownerless animal of domestic breeds. The word specifies mountain sheep, whence the Cimarron River, which heads in mountains once inhabited by aboriginal sheep, took its name. About 1840, a traveler in the Osage country found frontiersmen calling the wild horses *marrons* (or *maroons*), manifestly from *cimarrones*,[2] but this Americanism made no headway against *mustang*. In so far as I have found, the latter word was first written in 1807 and first printed in 1810.*

* June 3, 1807, after crossing the Rio Grande from Mexico into Texas, Zebulon M. Pike, as his journal reads, "saw some wild horses." June 4, near the Nueces River, "great sign of wild horses." June 5, "passed two herds of wild horses." June 6, "immense numbers of cross-roads made by wild horses."

Toward the middle of the 17th century Fray Bernabé Cobo, who observed the plants and animals of the New World with a fresh eye, wrote: "In many provinces of America there are a great many *caballos alzados al monte* [run away to mountains, woods, brush] or *montaraces* [mountain-wildings]. They are especially numerous in Española, [Santo Domingo], where I in traveling saw on plains and meadows great manadas of them, which upon sighting a person take fright and flee like wild animals. In much larger numbers they exist in Paraguay and Tucumán. There people take *potros* from these *caballos cimarrones* to tame and hunt them as they hunt the *jabalí* [peccary] and other wild beasts." [3] In the 18th century, Spanish travelers in Texas were using *alzado* as a synonym for *mesteño*,[4] but the word did not survive in popular usage.

In 1537, the Spanish government established the Mesta in New Spain, where it was reorganized in 1574. It passed laws regulating the branding of cattle and horses, disposal of unbranded stock, roundups, theft of livestock, slaughter houses, etc., but its influence was restricted and temporary, and never touched the frontiers.[5] The king, followed by the Mexican government, claimed all mustang cattle and horses, just as states of the American Union now claim game animals. Law defined *mesteñas* as wild, estrayed, branded stock, the owner potentially ascertainable, in contradistinction to *mostrencas* (or *mostrencos*), unbranded, wild, and ownerless.[6] In popular use, however, *mesteña* overcame the legal term.

The government disposed of its mustang stock by taxing the captors two bits (*dos reales*) per head. At Nacogdoches, San

June 17, east of the Colorado River, on San Antonio–Nacogdoches road, "immense herds of horses." June 20, on prairies west of the Trinity River, "passed through several herds of *mustangs* [my italics] or wild horses." In his journal-narrative of the 1807 "Tour through the Interior Parts of New Spain," Pike notes time and again wild horses up the Arkansas River and in Texas, but the entry for June 20 is the only one in which he uses the word *mustang*.

Antonio, and other outposts, the government maintained a *Fondo de Mesteñas*, Mustang Fund. The money was kept in a designated box. Frequently it was about all the money that a provincial post had. On October 6, 1807, for instance, officials at Nacogdoches took 2510 pesos out of the box for government expenses. The fund was often used to bribe Indians against running off domestic stock.[7]

The law required mustang hunters to obtain licenses from the alcalde within whose jurisdiction they lived. It limited the time for running wild horses to the period from the first of October to the first of March. During this period, colts were ripe for branding and the breeding season had hardly begun. Many Spanish-Mexican citizens saw no reason why they should pay for licenses. Some wanted to be out mustanging the year round, just as old-time hunters stalked deer the year round, law or no law. How many men anywhere have made a full rendition of invisible property for taxes? The *mesteñero* (mustanger) could brand an animal and the government, residing as far away as the throne of Heaven, would never know.

After Texas became a republic and then a state, the lawmakers continued with few changes the Spanish-Mexican laws regulating mustanging.[8] An honest frontiersman would post description of any wild branded horse he captured, and, if nobody claimed it, receive a fourth of what it brought at public auction. Many county lines existed only on paper, and mustangers generally paid no more attention to them than the mustangs paid.

In 1596, while waiting on the Río Nazas in Durango for *mañana* to come, before leading his colonial expedition into New Mexico, Oñate wrote the viceroy that during a period of thirty days more than 300 horses and mules, about a fifth of his animals, had strayed away. The country was so immense (*tan larga*), he said, and so full of wild mares (*llena de yeguas cimar-*

[96]

ronas), with which the strays ran, that he feared being left afoot.[9]

Ninety years later, according to negative evidence so strong that it is positive, wild horses did not exist anywhere north of the Rio Grande. Although La Salle and then Spaniards and other Frenchmen in search of him found a limited number of horses among Indians in eastern Texas, they did not report a single wild horse. Spanish occupation of the territory made wild horses inevitable, and as New Mexico furnished horses for the initial mounting of the Plains Indians, Texas became the main center of mustang increase.*

Late in March, 1689, General Alonso de León set out from Monclova in Coahuila with 114 men, including priests, muleteers and servants, and 720 horses and mules, of which 85 were loaded with packs. On the night of April 9, east of the San Antonio River, the horse herd stampeded. At daylight, 102 were missing, but by riding all the next day, which was Easter Sunday, De León's men brought them in from "various points." At night a week later on the Guadalupe River, the caballada stampeded again. This time 36 head were left to range free over the wide

* According to tradition (given me by Patricia Fent Ross of Mexico City, author of *Made in Mexico* and other books), the first horse to run feral on the American mainland was the brown mare's colt that had been foaled on ship not long before Cortés landed with his sixteen horses and set out to loot the Aztecs. The coastal marshes and woods afforded poor pasturage for the horses. By the time the caravan had climbed to Jalapa, the cold winds coming down after dark from the everlasting snow and ice of Orizaba, 18,000 feet high to the south, made the nights bitter to all thin-blooded exposed creatures. Climbing on through the rocks, the Spaniards met snow and freezing weather. Somewhere in the region the colt was left behind. Perhaps the mare was killed — like another from which the overwhelmed Indians severed the head and sent it around villages to show that horses were mortal.

Anyway, as tradition goes, said to be fortified by documents in Jalapa, soon after the Conquest, Spaniards as well as natives saw a horse running with deer on the lower slopes of Orizaba. An *hacendado* captured it and placed it with his other horses. It could not be tamed, however, and before long escaped and rejoined the deer with which it had grown up. Legend, adding itself to tradition, says that it is still occasionally seen in the wild lands, the sight of it bringing good luck to the glimpser. The color of it is white.

[97]

country. It is likely that the expedition's horse stock included mares as well as stallions.

Certainly De León's second expedition took mares. In the spring of 1690, accompanied by Father Massanet, he set forth to establish a mission on the eastern border of Texas, near the Louisiana line. According to the missionary, the soldiers "were for the most part tailors, shoemakers, masons and miners" who could not catch the horses they were to ride and who, once mounted, could not manage them. "Besides, their saddles could not have been worse." De León had orders to take 200 head of stock cattle and 400 head of stock horses to the mission site. On the night of April 17, between the Frio and Medina rivers, the horses stampeded; one infers from the record that 126 head were not recovered. At the mission, nine of "the king's horses," twenty cows and two yoke of oxen (bulls) were left. Many more must have been left along the route.[10]

The next year, 1691, Terán's reinforcing expedition lost 60 stampeded horses on the Rio Grande and 75 more on the Guadalupe River.[11] The mission was a failure, but before it was abandoned, St. Denis, the romantic Frenchman who reported lead mines never seen by anybody else, testified that "thousands of cows, bulls, stallions and mares" covered the surrounding ranges.[12]

Nacogdoches became the main Spanish ranching center east of San Antonio. In 1807 the commandant of the post reported that stampedes of garrison horses into the "infinite herds of mustangs" running over the country had, along with swarms of insects and poor grass, left his soldiers virtually afoot. The soldiers, he said, were riding down what horses they had, chasing runaways. Two hundred garrison troopers were out one day horsehunting. They would be better off with one horse and one mule each, fed lightly and kept in a herd under a bell mare. An official report to the Spanish crown in 1811 declared that largely on account of mismanagement the horses over all Texas had gone *mesteña*. The inhabitants of San Antonio were neglecting corn-growing to take hides from the "innumerable manadas of wild horses and wild cattle" for contraband trade with Louisiana.[13]

The reservoir for Spanish horses, as of cattle, in Texas was a great triangle of land between lines running from San Antonio southwest to the Rio Grande and southeast to the Gulf of Mexico. To set up the first mission settlement at San Antonio (1718), seven families, a military detachment and missionaries brought 548 head of horse stock, not counting mules, besides cattle, sheep, goats and chickens. Other missions, along with privately owned ranches, were established down the San Antonio River. Domesticated animals left on the range constantly reverted to the wild. Moved in herds, they frequently stampeded to freedom. For example, on August 11, 1806, a herd of 736 horses from Mexico was stampeded not far from San Antonio by shouts of men hunting *jabalí* (peccaries) with dogs, and 136 got away for good.[14]

A herd of horses, whether on trail or grazing grounds, was more likely to stampede than a herd of cattle. Being of a much more nervous temperament than cattle, horses are more subject to "panic terror," the Greek term for stampede. A terrified herd would run into anything, beating to death, trampling upon, smothering and mutilating each other with the madness that possesses a crowd of human beings rushing out of a burning theater. Stampeding horses would quickly disperse, whereas a cattle herd would run together for a long while or split up only in large units. A herd of mixed stallions and mares would scatter more widely than one of geldings or of only mares. Losses from horse stampedes were sometimes almost incredible. Out of a herd of five hundred that left Buenos Aires about 1830 for recruiting an army unit, only twenty head were delivered. The whiff of a panther one night, a clap of thunder another night, and something else the next had kept the herd running.[15]

Yet losses from stampedes were light compared with those from Indian raids and gradual straying as herds increased. Mustangs on a range of domesticated stock stole more insidiously and constantly than Indians.

When José de Escandón began establishing settlements along the Rio Grande in 1747, he found wild horses existing, but not numerous, on the Texas side. Eleven years later, an official inspector reported thousands of mares, horses, mules and burros in herds between Reynosa and Laredo. In 1804, a Spanish judge who rode from Reynosa to inspect land on the lower Nueces River reported mustangs so numerous that settlers could not raise horses among them; all went away with the wild herds. The only improvements he found on the land were ruined mustang pens.[16]

Long before this, mustangs in the Rio Grande–Nueces River territory had by sheer numbers become the wonder of travelers. On maps of Texas drawn early in the last century this vacant space was merely marked "Vast Herds of Wild Horses" or "Wild Horses." In 1777, Fray Morfi, a Franciscan missionary and a man of scientific curiosity, made the earliest observations on the multitudes of mustangs that I have found. He kept a diary while traveling with a large military party from Mexico City to San Antonio, Texas.

On December 20, between Monclova, in Coahuila, and the Rio Grande, he came into valleys "covered with *mesteñada caballar*." On December 26, north of the Rio Grande, the *mesteñadas*, or bands of wild horses, he wrote, "are so abundant that their trails make the country, utterly uninhabited by people, look as if it were the most populated in the world. All the grass on the vast ranges has been consumed by them, especially around the waterings." That evening, having ridden ahead of the escort, he waited to unsaddle at the camping place until the cavalry caught up and drove away *una gran manada de mesteños* occupying the grounds. They roped a fine colt.

On December 27, just north of the Nueces, another large band of mustangs ran into the remuda driven by the troops and took 70 horses with them. A horseman jerked off his saddle, so as to lighten the weight, and after a long run bareback, recovered all but six of the escaped animals. The six, presumably, remained free the remainder of their lives. That afternoon Morfi estimated that one congregation of wild horses along the route numbered 3000 head. A freezing norther was sweeping over the country, and when Morfi and other stiffened riders dismounted among coma trees to make a fire for warming themselves, a band of mustangs rushed up to them out of curiosity. While chasing it away, soldiers roped a very beautiful mare and colt. The next morning, mustangs surrounding the campers had so much interest in their mounts that considerable effort had to be exerted to scare them away. They kept the water muddy in ponds where they drank and pawed.

As Morfi traveled on north, he noted that between the Atascosa and Medina rivers mustang horses gave way to mustang cattle, "so numerous that they had no number." On returning to Mexico in January, 1778, over the same route, he saw again the great *mesteñadas*, intermixed with manadas of antelope, deer and wild turkeys, but of the wild creatures — the only creatures on the land — the wild horses were the most striking and the most beautiful.[17]

In 1828, the Mexican government sent a commission to report on the boundaries between the United States and Mexico, of which Texas was still a part. Three *científicos* accompanying it made notes on the fauna, flora, and physiography of the country.[18]

Approaching Laredo on the Rio Grande from the south, they "saw herds of deer and a great number of wild horses and mares that pasture peacefully on the immense deserted plains." On the hundred and fifty miles between Laredo and San Antonio there was not a habitation. Travelers over it were so infrequent that in some places the road was too grassed over to be distinguishable. The *grandes llanuras* — the great prairies, later to be a brush thicket — "were covered with deer; the margins of the rivers abounded in wild turkeys, and the whole land in *caballos silvestres.*"

At camp on La Parida, south of the Nueces, the chroniclers were hearing their first bullfrog. "At sunset and in the silence of night is when the creature bellows, interrupted only by the arrival of *caballos salvajes* to drink, according to their custom early in the night. . . . The prairies are crossed and recrossed by a network of mustang trails that lead nowhere. . . . Indians reduce the herds of both deer and mustangs."

In prickly pear country and on rolling hills between the Nueces and the Frio rivers, "Immense herds of *mesteños* presented themselves in all directions. After camp was made, soldiers, always eager to chase these animals, roped two mares, but because of their old age freed them. First, however, they roached their manes and tails so that anybody who sees them henceforth will know they are valueless." Three days later, the soldiers "roped two colts following their mothers amidst large bands of *mesteños*. They butchered one and at night ate the tender and savory meat."

The travelers found "bulls and cows, though not so numerous as *mesteños*, reverted to primitive wildness. In the regions around San Antonio *mesteño* cattle, along with wild burros, horses and coyotes, flee at the approach of man. In winter time buffaloes migrate to these ranges from the north, but the wild horses live there the year round."

Ulysses S. Grant was no romanticist, but in youth he used to stand for long whiles looking intently upon horses — looking into their natures. In taming horses, always with kindness and patience, and in riding skill he was perhaps as good a horseman as ever came out of West Point. When General Taylor's army broke camp at the mouth of the Nueces River in March, 1846, to invade Mexico, Lieutenant Grant accompanied it on a freshly caught mustang, priced at three dollars.

"A few days out from Corpus Christi," he wrote long afterwards, "the immense herd of wild horses that ranged at that time between the Nueces and the Rio Grande was seen directly in advance of the head of the column and but a few miles off. It was the very band from which the horse I was riding had been captured but a few weeks before. The column halted for a rest, and a number of officers, myself among them, rode out two or three miles to see the extent of the herd. The country was a rolling prairie, and, from the higher ground, the vision was obstructed only by the earth's curvature. As far as the eye could reach to our right, the herd extended. To the left, it extended equally. There was no estimating the animals in it; I have no idea that they could all have been corralled in the State of Rhode Island, or Delaware, at one time. If they had been, they would have been so thick that the pasturage would have given out the first day. People who saw the Southern herd of buffalo, fifteen or twenty years ago, can appreciate the size of the Texas band of wild horses in 1846." [19]

In October of that year another traveler over the prairies between Corpus Christi and the Rio Grande estimated one aggregation of mustangs at 5000 head, though his companions put the number at 7000. "On our approach," he says, "the stragglers and sentinels on flanks and outposts retreated to the main body, which, almost as if by magic formed on a high piece of ground, with all the precision and regularity of a well-trained troop of cavalry. Each band was headed by its own leader." Between itself and the bands on the right and on the left of it, each "preserved an open space about equal to that occupied. This was, in Mexican phrase, their 'wheeling distance.' When we approached within four hundred yards, the signal of ' 'Bout face' and off was given. . . . For three miles they were in full view, tossing their proud necks and flowing manes into the air and coursing with the speed of the wind." [20]

In 1847, Thomas A. Dwyer, weary of practicing law in London and Dublin but still delighting in Horace and Byron, established a horse ranch on the lower Nueces River. He bought native mares on the Rio Grande and crossed them with blooded jacks and stallions. Setting down some of his recollections a quarter of a century later, he said:

"I well remember when I first came to Texas seeing thousands and tens of thousands of wild horses running in immense herds all over the western country, as far as the eye or telescope could sweep the horizon. The whole country seemed to be running! While traveling through it, I have had my gentle pack mules cut off by mustangs circling and circling around us and gradually closing in until, by a rush, they darted away with them. . . .

"Time and again I have had to send out my best mounted men to scare away the immense masses of mustangs (charging around and threatening to rush over us), by yelling and firing at them. Then the mustangs would wheel and go thundering away as Byron grandly describes the hundred thousand wild Ukraine horses in *Mazeppa*. . . . The supplies of wild cattle and horses then seemed so abundant as to be inexhaustible." [21]

While with a company of rangers pursuing Indians into the "Mustang Desert" along in the '40s, John C. Duval, who had escaped the Goliad Massacre and was to write the extraordinary narrative of his experiences, saw "a drove of mustangs so large that it took us fully an hour to pass it, although they were travelling at a rapid rate in a direction nearly opposite to ours. As far as the eye could extend on a dead level prairie, nothing was visible except a dense mass of horses, and the trampling of their hoofs sounded like the roar of the surf on a rocky coast." Again, in a narrative somewhat fictionized as to characters and episodes but not as to nature, Duval described this mass of mustangs as strung out for "four or five miles." Bigfoot Wallace, as quoted by Duval in another book, found that while his Virginia kinfolk swallowed all his whoppers about "cow killers" and other deadly varmints in Texas, they would not believe he had seen 30,000 or 40,000 wild horses in one herd.[22] Perhaps that is "too much pepper."

In December, 1852, John R. Bartlett was proceeding with a wagon train from the Rio Grande to Corpus Christi. As he gazed one day across the trackless grass, "the prairie near the horizon seemed to be moving, with long undulations, like the waves of the ocean." A telescope revealed "the whole prairie towards the horizon alive with mustangs." Before long they were nearing the wagons, the herd "extending as far as the eye could reach." The great stream of wild runners stampeded some of the mules. The wagons had to be placed in corral formation and the wheels locked; the men even thought it necessary to fire at the "avalanche of wild animals sweeping like a tornado" in order to deflect it.[23]

For more than a hundred years the far-stretched pampas of South America supported more wild horses than North America ever contained at one time. On a long ride made in 1744, Thomas Falkner, the English Jesuit, saw the *baguales* * "in such vast numbers that during a fortnight they continually surrounded

---

* Until recently historians propagated a myth as to the origin of these horses. It is true that Pedro de Mendoza landed horses at the mouth of La Plata River and in 1541 sailed away with his starving people. As Madeline W. Nichols proves (in "The Spanish Horse of the Pampas," *The American Anthropologist* for 1939, 41, 119–129), the Spaniards would never, as the myth goes, have released five mares and seven stallions to breed upon the prairies while they themselves were starving to the extremity of eating shoe leather. Yet when Buenos Aires was re-established in 1580, wild horses abounded on the adjacent pampas. They were called *baguales*.

me. Sometimes they passed by, in thick troops, on full speed, for two or three hours together, during which time it was with great difficulty that I and the four Indians who accompanied me preserved ourselves from being run over and trampled to pieces by them. At other times, I have passed over this same country without seeing any of them. . . . They were wont to go from place to place, against the current of the winds." A half century following Falkner's rides, the naturalist Azara reported congregations of *baguales* amounting "without exaggeration to ten thousand," though the "squadrons" composing any such herd maintained their identity under dominating stallions. During the first quarter of the 19th century as many as 500,000 of the superfluous feral and semi-feral mares in Argentina were slaughtered annually.[24]

The Columbia River basin held many wild horses. About 1816, in the region dominated by the Nez Percé Indians, Ross Cox estimated "from seven hundred to a thousand" in one band. Some of his fellow explorers reported bands of from 3000 to 4000 head in the Snake Indian country; one of 200 head verified by Cox sounds more realistic.[25] The San Joaquin valley of California was intensively stocked, with perhaps 20,000 mustangs.[26] They were numerous along the Arkansas; large numbers ranged on other areas of the plains and up from the coastal prairies of eastern Texas; but nowhere else in North America were there the multitudes that gave their name to the Mustang Desert between the drainages of the Nueces and the Rio Grande.

When Texas won the war against Mexico in 1836, titles to land owned under the Spanish and then the Mexican government were confirmed by the new republic, but — without official action — the horses and cattle belonging to Mexican ranches between the San Antonio River and the Rio Grande became virtually free to raiders. Some rancheros abandoned their claims, fleeing behind the defeated Mexican army across the Rio Grande.

The swift raiders, called "Cow Boys," took only the more manageable animals, leaving the others to run wilder than ever. The sparse English-speaking settlements were far east of "the Spanish country." Until the end of the Mexican War in 1848, wild horses multiplied, reaching about this time their numerical climax. Even after tens of thousands had been captured and killed, many remained until the land was all fenced in.

The coming together of many bands was only occasional. Perhaps fright, by man, wolf or panther, converged the runners oftener than any other cause. "A badly scared bunch would generally run towards any other animals in sight, whether antelopes, wild cattle, or another bunch of mustangs." As late as 1881, in a great brush-rimmed prairie between the Nueces and Frio rivers, John Young sat on his horse and watched "fully a thousand mustangs" running together from many directions ahead of a big roundup of cattle. "When they left the plain where they had gathered, they all left at once in one direction. The rumble from their running was deafening and they fairly shook the earth. A stampede of five times as many cattle could not have caused such disturbance." [27]

Sheer animation, contagious curiosity, some special urge of the herd instinct, and other factors no doubt drew running bands together. Whether the bands maintained their identity during a run or disintegrated in mass flight, after a run was over they separated for normal pastoral life. Every stallion commander knew his own, and each could be seen cutting out of the general herd what belonged to him. [28]

Never anything like so numerous as the tens of millions of buffaloes, the mustangs ranged more widely. Buffaloes barely reached the coastal prairies and did not compete for grass in the wild horse country between San Antonio and the Rio Grande. The mustangs browsed, though not like deer. Swampy land ruined their feet and stunted their bodies. Their instinct was to get away from sappy grasses and soggy ground, for "your water is a sore decayer" of hoofs as well as of "your whoreson dead body." But mustangs dragged their mud-matted tails into woods of eastern Texas and northern Louisiana where no buffalo ever pawed. Apaches snared them in mountain canyons hundreds of miles beyond the western range of buffaloes, and to this day a few of their crossbred descendants manage to exist in the sage lands of Nevada.

No scientific estimate of their numbers was made. Plainsmen in the '70s guessed the number between the Palo Duro in the Texas Panhandle and the Salt Fork of the Brazos at 50,000 head. The guess was not based on any system of computation. All guessed numbers are mournful to history. My own guess is that at no time were there more than a million mustangs in Texas and no more than a million others scattered over the remainder of the West. Wherever they ranged, they were exceedingly visible. Mention of them by travelers over the plains is frequent, but the total number enumerated by many a chronicler during a month's time is surprisingly low.*

* For example, the journal of Captain Nathan Boone, U. S. A., kept during a tour over the prairies of the Southwest, May 14–July 31, 1843, has the following entries pertaining to mustangs. June 23, after mentioning buffalo several times, Boone saw in the upper Arkansas River country, "perhaps 10,000 Buffalo feeding on the plain below as far as the eye could reach. Here we saw a herd of wild horses of a dozen in number — They ran off through the herds of buffalo, which did not seem to mind them." June 24, "Started a wild horse to day, and one of the officers chasing it fell in with a herd of about 30. Saw plenty of Buffalo to day, and Elk came near our camp this evening." June 25 and 26, buffalo. June 28, "Saw buffalo and one herd of wild horses." June 29–July 11, in roughs of upper Cimarron and Canadian rivers, buffalo generally sparse; no horses until July 12: "Grass excellent — Saw 7 wild horses." Louis Pelzer, *Marches of the Dragoons*, Iowa City, 1917, 214–227.

VII

WILD AND FREE

NO ONE who conceives him as only a potential servant to man can apprehend the mustang. The true conceiver must be a true lover of freedom — a person who yearns to extend freedom to all life. Halted in animated expectancy or running in abandoned freedom, the mustang was the most beautiful, the most spirited and the most inspiriting creature ever to print foot on the grasses of America. When he stood trembling with fear before his captor, bruised from falls by the restrictive rope, made submissive by choking, clogs, cuts and starvation, he had lost what made him so beautiful and free. Illusion and reality had alike been destroyed. Only the spirited are beautiful. The antlered buck always appears nobler leaping the brush than he measures lifeless upon the ground. One out of every three mustangs captured in southwest Texas was expected to die before they were tamed. The process of breaking often broke the spirits of the other two.[1]

Out on the plains, Josiah Gregg relates, his party "succeeded in separating a gay looking stallion from a herd of *mesteñas*, upon which he immediately joined our *caballada* and was lazoed by a Mexican. As he curvetted at the end of the rope or stopped and gazed majestically at his subjectors, his symmetrical proportions attracted the attention of all; jockeys at once valued him at five hundred dollars. It appeared that he had before been tamed, for he soon submitted to the saddle, and in a few days dwindled down to scarce a twenty-dollar hackney."[2]

The aesthetic value of the mustang topped all other values. The sight of wild horses streaming across the prairies made even the most hardened of professional mustangers regret putting an end to their liberty. The mustang was essentially a prairie animal, like the antelope, and like it would not go into a wooded bottom or a canyon except for water and shelter. Under the pursuit of man he took to the brush and to the roughest mountains, adapting himself like the coyote, but his nature was for prairies — the place for free running, free playing, free tossing of head and mane, free vision. He relied upon motion, not covert, for the maintenance of liberty.

One early morning on the south plains of Texas, a surveying party[3] saw a great troop of mustangs galloping towards them fully two miles away. Not a tree or a swag broke the grassed level, but from pure wantonness of vitality the oncoming line, following the leaders, deflected here and there into a sinuous curve. Coming nearer, the phalanx charged straight. A hundred and fifty yards away, it halted, with a front of about a hundred horses. Heads tossing high, nostrils dilated, the wild and free stood in arrested animation. The bright light of the rising sun brought out details of prominent eye, tapered nose, rounded breast, and slender legs on small feet. It glistened on sleek hairs of bay and sorrel, brown and grullo, roan, dun, and gray, with here and there black, white and paint. Now with loud snorts, they wheeled and dashed away like a flight of sportive blackbirds, adding symmetry of speed to symmetry of form, contour of individual blending with contour of earth-skimming mass.

Only by blotting out the present can one now see those wild horses of the prairies. They have gone with the winds of vanished years. They carried away a life and a spirit that no pastoral prosperity could in coming times re-present.

Mustangs never migrated from north to south and back like the buffaloes.* Nor did they migrate sporadically in the manner of squirrels, wolves and some other quadrupeds. They did not drift before winter winds as Longhorn cattle on the open range sometimes drifted. Had they habitually kept together in vast droves, depletion of grass would have made constant change of grazing grounds necessary. Drouths and scarcity of grass from excess horse population caused irregular shifting. If rain fell on a restricted area, mustangs from far away would find the fresh grass. Perhaps the movement of bands near it communicated what they had sensed to other bands. With a continent over which to roam, every band of mustangs habitually kept to a range seldom more than twenty miles across. Charles Goodnight, who during the Civil War scouted over the Texas plains far beyond all frontiers, told me that whenever he saw a mesquite bush he expected to find water not more than five miles away. The then sparse mesquites were planted by beans carried through the stomachs of wild horses, and the horses did not habitually graze out more than five miles from water. Unless severely disturbed, they watered at the same spot day after day. Even if ranging along a river, they would walk miles to come down the bank at a certain place and drink at a certain spot.

* "The genuine wild species is migratory, proceeding northward in summer to a considerable distance, and returning early in autumn. The mixed races [feral horses] wander rather in the direction of the pastures than to a point of the compass." — Charles Hamilton Smith, *Horses* (Vol. XX in Jardine's *The Naturalist's Library*), Edinburgh and London, 1854, 165.

While out of view, they often smelled travelers and their horses and came pellmell to investigate. If they could see but not smell strangers, they were not satisfied until they had circled into their odor. "Their playfulness rather than their fears seemed to be excited by our appearance," one early explorer wrote. "We often saw them more than a mile distant leaping and curvetting, involved by a cloud of dust, which they seemed to delight in raising." [4] They were free to satisfy curiosity. "When our horses were feeding fettered about our encampments," observed John B. Wyeth in Oregon, "the wild horses would come down to them and seem to examine them as if counting them." Occasionally one horse — "the spy" — came alone from a band to inspect strangers and snort the signal for flight. [5]

The snort was often startling, audible hundreds of yards away. In cowboy language, the mustang had "rollers in his nose." Mexican soldiers on the road from Laredo to San Antonio managed to rope a slow, pregnant mare out of a band of mustangs and brought her to the evening camp. "She made so much noise snorting" that nobody could sleep until she was released. [6]

"The vulture's eye," wrote W. H. Hudson, "with all the advantage derived from the vulture's vast elevation above the scene surveyed, is not so far-reaching as the sense of smell in the pampa horse." Many times in desert country, range horses have smelled distant water and saved their riders. While Zenas Leonard and his men were perishing from thirst and heat on a California desert, their Spanish horses suddenly became unmanageable. The crazed men were bent on going one direction; the horses persisted in going the opposite. They made straight over rough ground for a stream of clear water, hidden from the eye until the animals were almost upon it. [7] Yet there are perhaps more instances of water-finding by burros and mules than by horses.*

* "In the spring of 1849, W. C. S. Smith and three other men on their way to California gold, landed at the lower end of Baja California and set out over

Among horses, as among men, the primitive and the highly cultivated have in common some pronounced qualities that are dead or dormant in the great stretch of mediocrity lying between. The keen sense of smell in feral horses of Spanish blood was a mark of both primitive and Arabian ancestry. One day an officer of the military school at Saumur accompanied a lady through the grounds. An old Arabian horse that she caressed demonstrated his pleasure in the perfume of her handkerchief. She came no more, but the officer often visited her. If he neared the old horse after a visit, the horse would neigh and otherwise show delight at sensing the aroma associated with the lady. Except when the officer brought that aroma with him he gave no notice of sensory stimulation.[8]

Careful mustangers avoided altering their odor by a change of clothes, especially of underwear, while following a band of wild horses and trying to get them used to their presence. A tamer who changed clothes while breaking a captured mustang

---

that desert land. An extract from Smith's diary emphasizes the burro's sense of smell.

"'On the 9th [of May] the trail was over a dry desert where tracks left but a dimple in the hot sands. Neither water nor grass all day. At night we threw down on the plain, tied the animals to cactus. We divided and drank our last few swallows of bitter water. We could not eat, could not sleep from thirst. We started in the morning early. The sun came up as a great ball of fire. To the east was a range of hills, the only chance for water. We traveled for them. About noon, two horses laid down and died. We came to a dry cañon. The heat was intense and our tongues were so swollen we could scarcely speak. Presently the cañon grew narrow. A high rock threw a few feet of shade on the burning sand. All, men and animals, crowded into this shade, but this would not do. Van and I drove the animals out. Nye and Miller lay down under the rock and could not come. There was no time to lose. It was simply find water or die. We left them and we had not gone far when a Jackass — one we had brought from the Rancho Colorado — pricked up his ears, gave a loud bray and started on a run, square off, up the steep side of the cañon. All the other animals followed pell mell up the hillside, over the ridge and out of sight in a cloud of dust. Van and I climbed slowly after them to the top and there looking down we saw a little green valley, a brook, and the mules and horses standing in the water drinking. . . . The instinct of a Jackass [had] saved us.'" — Robert Glass Cleland, *A History of California: The American Period*, New York, 1939, 492.

For mule instinct for water on desert journeys, see Frances Fuller Victor, *The River of the West*, Hartford, Conn., 1870, 145.

would have to do everything over again. After Californians ran mustangs into a pen, they would dismount and walk around and around the fence in order to accustom the animals to human odor before entering to rope them.[9] A Texas rancher whom I knew rode a primitive-natured horse that was gentle for him but for nobody else. One day after saddling the horse, he drew on a pair of new leggins before mounting. The horse would not allow him near until he had removed the foreign-smelling leather. If Indians on a horse-raiding expedition killed and ate a horse, they washed themselves thoroughly in sand or in mud and water before approaching the enemy's camp. The horses were so sensitive to the smell of blood and fat of their own kind that they would not allow a man bearing it to come near them.[10]

The pampas were perforated by burrowings of the viscacha very much as the plains were by prairie dog holes. Captain Head, vivid reporter of Argentine life, wrote: "I have often wondered how the wild horses could gallop about as they do in the dark. I believe they avoid the holes by smelling them, for in riding across the country in darkness that prevented my seeing my horse's ears I have constantly felt him, in his gallop, start a foot or two to the right or the left, as if he had trod upon a serpent, which I conceive, was to avoid one of these holes." At a narrow pass of the Andes, slippery and covered with loose stones, Captain Head observed the lead pack mule of his outfit "literally smelling his way." [11] I have seen a Mexican mule in the Sierra Madre do the same thing and have watched horses both ridden and loose test boggy ground with their noses while being forced into it. What makes the hole of a rodent detectable to their noses may be the smell of the rodent itself.

About 1830, Gideon Lincecum, then living in the wilderness of Mississippi, hunted on a small black Indian pony that "could track a deer equal to the best trained hound." [12] An old range man of the Texas brush country told me that he once had a Spanish horse that often gave notice of a rattlesnake smelled many yards away. In a very arid, rough part of Sonora I once went javelina (peccary) hunting with a Mexicanized Indian who claimed to be able to smell the animals as well as his curs could. Looking at the curs, I could believe him. I won't say that he could not smell as keenly as the little brown Mexican pony he rode, but when he announced javelinas in the brush, off to one side from where the dogs were hunting, I noticed the pointing of his horse's ears. Elsewhere I have told of old-time Spanish brush horses that could trail a maverick with hound-like accuracy. John Chapman of Wyoming lost a saddled horse and a year later found him running with a herd of elk, still wearing the skeleton of the saddle. He had grown very wild. The bell mare for Chapman's pack outfit had a young colt. He staked the mare as near the elk as possible, led the colt off some distance and hobbled it with gunny sacks. The animated nickering between mare and colt eventually brought the wild horse to them, away from the elk. He found a cupful of salt near the mare, and after two days of maneuvering by Chapman, followed mare and colt into a corral. He came to be noted as an elk-hunter. He could smell elk and would indicate his recognition of the smell as soon as he got in their range.[13]

Frontiersmen claimed that mustangs were alarmed by the smell of Indians. Indians took warning from mustang behavior in the vicinity of white men. Actually, horses used to the odor of either white man or Indian were alarmed by that of the other. "The gaucho horse manifests the greatest terror at any Indian invasion," Hudson wrote. "Long before the marauders reach the settlement (often when they are still a whole day's journey from it) the range horses take the alarm and come wildly flying in. The gauchos maintain that the horses smell the Indians. I believe they are right, for when passing a distant Indian camp, from which the wind blew, the horses driven before me have suddenly taken fright and run away, leading me a chase of many miles."[14]

Many a pioneer Texan relied on his horses — American as well as Spanish — to give warning against Indians. One family on the

Sabinal River was awakened repeatedly at night over a period of years by a horse that would run up on the porch and paw and neigh at the smell of Indians. A few frontiersmen with the help of friendly Indians trained horses to fear Indian odor.[15]

It was not solely to detect enemies and water, to trail dim scents and locate far-off oases of grass that the nostrils of the mustang worked. When spring opened and the south wind blew over new grass and nectared flowers, he inhaled the air with a gusto and exhaled it in elated whinneyings, now delicate, now expansive, that plainly bespoke enjoyment of the earth's fragrance.

The mustang's eyes were as alert as his nostrils. The only way to approach a band that had been hunted was against the wind and under cover. Any rider who sighted a lookout mustang silhouetted on high ground two or three miles away knew that he had been seen. Indians claimed that if a man crept up a ridge to look through grass or bushes at wild horses in the valley below, a sentinel would detect his presence. Even antelopes took warning from mustang behavior.

One need not have observed mustangs to know that they were sociable; sociability is a characteristic of the species. In my mind's eye I see Snip and Snap, a pair of bays, standing side by side, head to tail, each switching flies and gnats from his own rump and his comrade's face. I see Canelo, a meek red roan, freshly unsaddled, approach the remuda, whence his devoted friend, a broad-hipped dun as yellow as ripe corn, steps forth nickering low to greet him. Then after they have affectionately rubbed noses and said something no man will ever know, I see the two grazing in a harmonious contentment that memory makes a benediction. I see a narrow-chested, nervous little bay Spanish pony named Cardinal, after being released into the horse pasture, shortening his drink to trail down his fellows. He trots with nose to ground, smelling tracks, smelling dung. He nickers now and then, but there is no response. Nor does any horse notice him when he approaches the bunch, but fulfillment of his desire to be with his kind sets him at ease.

A solitary mustang seemed always to be seeking company. Now and then one took up with buffaloes. The chronicler of Long's expedition made this entry in August, 1820: "A few wild horses had been observed in the course of the day, and towards evening one was seen following the party, but keeping at a distance. At night, after our horses had been staked near the camp, we perceived him still lingering about, and at length approaching the tent so close that we had hopes of capturing him alive. We stationed a man with a noose rope in the top of a cotton-wood tree, under which we tied a few of our horses, but this plan did not succeed.

"On the following morning, one of our hunters discovered the horse standing asleep under the shade of a tree, shot him, and hastened to camp with the intelligence. We had all suffered so severely from hunger, that we ate greedily of this unaccustomed food. Yet we felt a little regret at killing a beautiful animal who had followed us and then lingered with a sort of confidence about our camp." [16]

A man-driven caballada was sometimes joined by a lone stallion. One morning in 1884 a bright chestnut stallion with head thrown up and "long mane and tail floating out in the air like liquid gold" dashed into a herd of 500 Spanish mares and colts and a few stallions trailing north from southern Texas across the Indian Territory. He whipped four stallions and virtually took control of the herd before cowboys roped, threw, deprided and then cast him out. [17]

The habit an occasional ranch horse has of depositing his dung at a certain spot is a relic of primitive ancestry. The range of the aboriginal horse called Prjevalsky's in the Great Gobi Desert was indicated by "enormous heaps of dung" along trails leading to water. Guanacos in South America heaped their dung day after day into mounds that measured up to eight feet in diameter.

Traveling across the pampas, Azara marveled at bulky cones of wild horse dung lining trails for leagues. He counted up to fifty accretions in some cones. A generation after him, Darwin was struck by the "richly manured" grass along the "channels of communication" across the pampas. To riders across the plains in early days, mounds of freshly-topped manure were the main mustang sign. Washington Irving was too elegant to mention the crudity in his account of mustangs, in *A Tour on the Prairies*, but Henry Leavitt Ellsworth, who accompanied him, noted "pyramids of manure often 2 or 3 feet high." Zebulon Pike, ahead of Irving, saw "ground covered with horse dung for miles around." Campers on New Mexico plains west of the buffalo range burned wild horse dung instead of the usual "prairie coal." One forty-niner found piles "measuring several bushels" each. Stallions were the main accumulators. A stallion's addition to his private "pyramid" was a notice to other stallions that he had been there. He looked and smelled for notices left by other stallions.[18]

No English word translates *querencia* (from *querer*, to love). It denotes not only the haunt, the lair, the stomping ground of animals, but their place-preference for certain functions. Some attachments to the *querencia* remain a kind of mystery. In their primitive state in the Rocky Mountains — before they were hand-fed for the benefit of sportsmen and tourists — bull elk occasionally congregated on certain grounds to shed their antlers. Hummingbirds are among the most astounding migrants of earth and air, but the constant adherence of one rare species to its *querencia* is as extraordinary as the longest flight of other species. On Chimborazo, the tallest mountain of Ecuador, more than 20,000 feet high, lives a vivid hummingbird known to ornithology as Chimborazon Hill Star. It is found nowhere else in the world. No example of the bird has been seen even an hour's flight from Chimborazo. Its only change is to range down the mountain in cold weather, ascending with ascending temperature. The composite flower on which it seems to feed exclusively is found on other mountains.[19]

Who will explain this *querencia*, this attachment of a parcel of living flesh for a particular parcel of earth? For ten thousand years the dying guanaco in southern Patagonia walked and crawled to certain bone-littered Golgothas on the banks of the Santa Cruz and Gallegos rivers to lie down for the last time. This is not to say that guanacos did not die elsewhere. They did, but they had their *querencia* for death.[20]

Only the sense of being in place gives natural horse or natural man contentment. A range mare drops her colt year after year in the same place. Old-timers of south Texas who had driven horses far north and east used to tell of mares that in the spring came back to their stomping grounds to foal. One fall a rancher named Adams near San Antonio sold a little fifteen-year-old red roan mare to a vaquero to ride to his home in San Luis Potosí, Mexico, 600 miles southward, not a fence or a bridge between. The next April the mare came pacing up to the gate in front of the Adams ranch house and asked to be let in. The other horses, some her own offspring, greeted her with demonstrations of affection. A week later she brought her colt. According to a letter received from the vaquero, the mare had been about three months making the trip home.[21]

In desert fashion, the mustang bathed in sand or other loose earth by rolling. At the same time he was a disturber of the waters, pawing them, pawing also through ice to drink. In swimming rivers, the colt placed itself on the downstream side against its mother, for a breakwater. Sometimes a colt would place its head over the back of an adult animal and float across a stream.[22]

The power of Spanish horses, both mustang and tamed, to go without water has been exaggerated.* Their thirst-resisting

* Exaggeration was a part of their inheritance from Arabia. According to legend, Mohammed was once compelled to lead his army of 20,000 cavalrymen for three days without a drop of water. Towards the end of the third day, he and other leaders saw from a hill a line of trees. Mohammed ordered his trum-

power was, nevertheless, remarkable. Gauchos, on the word of Azara and others, sometimes rode their horses three or four days without food or water. Yet during drouths wild horses of the pampas became so frantic that upon finding a waterhole they piled into it on top of each other, drowning and trampling to death great numbers. At one lake south of Buenos Aires, Azara saw "more than a thousand skeletons of wild horses thus killed." [23]

One dry June my friend Rocky Reagan of the brush country took all the stock, except seven or eight *ladino* horses that could not be caught or shot, out of a 4000-acre pasture in which the dirt tanks, the only source of water, had gone dry. After September rains, he rode into the pasture and found horse tracks; he saw where horses had pawed down the trunks of prickly pear and chewed the fiber for water. Two or three of the horses had perished, but the others were in good condition. During drouths on the open range, some mustangs not only chewed prickly pear but broke through the defenses of the Spanish dagger to eat the

---

peter to blow the order to dismount and loose the all but spent mares so that they could go on to water. They had already smelled it. Twenty thousand released mares set off to drink.

Then arose the alarm of a sudden ambush. "To horse! To horse!" Mohammed's trumpeter blew the order, repeated by other bugles.

But the mares, all of them trained to obey the signal as well as the soldiers were trained, now paid no heed to it. Mad thirst was their only commander. Only five mares responded. They turned in their tracks and came back to their riders, resisting their awful torment.

"The alarm proved to be false and the five mares were at once released again to drink. But they had selected themselves to become breeders of the best Arabian horses of the world. Mohammed took them for his own mount; they became the dams of the greatest equine race the deserts of the world have known." — Theodore A. Dodge, *Riders of Many Lands*, New York, 1903, 408–409.

On an excursion into the desert in 1897, a Soudani assured Wilfrid Scawen Blunt, who wanted to believe him, that at a certain place in Arabia horses of pure blood ran wild. "The Arabs," Blunt reported, "catch them at their watering places in pitfalls or traps which catch them by the leg. They keep these horses tied up fast for three days, then put bits into their mouths and ride them. They can go ten days without water. This he told me in almost the same words as those used by Leo Africanus 400 years ago." — Wilfrid Scawen Blunt, *My Diaries*, New York, 1932, 260.

flowering stalk.²⁴ Many cattle of Spanish blood have survived drouths on water from cactus, but the mouths of horses are generally too tender to overcome the spines. Once while I was riding across the Bolsón de Mapimí, the most forbidding desert of northern Mexico, my guide, a vaquero who had ridden with Pancho Villa, pointed out, many miles away, a low mountain where Villa and a remnant of his men had singed thorns off prickly pear for their horses to eat — and drink.

Over the greater part of North America, the only formidable natural enemies met by the Spanish horses, aside from flies, mosquitoes and screw worms, were the panther and the lobo — the timber, or buffalo, wolf. All horses are afraid of bears, but grizzlies in California, where they were most numerous, killed few horses. Living on the prairies, the wild horses were comparatively free of insect pests.

Wolves in packs followed the buffalo herds, cutting off and bringing down stragglers. They sometimes attacked mustangs also, but horse flesh was never their main diet. After cattle took the place of buffaloes, they continued to prey more on cattle than on horses. The defense of a solitary horse against them was limited. A band upon being threatened formed a circle, heads out, colts in the center. Running away meant exposure of the hindmost to the enemy. They did not run. Safety lay not only in numbers but in standing. A mustang in a threatened bunch would grab an over-bold wolf with his teeth and beat him to death with his front feet. Sometimes the mustang chased the wolf, seized it by the back, tossed it into the air and then stamped it to death. The object of the wolf was to hamstring his quarry.²⁵

Alexander Ross, who knew well the big wolves of the north, asserted that seldom more than two began the assault on a horse, although a score might be in the "gang." These two, he said, "approach a horse in the most playful manner, lying, rolling and frisking about until the too credulous victim is completely put off his guard by curiosity and familiarity." Meantime the other

wolves waited in the distance. Finally one of the two actors slyly neared the horse's head, the other his tail. They sprang at the same instant, "one to the throat, the other to the flank," holding on. "Instead of springing forward or kicking to disengage himself," the horse turned round and round until the forward wolf dashed to the rear and cut the horse's leg sinews. His fall was a signal for the pack to rush to the feast. A wolf attack, according to Alexander Ross, paralyzed a horse's sense in the way that fire paralyzes it. Bewildered in the smoke of a prairie fire, horses "turn round and round, stand and tremble, until they are burned to death." [26]

The panther lives now mostly in broken country, but he was once common in brush and timber contiguous to mustang-inhabited prairies. His natural prey is deer, but once he has eaten horse meat, especially colt, he rates it above any other flesh. In 1926, I was on the Rio Grande with a rancher who that year raised only three or four colts from 400 Spanish mares pasturing on mesa range in Mexico. The others had been devoured by panthers.

This rancher, Asa Jones, has seen many a mare with a clawed face, indicating that she had tried to protect her colt and been slapped back. One of his stallions came in with nose bitten off. Few men have seen the attacks, which are mostly at night, but claw marks indicate that the panther either leaps directly for the head or springs on the back of its victim and, digging hind claws in for a purchase, bites into neck and throat. Some mustang stallions were no doubt aggressive towards panthers.

Years ago now, John E. Hearn, a trapper in the brush on the Texas border, rode an old dun horse — a coyote dun, with line down his back — that had been brought across the Rio Grande and left by tequila smugglers. One day while trailing a panther dragging a steel trap, Hearn cornered the animal in a large clump of prickly pear, shot it dead from the saddle, and then got down and pulled the carcass out onto open ground with the intention of loading it on Old Dun to take in for skinning. Dun was thoroughly gentle, but when led up, he let out a squeal louder than a panther scream and the next instant was pawing, kicking and biting the carcass. Hearn blindfolded him, but he would not allow himself to be loaded with a panther. Hearn rode to a ranch for help. When he returned to the carcass, Old Dun tried to seize it in his mouth like a bulldog. "The way," said Hearn, "to keep a horse from being skittish around panthers is to rub his nose in some panther blood." [27]

One noon, along about 1880, Jim Tanner, another rider of the brush country, staked his cow pony to his saddle horn and, using the saddle as a pillow, lay down under a mesquite tree to take a nap. He awoke to find the horse standing directly over him, legs trembling. On the ground about twenty feet away he saw a panther stretched out, swishing his tail, apparently ready to leap. At movement of the man he vanished. Jim Tanner regarded the horse as a protector; I think he came to his master for protection. I never heard of a mustang's using the tactics against a panther ascribed to a burro.*

Victor Lieb, of Houston, told me that while he was mining in the Sierra Madre of Chihuahua before the Madero revolution of 1910, he became the friend of a little ranchero who owned a stallion named Chinaco. He was a blood red — the color of the uniform worn by Don Porfirio's *rurales* (mounted police), known as *chinacos*. Black points and short coupling bespoke his

---

* In a puma-infested region of the Argentine, A. F. Tschiffely, who made the noted ride on two *criollo* horses from Buenos Aires to Washington, met a settler who claimed that native burros were safe from attack. To demonstrate burro tactics, he tethered one to a bush on a hollow and then with Tschiffely took a stand about a hundred and fifty yards away to watch. The night was bright. For about two hours there was no indication of puma life. Then the burro doubled his legs and rolled over on his side while a puma came into view, creeping towards its intended prey. Soon the burro "rolled right over on his back and started to kick wildly with all-fours, at the same time making noises terrible to hear. The puma made a large circle around him, slowly slunk away and disappeared." The settler explained that the puma would attack an animal only by leaping on its neck. — A. F. Tschiffely, *Tschiffely's Ride*, New York, 1933, 40–41.

Arab-Barb origin. His neck and face bore scars from clawings by a panther that had leaped upon him while he was a colt. He had had other encounters with the *león* — mostly, after he was grown, of his own seeking. His owner said that if a man were riding him when he smelled a fresh track, the only thing to do was to dismount, remove saddle and bridle, and turn him loose. He was too powerful to manage in a frenzy of hate. He had all the bottom that generations of toughness could transmit. He was a family pet, very gentle with children. His owner would not sell him.

But he owed a note to Don Luis Terrazas, whose haciendas covered millions of acres and who dominated thousands of peons. Now it was either pay the note or enter into a peonage extendable even unto the third and fourth generations. Victor Lieb paid the note. The next day Chinaco was led to his camp. He would not accept the horse to keep but only for riding while he remained in the region.

One early morning he rode out after venison. He was on a short stretch of softish mountain trail when Chinaco began to sniff and grow excited. Examining the ground, Victor Lieb saw a fresh panther track. Chinaco was already straining to go on. Lieb removed saddle and bridle, turned him loose and followed afoot. He could not see how the fight started, but when he got around the mountain he saw Chinaco rushing with extended head upon the dead panther's body, grabbing it by the neck, shaking it, flinging it to the ground and striking it with both forefeet at once. After he was satisfied with his conquest, Chinaco showed great pride. He had received no wound. Without even a hackamore, he bore Victor Lieb bareback to where saddle and bridle had been left.

Even in rough, panther-infested country where he made his last stand, man and not panther proved to be the mustang's fatal enemy.

VIII

THE STALLION AND HIS MARES

NO MALE among wild animals outside the genus *Equus* exercises despotic mastery over a band of females in the manner of the stallion. In some species, male and female pair off; in the bovine, deer and certain other families, males consort promiscuously with the females for a season and then are indifferent to them. The mustang stallion was both polygamous and constant. Guarding his mares the year round against all enemies and keeping them for himself against all opponents made him fiercely possessive and domineering. His band was the normal mustang unit. In the Southwest it took the Spanish name, *manada*.

Only at foaling time did the mares drop out to be alone, often for hardly a day, until their colts grew strong enough to run. The identity of the manada endured as long as the vigor of its master endured. Depending upon his vigor and aggressiveness, it might number anywhere from three to fifty. Perhaps, as old tales tell, a rare master-stallion now and then assembled a hundred or more mares. A band of thirty was considered extra large; one of from fifteen to twenty was usual, but bands of a half dozen or so were common. The number fluctuated, for the stallions were constant contenders with each other for mares, the old giving way to the young, the young dividing up their inheritance, not because they wanted to but because they were powerless to maintain monopolies.

Since colts are born about equally male and female, many stallions could have no harems, not even a single mare. The outcasts kept company with each other to an extent but formed no cohesive unit. They came together like buck deer when they are not bucking, in twos, threes, and other small numbers, though as many as seventy-five in a bunch were reported.[1] Pursuit of a group would scatter them, whereas a manada ran as a unit to either freedom or captivity. The mareless stallions were of three classes: the immature, the declining, and the mediocre who had never tasted and would never taste power.

Virtually all stallions were wanting mares. Even the impotent, like geldings, wanted them for company if nothing else. Few stallions with mares had so many that they did not desire more. Every herd-stallion had to combat constantly against other leaders as well as against the ever-hungering outcasts.

Although the contests might occur at any time except when winter cold and starvation shriveled vitality to the minimum, they were naturally more frequent and fierce during the breeding season. The scent of a mare in heat can be detected by a stallion far away on a cool breeze. She leaves notice of her condition in frequent urinary excretions. The lust-sensitized and the lust-emboldened have-nots dogged unremittingly the trails of the haves. They came by night to the grazing ground; they haunted the waterings.

Although wild horses cooperated in many ways, mareless stal-

lions did not combine with each other to overcome a possessor of mares. Sometimes while two herd-masters were contending midway between their passive bands, a bachelor tried to steal a mare, but as soon as her master became aware of the thief he broke away from the fight to retrieve his property.

Immediately before an engagement, the stallions, tails straight out or raised to an angle of about forty-five degrees, would prance, rush back and forth, nicker and whistle with a shrillness that could be heard a mile away. The combatants met each other walking on hind legs, striking with forefeet, ears laid back, mouths open, teeth bared. They raked the hide from each other, made deep cuts. They screamed. Their teeth slipping off firm flesh clicked together. They sought jugular veins. They lunged their whole weight against each other. Now one or both whirled with catlike rapidity and kicked like a pile-driver. A pair of flying heels hitting against another pair of flying heels cracked like a whipsnap of lightning. Those heels could crash a hock or cave in a rib. Unless the weaker ran — and he often chose the better part of valor — he went to the ground, there to be pounded with iron-hard clubs and lacerated between steel-strong, ivory-spiked jaws.[2]

After going to the ground, a stallion was lucky if he could regain his feet and run. The victor might follow a runaway for a mile, tearing at him with every jump. If the runaway had mares, some might escape with him, but the conqueror was likely to take some. Sometimes the fighters were evenly matched. Cheyenne warriors once rode up on two stallions, each the dominator of a band of mares, too exhausted from long fighting to run away. Great strips had been jerked from their hides, and the nostrils of one had been torn off.[3]

Perhaps no wild animal had to stay on guard more unremittingly than the mustang stallion. On approaching water, he tested the ground around it before allowing the mares and colts to drink. He smelled for the dung of a competing stallion, for sign of lurking panther or man. If something aroused his faintest suspicion, he stood, advanced, retreated, waited, looked a long time. If assured of danger, he ordered immediate retreat. Only at his signal did the band enter the water. They came eagerly, drank deep; some pawed and rolled. Their monarch gave the signal to race to clear ground.[4]

While grazing, he occupied the highest ground adjacent to his band; on flat plains, he maintained a lookout position to one side. Between bites of grass, he often raised his head as high as neck would reach, looking and smelling. He was the eagle of the turf. With some manadas, however, the chief sentinel was a mare or a mule. As lookouts, mules were as useful to wild horses as antelopes were to buffaloes. Stallions recognized mules and geldings as non-competitive and tolerated their company.

In rapine, cajolery and gallantry the mustang stallion was as bold with domestic mares as with the *cimarrones*. While horse-ranching and killing off mustangs on the Staked Plains of eastern New Mexico in the 1880's, Thomas Carson and some other men penned a small bunch of gentle mares and colts one evening and the next morning found that a mustang stallion had torn down the gate poles in the night and taken off the whole caballada. The ranchers rode thirty miles before getting sight of the stock. Another plainsman saw a stallion gallop up to a domestic herd of horses and select a mare that did not want to go with him. She lay down and refused to rise until he had bitten her severely. Then with ears laid back and jaws open he drove her to his manada, which she had to accept — and no doubt before long was devoted to the new way of life.[5] I incline to classify as folk-lore the account of a wild stallion's habit of chewing in two the picket rope on a mare in order to steal her.

Like all wild creatures, wild horses feared man above other enemies and wanted to get away from him. Now and then, however, some lord of a mare-harem, instead of running from an approaching rider, would trot out a short distance to meet him, stand with head held high, and look steadily until assurance of danger made him waver. Then with a mighty snort he would wheel and, squealing and biting, set the mares off on a run. Bolder stallions would run only so far before turning on the chasers. A heavy black stallion with only the stubs of his ears remaining that ranged long ago on the Republican River of Kansas would invariably turn on Cheyenne riders when they neared his band. No mounted horse could be forced against him. He and his always got away. Another stallion, a strawberry roan, chased by the Cheyennes acted in a similar way. Any horse so brave must have "strong spiritual power," and killing him would bring bad fortune to the killer.[6]

If roped, a fighter stallion was likely to turn on his captor with a ferocity that only a bullet could quell. Frank Collinson, one of the most powerful men I have ever met, came in young vigor to Texas soon after the close of the Civil War and ranged as far west as grass grew. In the fall of 1874, he went to a camp of buffalo hunters on Double Mountain Fork of the Brazos River and, while waiting for troops to clear the Comanches off the range, threw in with a hide hunter named Louis Keys. Both had worked as cowboys and both rode the best of cow horses.

Mustangs were comparatively scarce in that part of the country, but along Deep Point Creek, a magnificent-looking red-sorrel stallion guarded his band of mares. The buffalo hunters had no use for mares but wanted the stallion. Deep Point Creek has steep banks, lined by elm trees and other growth. If the mustangs were on the south side of the creek and took alarm, they ran to an old buffalo crossing and crossed to the north side. If anything disturbed them on the north side, they ran to another crossing and got on the south side.

Frank Collinson and Louis Keys decided that the first time they located these mustangs south of the creek, one would haze them across while the other waited on the north bank to rope the stallion when he came up. He would give a tremendous jerk when he hit the end of the rope; as Collinson rode the heavier horse, he was to do the roping. After Keys got the mustangs headed for the crossing, he was to fire his Winchester as a signal. Their chance to capture the stallion came as planned.

"Soon after I took my stand, beside the topping-out place on the trail," Frank Collinson said, "I heard the shot. Next I heard the plunging hoofs. The animals were running as hard as they could run. The first one up the trail was a big mare who always led the runs. The sorrel stallion was behind. I could not see him, but Keys later told me that he paused for a minute on the south rim to take a look at his enemy only a few hundred yards behind. He plunged up the bank like a big buck, in long jumps. Just as his head was clear, I shot my loop. I couldn't have made a neater catch.

"I thought he would run to the end of the rope, but before he tightened it he headed straight for me, ready to grab. He came pawing and caught my right thigh down towards the knee between his teeth. They peeled off pants, skin and a layer of flesh, and when they hit together they sounded like a sprung steel trap.

"I grabbed my sixshooter, and before he could charge a second time, shot. The flash of the discharge right in his face must have scared him. He wheeled. I had missed his head. While he was turning, I shot again and hit him near the root of the tail. He lunged to the end of the rope with all his might and jerked my horse down. I fell clear, but here he came again full speed, ears back and mouth open. His eyes were literally blazing. Just at this time, Keys topped out. He jumped off his horse, Winchester in hand, and shot. He hit the stallion in the shoulder, breaking it. That stopped him. The next shot hit him square in the head. He fell within a few feet of me. The rope about his neck was still tied to my saddle horn. I could hardly have reached the bluff for a jump. If Keys had not come up at the right instant, the stallion would almost certainly have killed me.

"I have roped some bad maverick bulls with wrinkles on their horns. They were tame compared to a savage mustang stallion. In his rage he was the most vicious animal on four legs. By the time we got back to camp my boot was full of blood. Our cook, an old soldier of the Civil War, salted some hot water, bathed the wound and kept hot blankets on it. My whole leg turned black, but after limping around a few days, I was all right." [7]

When buffaloes became scarce on the Texas plains, two hide hunters named Havie and Wilkinson turned to mustanging. They had three or four saddle horses in addition to a stallion that helped pull their wagon. They fed him grain and sometimes rode him. After they had captured a number of mustangs, selling them to horse traders who rode into the country as hide buyers had ridden before them, they began following a band of extra good mares dominated by an especially domineering stallion. He took a stand several times as if he intended to be driven no farther, but until his band was pretty well tired out always retreated. Then he refused to go on. No matter from what direction the mustangers approached the band, the stallion would lay back his ears, open his jaws and charge. They scared him again and again by shooting near him, but still could make no headway in directing his band towards a corral.

They decided to kill him and use their gentle stallion to help bring the mares in. Their stallion was rather small, but he was strong enough and exceedingly ambitious. As he was led near the wild bunch, he began nickering, and here the mustang stallion came with blood in his eye. Wilkinson shot him dead. Upon being released, the gentle stallion raced among the mares, scattering them badly, finally running off after three or four. The whole bunch was lost. Their horses utterly run down, the mustangers had to rest in camp several days before starting after a fresh band of wild horses. One morning their pet stallion came limping up to the wagon, cut and kicked from head to tail. His hide was torn in many places. He looked as if he had been run through a wringing machine. Wild stallions had cooled to zero his ambition to consort with their mares.[8]

To kill the master stallion was to throw away the chance to capture the manada. As soon as the mares lost their commander, they scattered beyond all control. However, one group of un-hurried ranchers in Nebraska killed off the wild stallions, re-leased domesticated stallions, and waited for them to gather the mares.[9]

It is natural for a domesticated stallion to claim and keep mares. The Spanish *modo* of horse-raising was to deliver about twenty-five mares to a stallion and herd the manada during the day, penning them at night, until the bunch was well cohered and the stallion had shown himself master. Then he was left to herd alone. If he failed to demonstrate mastership, he could be of no use on the open range and was, accordingly, castrated. A man without a cowwhip could not ride up to the mares under a fierce herd stallion. The Mexicans had a way of "fixing" a stal-lion — by an operation on the sheath — so that, while maintaining potency, he could not copulate. Often *un garañón dispuesto* — a fixed stallion — was put in charge of a band of mares to train them to stay together before delivery to a breeding stallion or a jack. Frequently a *ladina* * mare, perfectly willing to remain with the manada out on the range, would break away upon ap-proaching a pen. A good *manadero* — herding stallion — was more effective in forcing her into the corral than a dozen vaqueros.

The one gentle stallion I have heard of as being useful in cap-turing mustang mares had been a mustang himself.[10] Many years ago Julián Coronado was *caporal* (boss) on the Rancho del Salitre in northern Coahuila. It ran three or four thousand head of cattle and numerous manadas. Many branded mares were as

---

* No English word adequately translates *ladina*. *Outlaw* is not the word. Many a *ladino* saddle horse was absolutely docile after being penned. A *ladino* is an animal hard to catch or pen. The word is often applied to cattle and hu-man beings — wild runaways.

wild as anything that runs. Many, separated from their bands by wild stallions, were raising *mesteñas*.

A mustang colt that Julián Coronado caught and raised on milk grew to be a very gentle and very superior stallion. He became such a dominator of horses that he was named Comanche. His owner would give him a half dozen or so tame mares and drive the bunch to a part of the range where *ladina* mares were running. Within a short time the stallion would have them in his bunch. If, upon the approach of a man, the mares tried to escape, the stallion would force them to remain with his bunch. No slave-master could have been more severe on runaways. After being driven to the ranch corrals, the wild mares were roped and kept tied or staked until they were tamed; Comanche meantime was treated to salt, corn and petting.

Finally, Julián Coronado took Comanche to a part of the range where a blooded jack, as wild and wily as the wildest mustang, kept a manada containing two beautiful mules, paints and unbranded. Most of his mares had never been branded. Within a few days the mustanger stallion was in charge of the band, including the jack. Julián never allowed anybody but his son Santana to approach a manada dominated by Comanche. This was the finest catch he had ever made, and Julián knew better than to rush the difficult business of corralling them. Every few days he would ride near the manada, whereupon the mares would flee, led by the jack, while Comanche, paying no attention to the jack, would in his fiercest manner force the runaways to stop.

A drouth was on, and there were only three waterholes over a big stretch of country. Julián and his son fenced in two of the holes and camped at the third. Their camp equipment by itself was sufficient to frighten away the wild mares. They would approach the water and hold back while Comanche came in, drank, rolled in mud, and got a treat of corn. Then he would return to them fresh and lordly.

Early one morning after the manada had been kept from water

four days, the campers at the waterhole rode out to meet them. The mares ran, Comanche, followed by Santana, circling them back. Julián watched from a hill. Finally the whole band went into the water and drank. As they came out full and loggy, Julián rode nearer, lying down in his saddle and imitating the whinny of a colt. His horse was headed toward the ranch corrals, ten miles away. As he moved in that direction, Santana and Comanche pushed the wild band after him. He led in a long run, but within a short time the mares, sweating and blowing, began to slow down. Comanche kicked and bit their already scarred shoulders whenever one tried to break away. All but the jack were brought into the big pen. There were twenty-odd brood mares, eight or ten sucking colts, and an equal number of fillies, besides the two beautiful paint mules. Comanche was feasted.

In fiction the proud stallion always "troops it at the head of his band." An exceptional stallion did, in fact, sometimes lead the runners. He might run clear away from them, leaving them to scatter and shift for themselves. Among the true wild horses of Asia, it is said, the stallion in case of danger runs forward "only if the herd contains no foals." [11] One experienced mustanger of the old days — dead now like all of his kind — told me that he learned not to bother with a manada which the stallion led instead of driving; he could not be trusted to keep it together. [12]

The typical stallion was both driver and rear-guard defense. He punished laggards unmercifully, sometimes forcing mares to leave colts unable to stand the pace, even on rare occasions killing colts so that they would not impede the manada's flight and cohesion. [13] He raced up and down the sides of his band, ramming into the ribs of one mare with his hard crest, kicking this one, raking that one with his teeth or nipping her ear, grabbing into the haunch of another. Once in a while he had to force the leaders to swerve in the direction he wanted to go. One chaser of a hard-pressed manada saw the stallion upon approaching breaks at the edge of a prairie "cut through the middle of the herd, squealing at a great rate, scattering the mares into broken, wooded country." [14] He could reassemble them later.

Sometimes, seemingly from whim, though the result was discipline, a stallion dictator kept his band in a huddle, going around and around them until he beat out a trail. Some stallions seemed to choose certain grounds for frequent practice in close-herding. [15]

Because they are intelligent, horses vary from each other in conduct. Occasionally more than one stallion ran with a manada, for a while at least. A band of about seventy chased by one plainsman included eight or ten young stallions subservient to an old one. Another band of about thirty was rear-guarded on a chase by an old stallion but led by two young ones. [16]

Wild burros must have been responsible for some of the mules frequently found with mustangs, though the intervention of man is often necessary for crossbreeding between jack and mare. Most of the mules were runaways. No spirited domestic horse was ever more eager to join the wild and free than a work mule. During times when army posts dotted the Indian frontiers, many a manada was led by a government mule, sometimes wearing a halter. [17] Mules are so devoted to mares that fifty of them will follow a single mare across the continent. For hundreds of years every big pack outfit of mules in the mountains of Spanish America has been led by a belled mare. "As crazy as a mule over a colt," an old saying goes. Many a mare mule has tried to steal a colt from its mother.

The mule might be a wiser general than the stallion. A "yaller" line-backed mule that had been raised by a mustang mare kept a certain band of wild horses free for years. Finally, however, Pony Campbell and some other men had the manada almost in the pen, and the stallion was doing his best to keep the mares together, when the mule split them up worse than a covey of flushed quail. Only one mare and colt were penned, along with a considerable number of unbroken range horses. The next morning the mule was out on a flat about a quarter of a mile away braying and the colt beside its mother was nickering in response. Then the mule disappeared. After the horse stock had been "worked over" and held in the pen for three days, they were let out to be driven to another range. All went well until the caballada was passing through a stretch of post oaks. There the lead man saw a flash of yellow, and before anybody could do anything the line-backed mule had cut out the mare and colt and was disappearing with them in a cloud of dust.[18]

The common idea that wild horses gradually degenerated through uncontrolled breeding is contrary to fact. Only the fittest stallions had a chance to breed. The defect of their natural system lay in the non-selection of mares. The stallions were as lacking in discrimination as the old cowman who declared he had never tasted bad whiskey or seen an ugly woman. When colts were a year or so old, the stallions generally cut them out of their manadas, males and females alike.[19] Some ignoramuses, but nobody else, said that they tom-catted young males to prevent competition.

Until the white man interfered, mustang stock did not degenerate any more than deer, antelopes, buffaloes and other wild species left to themselves degenerate. During the early part of the 19th century some observers thought the general run of mustangs in semi-arid parts of Texas superior to the general run of branded Mexican horses south of the Rio Grande. After professional Mexican and Anglo-American mustangers began, in the 1840's, corralling mustangs in large numbers, taking all choice animals and releasing the dregs to breed, deterioration was inevitable. Always, however, certain of the hardiest, fastest, most enduring and most intelligent individuals escaped.

Variations in color struck everybody who saw the wild horses. The colors were not, as has often been said, "of the rainbow."

[139]

They blended with the earth rather than with the sky. In some areas, certain colors dominated. In parts of southwest Texas, about 1880, blacks and browns are said to have prevailed. Before mustangs were much chased, occasional bands were of one color — whites, blacks, bays, roans, duns, etc.[20] Perhaps, like many human beings, some stallions and mares — though the mare was powerless to exercise her preference — had an affinity for the opposite sex of their own color. Only on this theory can a wild stallion's keeping a band of mares of one color be accounted for.*

Spanish-Mexicans raised horses for color as much as for any other quality, and to a limited extent early English-speaking ranchers in the Spanish zone of Texas adopted their ways. Twenty-five black fillies, say, would be delivered to a black stallion, twenty-five bays to a bay stallion, and so on. Scores of these manadas, each of uniform color, racing at roundup time from all directions to a common point and there mingling in broken color patches, made a sight fraught with life and beauty. And this was while mustangs still ran free.

A horse roundup on Mission Prairie in the late summer of 1875 highlighted this wild mixture. Mission Prairie stretched forty miles between the San Antonio River and Hines Bay on the Texas coast. All ranchmen in the country were at the time raising horses. Some had brought in blooded stallions from Tennessee and elsewhere. Wild stallions were fighting the blooded stallions off. Branded stock were badly dispersed. Stray horses, many of them outlaws, many in brands unknown, ranged the land. Jim Reeves, who owned about fifteen manadas on the prairie, took the lead in organizing the roundup. About a hundred and fifty riders, some representing remote ranches, joined in.

* Wild cattle on the Falkland Islands, free to mingle with each other, kept themselves in three color groups: mouse or lead-colored, dark brown, and white with black heads and feet, though black and spotted cattle occurred in all three groups. Observing them in 1832, Darwin thought that if the herds were left undisturbed for several centuries "one color would in all probability prevail over all the others."

The plan was to drive all horses towards San Nicolas Lake, about the center of the prairie, from all sides simultaneously. The riders were disposed and camped on the edges of the prairie the afternoon before the drive was to start. About daybreak they began the great run. All were armed. They had orders to kill any stallion that broke through the lines. Not until the horses approached the roundup grounds were they aware of any other riders than those they fled. For twenty miles many bands hardly broke a gallop. Cattle were left behind. Deer converged into herds numbering up to three and four hundred before breaking back. From a distance the dark running lines, flecked by the light from the sky, resembled the swaying of low-flying ducks in vast flocks.

Before the diameter of the herd had been lessened to a mile, many stallions and outlaw horses were breaking through, and at times the shooting sounded like that of a battle. Colts, old mares and old horses were trampled to death in the melee. It was estimated that 15,000 horses came together. Unless one has worked with livestock, he can hardly envision 15,000 running, milling horses. About 200 stallions were killed, some branded as well as straight mustang. It took three days of herding and separating to get order out of the mass. Many stray horses were left to their freedom. Scores of bunches were driven back to their proper ranges. Several thousand horses were held to be driven north and east for sale. "I have worked cattle from the Rio Grande to Montana," said George W. Saunders, "but this round-up of horses was the greatest sight I have ever seen on any range." [21]

Before the present generation reformed their ideas, range men had only three uses for mares: for breeding, racing an occasional runner, and belling some gentle individual — the *caponera*, or remuda mare — to keep the saddle horses together. A cowboy was as reluctant as any conquistador to ride a mare. An American in Monterey at the time California was seized from Mexico bought a fine mare for nine dollars and then, riding through town, heard the taunts of girls following him: *"Yegua! yegua! yegua!"* (Mare, mare, mare!).[22] When I was a boy my father gave me a little bay Spanish mare he had bought from a Mexican passing through our ranch. She was the most nervous, lightsome and energetic animal I have ever ridden; she would have kept going long after any man of not too much weight was dead tired from riding her. For shame at being seen on a mare, I almost never rode her off the ranch.

Mustang lore is as short on mares as German history is on women. Almost without exception the horse notabilities of the West have been mustang stallions and cow horses — geldings. The one great legend of the mustang world is of a stallion.

IX

*THE LEGEND OF THE PACING
WHITE MUSTANG*

EVERY SECTION of the mustang world had its notabil-
ity — the subject of campfire talk and the object of chases.
Supreme above all local superiors was the Pacing White Mustang. A superb stallion of one region in the beginning, he became
the composite of all superb stallions of his color wherever wild
horses ran. The loom of human imagination wove him into the
symbol of all wild and beautiful and fleet horses. Riders everywhere over a continent of free grass came to know of him and
many to dream of capturing him. His fame spread beyond the
Atlantic. He passed from the mortality of the bounded and aging
into the immortality of the legended.

It is now nearly thirty years since I took the trail of this ubiquitous stallion. Looking back, I am astounded at the sign he left and at my own trailing. The record is a kind of epic.[1]

The great horse went under varying names — the White Steed of the Prairies, the Pacing White Stallion, the White Mustang, the Ghost Horse of the Plains. His fire, grace, beauty, speed, endurance, and intelligence were exceeded only by his passion for liberty. He paced from the mesas of Mexico to the Badlands of the Dakotas and even beyond, from the Brazos bottoms of eastern Texas to parks in the Rocky Mountains.

1. Literary Prologue

The earliest account of the Supreme Mustang, so far as I have found, is in Washington Irving's *A Tour on the Prairies*. On October 21, 1832, somewhere west of the junction of the Cimarron with the Arkansas, he made this journal entry:

"We had been disappointed this day in our hopes of meeting with buffalo, but the sight of the wild horse gave a turn to camp conversation for the evening. Several anecdotes were told of a famous grey horse which has ranged the prairies of this neighborhood for six or seven years, setting at naught every attempt of the hunters to capture him. They say he can pace . . . faster than the fleetest horse can run."

In 1841, nine years after Irving's tour, the Republic of Texas sent out what is known as the Santa Fe Expedition to annex New Mexico. It became lost in Texas territory and, when its members reached Santa Fe, they were prisoners on a walk to Mexico City. Among them was a New Orleans journalist named George W. Kendall. The most important result of the expedition was his journals, published first in the New Orleans *Picayune*, 1842, and then two years later in book form: *Narrative of the Texan Santa Fe Expedition*.

One evening after a drove of mustangs had galloped up near the Texan camp, stood with raised heads, wheeled and dashed off, Kendall heard "the older hunters tell of a large white horse often seen in the vicinity of the Cross Timbers and near Red River. . . . As the camp stories ran, he has never been known to gallop or trot, but paces faster than any other horse sent out after him can run; and so game and untiring is the White Steed of the Prairies, for he is well known to trappers and hunters by that name, that he has tired down no less than three race-nags, sent expressly to catch him, with a Mexican rider well trained to the business of catching wild horses. . . .

"Some of the hunters go so far as to say that the White Steed has been known to pace his mile in less than two minutes, and that he can keep up this pace until he has tired down everything in pursuit. Large sums have been offered for his capture, and the attempt has been frequently made. But he still roams his native prairies in freedom, always alone. One old hunter declared that he was too proud to be seen with other horses, being an animal far superior in form and action to any of his brothers. This I put down as a rank embellishment, although it is a fact that the more beautiful and highly formed mustangs are frequently seen alone."

Writers about a country, whether travelers or residents, usually note what their predecessors have noted. Kendall's *Narrative* was the most popular work pertaining to Texas published in the 19th century. For years after its appearance both fictionists and nonfictionists writing on the Southwest felt obliged to include the White Steed, sometimes alluding to him as "Kendall's." Even before Kendall's journal got into book form, Captain Marryat of *Mr. Midshipman Easy* fame plagiarized the story of the White Steed and clapped it into his rambling *Narrative of the Travels and Adventures of Monsieur Violet in California, Sonora and Texas.* Meantime J. Barber had been inspired to a ballad: [2]

Fleet barb of the prairie, in vain they prepare
For thy neck, arched in beauty, the treacherous snare;
Thou wilt toss thy proud head, and with nostrils
    stretched wide,
Defy them again, as thou still hast defied.

Not the team of the Sun, as in fable portrayed,
Through the firmament rushing in glory arrayed,
Could match, in wild majesty, beauty and speed,
That tireless, magnificent, snowy-white steed.

Josiah Gregg had gone west over the Santa Fe Trail in 1831. He looked at life steadily and reported it faithfully. His *Commerce of the Prairies* appeared in 1844, the year Kendall's *Narrative* was published. He had heard, he wrote, "marvelous tales" of a "medium-sized mustang stallion of perfect symmetry, milk-white, save a pair of black ears, a natural pacer. The trapper celebrates him in the northern Rocky Mountains; the hunter on the Arkansas; while others have him pacing on the borders of Texas."

Among the "veracious memoranda" of François des Montaignes "taken during an expedition of exploration in the year 1845," the "celebrated snow-white pacer of the Canadian" has taken on the power of making himself "visible only to special and favorite individuals." [3]

With the appearance of *Moby Dick*, in 1851, the White Mustang entered with thundering hoofbeats into the ranges of true literature. In that great chapter on "The Whiteness of the Whale," wherein Herman Melville reviews the white objects of the earth, ranging from the snowy Andes to the sacred elephants of India, he reaches his climax in a panegyric on the White Stallion.

"Most famous," he exclaims, "in our Western annals and Indian traditions is that of the White Steed of the Prairies; a magnificent milk-white charger, large-eyed, small-headed, bluff-

[146]

chested, and with the dignity of a thousand monarchs in his lofty, over-scorning carriage. He was the elected Xerxes of vast herds of wild horses, whose pastures in those days were only fenced by the Rocky Mountains and the Alleghenies. At their flaming head he westward trooped it like the chosen star which each evening leads on the hosts of light. The flashing cascade of his mane, the curving comet of his tail, invested him with housings more resplendent than gold- and silver-beaters could have furnished him. A most imperial and archangelical apparition of that unfallen, western world, which to the eyes of the old trappers and hunters revived the glories of . . . primeval times. . . . Whether marching amid his aides and marshals in the van of countless cohorts that endlessly streamed it over the plain, like an Ohio; or whether with his subjects browsing all around at the horizon, the White Steed gallopingly reviewed them with warm nostrils reddening through his cool milkiness; in whatever aspect he presented himself, always to the bravest Indians he was the object of trembling reverence and awe."

Melville had never seen mustangs or talked with mustangers; he had the transporting power of imagination. Mayne Reid, on the contrary, had firsthand experience with the mustang world. He was an Irish Protestant twenty years old when he landed at New Orleans in 1838. He went out on the plains with traders, served as soldier of fortune with the American army in the Mexican War, and then, according to report, spent some time in southwestern Texas. Before he became an exceedingly popular inventor of adventure stories, he was well fortified with frontier traditions and with knowledge of native plant and animal life. In 1861, twenty-nine years after Washington Irving heard the first "anecdotes" of record concerning the Pacing Stallion, Reid published *The War Trail, or the Hunt of the Wild Horse.** The

* "On this wonderful Sunday, I found the opening of a serial story called *The War Trail*, by Captain Mayne Reid. I did not know what a war-trail might be; I looked at the beginning: and then suddenly found that I was in a world of beauty and romance, a world that I understood from of old, where

scene is laid more or less along the Rio Grande, and the story of the book-long chase is told in the first person.

"I had heard of the White Steed of the Prairies," the narrator begins his description. "What hunter or trapper, trader or traveler, throughout all the wild borders of prairie-land has not? Many a romantic story of him had I listened to around the blazing campfire — many a tale of German-like *diablerie*. . . . That there existed a white stallion of great speed and splendid proportions — that there were twenty, perhaps a hundred such — among the countless herds of wild horses roaming over the great plains, I did not for a moment doubt. I myself had seen and chased more than one magnificent animal, but the one known as The White Steed of the Prairies had a peculiar marking that distinguished him from all the rest. His ears were black — only his ears, and these were the color of ebony. The rest of his body, mane and tail, were white as fresh-fallen snow."

In almost the last novel, *The Boy Hunters, or Adventures in Search of a White Buffalo*, that Captain Mayne Reid wrote, he was still chasing the White Steed of the Prairies. Only as samples of other iterations do I name *The Backwoodsman, or Life on the Indian Frontier* (1864), by Sir C. F. Lascelles Wraxall, Bart., in which the White Steed leaps a canyon forty feet wide; *The White Mustang* (1889) by Lieut. H. R. Jayne (Edward S. Ellis); *Wild Horses* (1924) by Henry Herbert Knibbs, wherein, "his mane like new-spun silk lifting in the breeze," the untamable stallion, gray now, still paces. The Zane Grey assembly line and pulp magazines have published stories on the horse without end.[4]

An exception to mere iteration is "The Pacing Mustang," by Ernest Thompson Seton in *Wild Animals I Have Known* (1898), which is beautiful and true to range men as well as

---

the landscape led on and on, and men rode with comrades seeking, and villainy tried to thwart, and savagery tried to scalp, but how could either triumph over comrades and beauty? I was in an extraordinary world that would be mine forever." — John Masefield, *So Long to Learn*, The Macmillan Company, New York, 1952, p. 40. Quoted by permission.

horses. "The Ghost Horse," by Chief Buffalo Child Long Lance.
in *Long Lance* (1928) is true also to mustangs and is in the best
tradition of the Blackfoot Indians.

2. *Frontier Tales*

Before the Mexican War brought so many listeners and look-
ers to Texas, the White Pacer had changed his range from the
plains to regions far east and south. When, as descendants remember, J. L. Rountree [5] settled in Milam County on the Brazos
River in 1839, the stallion and his band were ranging on adjacent
prairies, never entering bottom woods. It was not long before
Rountree joined with two other men to run him down. The
horse's circuit was well known. The mustangers placed three relays of horses along it and added three packs of hounds. On the
third day an expert Mexican roper on the fastest horse in the
country was brought into the chase, but the White Stallion could
not be made to break his pace. He simply tired down everything
after him. The hunters set snares for him under trees where he
was accustomed to stand in the shade in the heat of the day, but
no device succeeded with the wary animal. He disappeared
finally without anyone's knowing whether he had been killed,
had died a natural death, or had left the country.

He had merely left the country. One of the veracious chroniclers with Taylor's army on the border was Captain W. S.
Henry. In his *Campaign Sketches of the War with Mexico*, he
recorded that in October, 1845, among numerous mustangs
brought in to mount the troops at Corpus Christi, was one "reported to be the celebrated 'White Horse of the Prairies.' He
was a fine flea-bitten gray, fourteen hands high, well proportioned, and built a good deal after the pattern of a Conestoga
No. 2. His head and neck were really beautiful, perfect Arabian; beautiful ears, large nostrils, great breadth of forehead, and

a throttle as large as any I have ever seen in a blooded nag. His white mane was two feet long. He looked about twenty-five years old. He had been driven into a pen with some hundred others and lassoed. Thus, by an artifice, was entrapped the monarch of the mustangs: no more will he lead the countless herds in their wild scampers of freedom; no more will be seen his noble form, with head up and eye dilated, standing on the prairie-knoll, snuffing danger in the breeze, and dashing off at lightning-speed when it becomes apparent."

Captain Henry no doubt saw a mighty fine stallion, but it was not *the* White Steed. A few years later, as a story of the brush country came down, the famous stallion led his mares into a mustang pen built at a lake, and a hidden mustanger shut the gate while they were drinking. Some ranch people said, however, that this horse was not a genuine mustang but a descendant of a white mare lost by Kentucky or Tennessee troops passing through the country on their way to join General Taylor's army.[6]

Rumors often circulated in one part of the country that the famous horse had been captured in another part far away. One drifting story had it that during the California gold rush a gambler offered a thousand dollars for the horse and that some frontiersmen crossing the plains saw him, captured him, and brought him to San Francisco, where the gambler rode him down the street every day and hitched him as an advertisement in front of his gambling house.

About the time Austin was established as the capital of the Republic of Texas, in the early '40s, John W. Young started ranching on Onion Creek ten miles or so to the southeast. He was a Kentuckian and raised horses. Not long after he settled, an extraordinary stallion appeared among the mustangs habitually watering on Onion Creek. His form was perfect; his alertness and vitality were superb. He was pure white. His tail brushed the short mesquite grass that carpeted the earth, and his tossing mane swept to his knees. His only gait out of a walk was a pace, and it was soon found that he never, no matter how hard pressed, broke that pace. His band of mares normally numbered from fifty to sixty.

He led them southward across the Blanco, the San Marcos and the Guadalupe. It was known that he even at times ranged down as far as the Nueces. He kept clear of the timbers, never crossed the Colorado to the east, and did not range into the rocky cedar hills to the west; he seemed to like the rich mesquite grass of rolling country edging the blacklands better than that on the blacklands themselves. Many men, alone or in parties, tried to capture him.

Because he usually moved southward when chased, it was generally supposed that he had come up from that direction. Some speculators held that he had been imported to Mexico from Spain or Arabia, had been brought up as far as the Texas border by one of the owners of the great horse ranches occupying that country, and then, after being established on this ranch, had quit it and the semi-domesticated horse stock to run with the mustangs.

No matter how hard or how far chased, he always in time came back to the waters of Onion Creek. The favorite point of view from which to see him was Pilot Knob, about four miles from McKinney Falls. Any mustanging party that proposed a chase generally sent a scout to Pilot Knob to locate their quarry. The White Stallion's color, his alert movements and the large size of his manada, all made him and the bunch he led conspicuous. If started, he would lead out pacing, the mares following at a dead run. In a mile's distance he would gain at least a hundred and fifty yards on anything behind him. Then he would stop and look back, keeping out of shooting, as well as roping, distance.

The Indians had spotted him and they gave him a few chases, but the most persistent chasers were from San Antonio. A certain doctor there who was a horse fancier heard of the White

Stallion, saw him in action, and offered five hundred dollars for him "delivered in sound condition." Five hundred dollars in those days amounted to a small fortune.

A Spaniard named Santa Ana Cruz determined to win the prize. He had a ranch on Onion Creek, kept several vaqueros, and was engaged by neighboring ranchers to put the quietus on rustlers. One day his vaqueros ran the White Stallion seventy-five miles south, and when they got back home two days later, found him grazing with his mares on the accustomed range.

To win the five hundred dollars, Santa Ana Cruz picked twelve riders, furnished each of them with two horses, and disposed them in the direction that the White Stallion was expected to run. A scout on Pilot Knob saw the manada go in to water and signaled. Soon after the mustangs had drunk, the nearest of the twelve men began the chase. The White Pacer took out in the direction of San Antonio. That first day, however, he did not

keep his direction, and before the morning of the second day he had circled back into his favorite range. On this second day he was crowded harder, his mares lagged more, and, leaving them behind, he crossed the Guadalupe. For three days and three nights under a full June moon the Santa Ana Cruz men ceaselessly pursued him.

By the end of the third day, every animal in his band had dropped away. He himself had not once lagged, had not once broken his rack, except to change from right to left and from left to right. Two men continued to trail him until he had crossed the Frio River, still pacing toward the Rio Grande. Then they quit.

He never returned to his old range. In time the Onion Creek country learned why.

South of the Nueces, the rolling land rises into rough hills cut by deep arroyos. About three miles from a waterhole in one of these dry arroyos was a Mexican ranch called Chaparro Prieto. The low rock house, with portholes against Indian attacks, and the adjacent corrals were located in a draw matted with mesquite grass. Nearby was a hand-dug well that supplied water for the ranch people and their saddle horses.

The arroyo waterhole was so boxed in by bluffs that only one trail led down to it, from the north. One hot afternoon a vaquero from the Chaparro Prieto saw a lone white horse approaching the waterhole at a slow pace. At the instant of observation he was hidden by chaparral and was considerably to one side of the trail the horse was traveling. The working of his ears and the lift of his muzzle indicated that he smelled water. He was gaunt and jaded, but still firm on his feet and alert. The wind was in the vaquero's favor. He slipped a hand over his mount's nostrils to prevent a possible whinny. As the horse passed, he recognized him from descriptions he had often heard as the Pacing White Stallion of the Mustangs.

Here was a chance to rope what so many riders had tried and failed to capture. The thirsty stallion would drink deep and come back up the bank loggy with water. After he had gone down the trail out of sight, the vaquero placed himself in position for a sure throw when the animal should emerge. He was riding a fresh pony.

Within a few minutes the long-sought-for lover of freedom emerged, his ears working, his body refreshed. He saw the man and made a dash so swift that he eluded the rope's throw. Quickly recoiling his reata for another cast, the vaquero spurred in pursuit. The Steed of the Prairies had come two hundred miles from his range on Onion Creek, besides pacing in great circles before he had finally headed straight for the Rio Grande. His marvelous endurance was at last wearing out; the water that had refreshed him now loaded him down.

The second loop thrown by the fast-running vaquero went over his head. But he did not run full speed on the rope and jerk himself down. His response showed that he had been roped before. He wheeled just as the rope tightened and with wide-open mouth rushed at his captor. He did not seem to see the horse ridden by the vaquero. He was after the man. He nearly seized him, but the agile cow pony had wheeled also. Fortunately for the vaquero's life, some scattered mesquite trees grew just ahead of him. He managed to get one of these mesquites between himself and the roped stallion. The mesquite served as a snubbing post for tying up the stallion. However worn by his long war of defense, he was, at close quarters, still magnificent.

The vaquero left in a long lope to get help. He returned with two other vaqueros. With three ropes checking the White Mustang's attempts to fight, they led and drove him to a grassy spot on the prairie near the ranch corrals. There they threw him, tied the ropes so that he could not choke himself to death, fixed a clog on one of his forefeet, and staked him. When night came, he was standing where they left him, not having taken a mouthful of grass. The next day they carried a sawed-off barrel, used as a trough, within the horse's reach and filled it with water. He did not notice it. For ten days and ten nights he remained there, grass all about him, water within reach of his muzzle, without taking one bite or one swallow. Then he lay down and died.

This story, in full detail, was told to me by John R. Morgan when he was past eighty-six years old. In 1868 he came from Kentucky to ride with his uncle John W. Young and learned the history of the wonderful horse from men who had chased him. To him it was a part of the Onion Creek land.[7]

In 1927 I got into correspondence with a frontiersman named Curly Hatcher then living at Myrtle Point, Oregon.[8] This is his story:

"While I was catching wild horses on the Kansas and Colorado line in 1868, I saw the famous mustang often. He never ranged with other mustangs but always alone. When I first saw him he was a beautiful gray with long mane and tail, and many a time

I ran him in an attempt to rope him. Always I rode the fastest horses I could get, but never one that could make this mustang break his pace. After I quit running him I heard of him drifting gradually south, through No Man's Land and New Mexico and then below the Staked Plains. He was known to many men of the frontier. In 1874 I laid eyes on him again.

"I was a Texas Ranger and while carrying dispatches came upon him about twenty miles east of Menard on the San Saba River. He was almost white now, but I recognized him immediately as the horse I had chased along the Kansas-Colorado line six years before. I took after him, but as usual got nothing but his dust. I had to go on and deliver the dispatches. The next day when I came back over the same trail I found him dead. Sign showed that a Mexican lion had jumped out of a live oak tree onto his back and bit him in the neck. The ground was torn up from a terrible struggle. I examined the beautiful horse closely but could find no brand or mark of any kind on him. I clipped his mane and tail and as soon as I got back to camp wove a small rope out of the hair. This I kept for years as a souvenir of the greatest mustang in the world. Some of the old boys yet living have no doubt seen the horse."

One of the "old boys" was Andy Mather, of Liberty Hill, Texas, long since dead. "Yes," he said to me, "I knew Curly Hatcher well and I know he was lying about finding the Pacing White Mustang dead in Menard County. In the early days I heard of that horse a thousand times but he was always on the plains and to the north."

Andy Mather was a hasty man. Another frontiersman, C. M. Grady, who rangered with Curly Hatcher corroborated him, in part at least. According to his testimony,[9] in 1875, he and some other men on a buffalo hunt sighted a band of wild horses near the Santa Anna Mountains, in Coleman County. "As we rode out towards them, the most beautiful stallion I had ever seen, iron-gray and a pacer, stepped into view. The race was on. The stallion took the lead, his long mane hanging on both sides of his neck. He skimmed through the air like a flying bird. We soon gave up the chase. . . .

"Months later we came upon his band again, and again he paced away, like a bird flying, like a spirit horse. After that, one day alone, I came upon him asleep at the edge of East Santa Anna Mountain. I drew rein and looked at him for several seconds. The thought came to me that as I could never hope to catch him I would just shoot him as he slept. I raised my gun to my shoulder, but could not find the power within me to shoot such a beautiful creature. We all wanted him. Two men, John and Will Hampton of Burnet County, quit our ranger company to try to catch him, but never succeeded. . . . All the settlers, Staffords, St. Clairs, Hardins, Livingstons and Robertsons, tried to catch the gray horse but in vain.

"The last I heard of him he had moved on west. His range lay west of Table Mountain, and he was seen there several years later by Curly Hatcher and others, who were still trying to catch him. He moved on into the Golden West and never more was seen on his old range."

Maybe Curly Hatcher just dreamed that the great steed had been killed by a panther. "He moved on into the Golden West." White Horse Plains in Colorado, south of Cheyenne, is named for him, they say. White Horse Plain, up the Assiniboine from Winnipeg, was named for him too, they say.[10]

In 1924 a veteran trail driver named J. L. Hill, then living in Long Beach, California, issued two meaty, paper-bound booklets entitled *The End of the Cattle Trail* and *The Passing of the Indian and the Buffalo* in which he said something about mustanging. I wrote to ask if he had ever come across the White Steed of the Prairies.

"I have heard many times," he replied, "of the Pacing White Mustang. When I heard of him first, in the seventies, I was a clabber-lipped cowboy. I was living in Bonham, Texas, just south

[157]

of Red River. Various riders of the country kept bringing in word about a band of mustangs led by the Pacing Stallion. At that time he was ranging between Fort Sill and the Washita River, in the Indian Territory.

"Dick Bragg of Bonham kept race ponies that he would run against anything in Texas or the Territory for stakes as high as any man wanted to put up. In the fall of '79, after the round-ups were over, an extensive party organized to capture the stallion. With them they took the fastest of Dick Bragg's race stock as well as everything else in the country that could run. Dick Bragg himself was along, hoping to add the champion race horse of the world to his string. A number of reservation Indians were in on the hunt.

"The boys found their Mustang all right. They laid all kinds of traps for him and tried all kinds of dodges to run him down or hem him in. But when he was crowded he would break off from his manada, they said, and pace away like the wind. According to their report, he was not pure white but of a light cream color with snow-white mane and tail. The Indians believed him to be supernatural and called him the Ghost Horse of the Prairies or the Winged Steed. When running at a distance he showed nothing but a fast-flying snow-white mane and snow-white tail that looked like wings skimming the ground. The boys who got nearest to him said he had a piece of rawhide rope around his neck. They thought he had been snared at some watering and that the experience had helped to make him what he was — the most alert and the wildest as well as the fleetest animal in western America.

"Mustang hunters kept after him, and later I heard that he had changed his range from the Washita to the South Canadian. Such a change showed wonderful cunning, for the ordinary mustang when chased would keep circling within certain limits until he was finally closed in. Some of the mustangers swore they would get the White Ghost of the Prairies even if they had to shoot him. Death from a rifle may have been his fate. I last heard of him in 1881."

The latest date I have is 1889. In that year, as a lost mine hunter with a "constructive memory" told me, down in the Sierra Madre, the White Steed was ranging out from Phoenix, Arizona. Some man in bonanza offered two thousand dollars for him alive and unharmed. When pursued, he always paced out into the desert wastes, where he could go without water for days. Finally a hunter creased him, haltered him, led him to a strong corral, and collected the reward. But no power could make the horse submit. He walked restlessly about the corral, gnawed on the logs, nickered occasionally to the far-beckoning mountains, and refused food or water until he died — the usual ten days after capture.

According to another story, P. T. Barnum offered a reward of five thousand dollars for the horse. This was at a time, as a frontiersman named George McNeill used to tell, when the Pacing White Stallion ranged along the Bosque River in central Texas — a region noted for good horses. About every three months fifty or sixty men would organize to win the reward. One day while George McNeill was running him, his horse fell in a badger hole, breaking McNeill's leg. With help from another rider he remounted and was angling towards the pacing stallion when he saw a man shoot to crease him — and break his neck.

In 1926 while I was attending a convention of cattlemen in Fort Worth — to write an article — I fell in with a former sheepherder from New Mexico named Sandy Morris. He had a guitar, about thirty cowboy songs in his memory, and sufficient powers of endurance to sing all day and nearly all night. He kept the lobby of the convention hotel musical as long as a single soul remained awake to listen. While he was resting between songs, we had considerable talk and later I received letters from him. This is one story he told me.

[159]

"Along about 1875, I was riding down a road in the Llano River country of Texas when I spied a newspaper on the ground half covered by sand. Of course I got down and picked it up. I paid no attention as to where it had been printed, but I can never forget the story it told of a snow-white mustang stallion.

"It seems that the stallion had been ranging in the vicinity of a frontier fort, when one day a soldier saw him against the corral fence. He went outside afoot to investigate. The stallion made a dash at him, caught him by the back of the neck and killed him. After that, cowboys joined the post cavalry in a hunt to take the stallion alive. Everybody knew him. They had got on to his way of running, and they placed men in relays every five miles over a distance of eighty miles. Well, the White Mustang struck the expected course all right — and he went through those eighty miles without breaking his pace, and not a man got close enough to swing his rope. Then some soldier shot him dead. Some of the men who knew his history had a superstitious turn of mind. They said he would show up on his old range the next day. Whether he did or not, I can't say."

This "superstitious turn of mind" belonged to the illimitable spaces of sky and grass, to the drifts of buffaloes, to the howls of the buffalo wolves and the star-tingling cries of the little coyotes that in the night intensified the silences, and to the glow of coals and the evanescence of grayish smoke where a few minuscular human beings camped. But not all mystery is superstition.

Along in the '50s, as the story goes,[11] a fiddling, yarning character called Kentuck reached Santa Fe and threw in with an Arkansas gambler under the name of Jake. They heard so much talk about the White Steed of the Prairies and Jake had such a run of good luck that he decided to take his partner and hunt down the horse. He bought pack mules, everything needed for a pack trip, and four New Mexican horses of speed and endurance.

[160]

"I don't know exactly whur to hunt," Jake said, "but we'll ride on the prairies till we find the hoss or till they are burned crisp by the fires of Jedgment Day." He had a kind of fever in his mind.

They rode east on the Santa Fe Trail, and then away north of the Arkansas plains; they criss-crossed the endless carpet of short buffalo grass back southward until they were on the Staked Plains of the Canadian. They shot buffaloes and lived on hump. They dodged Indians and met no white man. Wherever wild horse sign led, they followed. They saw many bands and many stallions without bands, with now and then a white or gray among them, but not the White Stallion.

Summer passed into fall and northers brought the fluting sand-hill cranes. Kentuck, who had not from the start had any heart in this wild-goose chase, yearned for bed and bed-warmer in Santa Fe. The longer Jake hunted and the more mustangs he saw, the hotter he grew on the quest.

"Go back if you want," he said with a fixed hardness to his partner. "Go and rot. I hev sworn to git what I come to git. If I don't git him, I'll keep on a-hunting till the Day of Jedgment."

The White Pacer and the Day of Judgment seemed linked in his mind, and nothing else in it came to the surface. As winter opened, he took it into his head that the White Stallion would appear pacing out of the southwest. Whether riding or camping, he seldom looked now in another direction.

One cold, misty day, visibility cut to only a few yards, their camp backed against a rise of ground to the north, near a lake, the men huddled and pottered about a feeble fire of wet buffalo chips. They existed only to ride on. About sunset the skies cleared. For an hour not a word had been said. Now, while Kentuck rustled for chips dry on the bottom side, Jake squatted in his serape, straining his eyes towards the southwest as if he expected to catch the movement of something no bigger than a

[161]

curlew's head in the rim of grass blades. The glow of the sun had melted and a full moon was coming up in the clear sky when he yelled, "Yonder," and ran towards his staked horse.

"I supposed it was Indians and grabbed my rifle," Kentuck later told. "Then my eyes picked up the white horse. He stood there to the southwest, maybe a hundred yards off, head lifted, facing us, as motionless as a statue. In the white moonlight his proportions were all that the tales had given him. He did not move until Jake moved towards him. As I made for my horse, I saw that Jake was riding without saddle, though he had bridled his horse and held his reata. We kept our rawhide lariats well greased so that they would not get limp from water and stiffen when dry.

"The White Pacer paced east, against the moon, and against a breeze springing up. He seemed to glide rather than work his legs, he went so smoothly. He did not seem to be trying to get away, only to hold his distance. He moved like a white shadow, and the harder we rode, the more shadowy he looked."

After the run had winded his horse, Kentuck called out, "Jake, I don't like this. There's no sense to it. I'm remembering things we've both heard. Let's stop. We can't no more catch up with him than with our own shadows."

Jake had lost his hat. His long black hair was streaming back. His set features were those of a madman. He screamed out, "Stop if yer want. I've told yer I'm a-going to foller till the Day of Jedgment."

Not another word passed between the two. Kentuck did not stop. "Riding on and on out there in the middle of nowhere, not even a coyote breaking the silence, it didn't seem like this world," he said. Then he made out a long black line across the ground ahead. "It'll soon be settled now," he thought, "and we'll know whether the White Stallion can cross empty space like a ghost." Pulling back his horse, he yelled to Jake, "Watch out for the canyon — the bluff."

The word "Jedgment" came to his ears and he saw Jake using his coiled reata for a quirt. Then he disappeared over the bluff. Kentuck was watching him so intently that he did not see what became of the Pacing White Stallion.

Kentuck walked from his heaving horse to examine the canyon brink. He could hear nothing below. Downward in the moonlight he saw only jags of ground amid the stubby growth called *palo duro* (hard wood). He called, but there was no response. He hobbled his horse and about daylight found a buffalo trail leading down the turreted bluffs. Soon after sunup he came upon what was left of Jake and his horse, a full hundred feet below the jumping-off place. He did the best he could for a grave.

In Santa Fe his story was no novelty. Some who heard it had known more than one man to come back from far away with his partner's horses and an explanation.

The "superstitious turns" of the legend are mostly Indian. The Kiowas were sure that neither fire nor lead could injure the great White Horse. A prairie fire might burn to death the mares and colts under his domination, but he would emerge from it unsinged; a bullet might pass through his body but would not injure it. At a reunion of Texas Rangers on the San Saba River in 1929, a veteran named Fred B. Hambledon, then living in Denver, told me a good deal about what he had learned from Utes and Comanches while he lived among them. Individuals in both tribes, he said, had traditions of the Phantom White Stallion. He had heard Uncle Dick Wootton, the Mountain Man who made Raton Pass noted, tell about the Stallion's leaping an immense chasm; Uncle Dick inclined to believe with Indians that he was a ghost horse. Many years ago, E. E. Dale, Professor of Western History at the University of Oklahoma, asked an old Comanche named Julián how his tribesmen came to own so many white-spotted ponies. "They all came from the White Stallion of the Plains," the old Comanche answered.

However he might entice after him the paramours of other stallions, the White Mustang was not of a malevolent disposition. Only in the tale that Sandy Morris found in a newspaper half buried in the sand does he so appear, and in an exaggerated narrative called *Wild Jim, the Texas Cowboy and Saddle King* that a certain "Captain" W. J. French printed at Antioch, Illinois, in 1890. Herein the stallion appears as a man-killer. His captor, who went by the modest title of "Champion Wild Horse Breaker of Texas," "laid out on the prairie a whole year" following the White Stallion and his drove of "a thousand or more" mares. Finally by an extraordinary ruse he captured the leader and then trained him to allow no other man to approach him and to fight any stranger "like a panther." He killed at least "half a dozen men," most of them horse thieves trying to cut his picket rope. But in the narratives of the soil the Pacing White Mustang is consistently generous and noble.

A half century back, Dr. J. O. Dyer of Galveston was pursuing an unsleeping passion for the lore of early days. Some of it he wrote down. Along in the '70s he heard the following story, which in his last years — and that was a long time ago, too — he transmitted to me. It was, according to Doctor Dyer, told by a woman who as a girl came with German colonists to settle in Texas, about 1848.

They were moving up the Guadalupe River in wagons. Gretchen's family, at the end of the train, had a gentle old gray mare that followed their wagon without rope or halter, stopping every once in a while to grab a mouthful of particularly lush grass. She was stupid and lazy and her ears flopped, but she was faithful. She carried two big sacks of corn meal so arranged that they made a kind of platform.

The wagon was running over with such things as German settlers carried — beds and bedding, pots and pans, mugs and plates, a heavy chest of drawers, a sauerkraut keg, and a great many children. Gretchen, eight or nine years old, was the live-liest of these. One day she asked her father to let her ride the old gray mare. He could see no harm in this; in fact, her absence might lessen the constant hubbub. So he lifted Gretchen up on the platform of corn meal sacks and tied her there with a rope in such a way that she would be comfortable but could not fall off. The old mare hardly batted an eye, and with Gretchen on her back continued as usual to walk and pick grass along behind the wagon.

That afternoon at a gully the tire of a wagon wheel fell away from the felloes, shrunken by dry weather, and several spokes were broken. When the halt was made for repairs, Gretchen was asleep, firmly tied on her pillion of corn meal. She did not know when the old gray mare grazed out of sight down a draw. Her father was busy with the wheel; her mother, like the old woman who lived in a shoe, had so many children that she did not know what to do; and so neither of them noticed. It was only after the wagon was repaired and the other children were counted into it and the train started on, that little Gretchen was missed. Then the old gray mare could not be found. None of the German men, so new to the frontier, could follow her tracks in the maze of mustang tracks they now discovered. They struck camp to search. Night came and no little Gretchen; the next day came and passed and no little Gretchen. Then on the morning of the third day the old mare brought her in, and this is the explanation the little girl gave.

After dozing she knew not how long, she awoke with a start. The lazy old mare had come to life and was lumbering along in a gallop after a neighing, pacing white horse with cream-colored mane and tail. She tried to stop the old mare, but she had neither bridle nor halter. She tried to jump off, but she was tied on and the knots of the rope were beyond her reach.

After the old mare had trotted and galloped until nearly sun-down, the white horse all the time pacing ahead "like a rocking chair," they came to a large bunch of mares. They came out full of curiosity to greet their new sister, and they were very cordial in their greeting.

The wild mares seemed not to notice little Gretchen at all. They were so cordial in their nosings of the old gray mare that soon their muzzles were touching the meal sacks. Probably the sacking was salty. Some of the meal had sifted through. The mares tasted it. No matter if it was the first taste of corn they had ever had, they liked it.

They began to nip at the meal sacks so eagerly that they nipped Gretchen's bare legs. She screeched. She expected to be chewed up right away, even if the mares meant no harm. But at her cry the Pacing White Stallion was with one bound beside her. He was as considerate as he was intelligent. He drove the wild mares off. Then he chewed in two the ropes that bound Gretchen. Next he took her gently by the collar of her dress, very much as a cat takes one of her kittens, and set her down upon the ground.

It was about dark now and the coyotes were beginning to howl. Little Gretchen howled too, but there was no danger. After a while she made a kind of nest in some tall fragrant grass near a Spanish oak and, having cried a while, fell asleep.

When she awoke, the sun was high and not a horse was in sight. She was hungry. She went down to a waterhole that she saw close by and drank water for breakfast. She had heard that a person lost away out in the wilds had better stay in one place until he "found himself" or until someone found him. She had no hope of finding herself; she wished her papa would come. She remained near the waterhole.

Noon came and still no horse or person appeared within sight. Gretchen was hungrier than ever. It was late spring, and she gathered some of the red agrito berries (called also wild currants) growing near, but the thorny leaves pricked her fingers so severely that she quit before she had eaten enough to satisfy

[166]

her hunger. Evening fell and she was still alone. She gathered some sheep sorrel down in the bottom of the draw and drank more water. Darkness came, the stars came out, the coyotes set up their lonely howling. Little Gretchen lay down in her nest again and again cried herself to sleep.

When she awoke the next morning, there standing over her, sound asleep, ears flopped down and lower lip hanging shapeless like a bag of curd, was the old gray mare. Gretchen was as glad as the redbird singing over her head. She jumped up and ran to the mare and tried to get on her. But the old mare was too tall. Then Gretchen grasped her by the mane and tried to lead her to a log that lay near at hand. If she could get the old mare beside it, she could use it as a stepping block. But the stupid old mare would not budge. After vainly pulling, coaxing, and jumping about for a long time, Gretchen began to wail.

She was leaning against the shoulder of the old mare sobbing, when she heard swift hoofbeats, rhythmic and racking. She looked up and saw the beautiful White Steed. The sunshine was on his whiteness. He came arching his neck and pacing with all the fire of a mustang emperor, but there was something about him that prevented Gretchen from being in the least frightened. On the contrary, she stretched her arms towards him and gave a childish "oh" of welcome. He paced right up to where she stood, gently grasped the collar of her dress and the scruff of her neck in his teeth and lifted her upon the mare. Then he must have told the old gray mare to go home. At least she went — went with Gretchen but no corn meal.

Home was the camp by the gully where the wagon had broken down. Gretchen's parents were so happy at having her restored that they did not mind the loss of the meal. After she had told her adventures, she showed the nipped places on her legs.

In after years she told the story many, many times. If her children and grandchildren seemed doubtful of the facts, she would in a pet pull down her cotton stockings and show the small, faint scars on her legs where the wild mares had nipped her. Then the children would have to believe.

3. Spanish Pacers and White Color

The Spaniards introduced a strain of natural pacers into the Americas. Describing the horses of Sonora as well-built, small-boned, comely, proud, swift and enduring, a historian who lived among these horses for eleven years in the mid 18th century classified them in ranchero style as *caballos de camino* (travelers) and *caballos de campo* (what later came to be called cow horses). The *caballos de camino*, he said, paced as fast as any other horse could gallop and some paced up with running horses. They were incapable of running or trotting. Their gait was so smooth that "the rider could hold a glass full of water in his hand without spilling a drop." [12]

The strain was better preserved in South than in North America. In 1888 the minister from the United States to Colombia wrote: "The native horses are rarely over fifteen hands high, and but few are of that height. They all pace from their birth." [13] Tracing directly back to colonial times, the *caballo nacional* of Peru still has a *paso* peculiar unto itself. Many of these small national horses are of a light color — gray, white, palomino, with black skins. [14] According to the best evidence, the Narragansett pacers of New England, famous long before the Revolutionary War and now vanished, were descended from a stallion imported from Spain.

Charles W. Webber, who is reputed to have been a Texas Ranger in the '40s and who was among the early writers on the Texas scene, admitted that he had never seen the White Steed of the Prairies, though he had "often heard" of him from mustang hunters. "All the white mustangs I have ever seen," he said, "were natural pacers." [15] How many white mustangs Webber had seen, nobody could swear. Most Spanish horses walked slow, trotted hard and galloped soft; some few had a running walk; fewer paced. Pacing horses have never been favored by ranch people; they are too apt to stumble.

A white mustang was never a rarity like a white buffalo. As late as 1882 a band of thirteen white mustangs ran between the Palo Duro Canyon and the Canadian River in the Texas Panhandle — so alert that nobody ever saw them standing. [16]

Indians liked white-spotted horses, which blend leopard-like with the earth, but not white horses. They are too easy to see, especially at night. One of the favorite nighttime ruses of the Pawnees against their enemies was to picket a white horse a little out from camp and then wait in ambush for thieves, who could be relied upon to spot that horse first of all. [17] As soon as it was dark a party of Mountain Men in the vicinity of hostile Blackfeet covered a white horse with blankets. [18] One day in 1932 while I was driving from Austin to San Antonio, I picked up an oldish man carrying a pack on his back. He told me that his father had been a ranger with Captain L. H. McNelly. This noted captain, he said, would not allow a ranger to ride a white horse or a horse with a white face. White would make a target for Indians and bandits. The idea was common all during turbulent times on the frontiers.

Belief was widespread, furthermore, that white horses lack endurance. In many minds they were associated with weak-eyed albinos, though the prejudice did not extend to grays. It included, especially among range men outside of California, palominos. Captain John G. Bourke observed that in General Crook's campaign of 1876 against the Sioux, white horses ridden by a certain cavalry troop stood up better, contrary to superstition, than all others. [19]

Overwhelming all prejudice against the color, is the association of the white horse with power, pride, glory, with feared conquerors and adored deliverers. Vishnu of the Hindus skimmed the world on his white horse long before St. John the Divine saw the seals opened and beheld a crowned one going forth upon a white horse conquering and to conquer, beheld Death upon a pale horse, and then later beheld one called Faithful and True upon a white horse followed by the armies of Heaven, all on white horses. Joan of Arc rode a white horse. In the old Confederate rhyme, "Jeff Davis rode a white horse." On gray Traveler, Robert E. Lee epitomized a holy cause. Buffalo Bill, last in line of the traditional Men on Horseback, showed himself to the millions of America and Europe always upon a white horse. For thousands of years white has been the color of supremacy, of sublimity and of mystery, the color most stirring to imagination.

Only this color from among hues of infinite variety that clothed the wild horses could have been sublimated into the legend that in space and time transcends all other animal legends of the Western Hemisphere.

When Washington Irving first heard of the great White Mustang in 1832 — though his color inclined to gray then — he had already tantalized wild-horse runners for "six or seven years," between the Arkansas and the Cimarron. From that time until 1889, when, according to story, he was captured near Phoenix, Arizona, and stood in a pen for ten days without touching food or water, his ears pointed to the far mountains of freedom, neighing his death song, is a long time for any king to reign.

The tradition represents a lost culture, the culture of the Horse Age, before machinery outmoded it. It embodies the ideals of peoples who lived by the horse. It belongs now with the memories of Pegasus and Bucephalus.

X

DEATH AND LIBERTY

1. Black Devil

WHILE Washington Irving was listening to prairie talk about the Pacing White Mustang, he heard "equally marvelous accounts of a black horse" on the upper Brazos River in Texas. For a time black somewhat rivaled white in fame. A diary-keeper with Kearney's army who knew wild horses only by fame's coloring was "too far away" from three runners on the Arkansas "to see whether the famous black, or as some say white, horse was among them." [1] About the same time, in the year 1846, a surgeon with Taylor's army at the capture of Monterrey heard of a jet-black mustang sixteen hands high, ranging over on the other side of the mountain, that could "outspeed the famous White Pacer of the Plains." [2] But in character, features and exploits, no black mustang ever emerged out of actuality into the renown that imagination wove around the White Stallion.

Perhaps in Texas, where Santa Anna flew the black flag to annihilate the last man of the Alamo, black became more closely associated with ferocity than elsewhere in the West. Nelson Lee's Black Prince "regarded a Mexican or an Indian with such intense hatred that in a fight his teeth and heels often rendered as effectual service as the armed rider on his back" — and this particular armed rider was death-to-the-devil. [3]

Tales about man-killing black stallions among the mustangs seem to be mostly Indian folklore. Some time before the Civil War, so one tale goes, [4] a strong band of Shoshones came from the north to raid horses among the Comanches on the San Saba River.* One night they awoke to the sounds of a great commotion among their horses. Rushing forth, they saw a monstrous black stallion gnawing the hobbles from the mares and turning them into his own manada, which stood to one side. The Indians shouted, but the marauder paid no attention. They shot their arrows, but the arrows glanced off the black skin of the target as

* I don't know if the Shoshones, or Snakes, of the Northwest ever came as far south as central Texas to steal horses. It is entirely possible and even likely that they did. Certainly the tale of the black stallion of the San Saba is in their style. Says Colonel Albert G. Brackett, in an article on "The Shoshonis or Snake Indians," *Annual Report of the Smithsonian Institution for 1879*, 332:

"In the long and dreary days of winter the Indians sit in their lodges, where there is a good supply of meat, and pass the time as best they can. They tell stories of their hunting expeditions and war parties, and embellish their narratives as much as possible. They tell of the Great Brown Bear of the Mountains . . . , of the Giant Big Horn . . . , of the ghosts . . . , of the Big Beaver . . . , of the Black Raven. . . . These stories and many more they tell each other, until, like children, they cower near the lodge-fires and are afraid to go out alone. Never were there more marvelous story-tellers, and never were there more willing listeners."

harmlessly as if it were obsidian. Then a few of the boldest warriors rushed upon him. One swung his long reata and cast the loop over the stallion's head. Squealing with rage, the black made for the roper, seized him in his mouth, and, carrying him as easily as a coyote carries a cottontail rabbit, disappeared into the darkness, his mares fleeing before him.

The trail lay plain under the moon. The Shoshones followed to the rescue. At daylight they came into the rank grass of a dried-up lake. There they saw the stallion, amid his mares, eating the flesh of their comrade.

The next night Black Devil, as he came to be called, returned to the Shoshone camp and gnawed the hobbles off sixteen other mares. Better to lose another life at his jaws than be left afoot. The braves painted themselves for the warpath and with a medicine man at their head set out to recapture the stolen stock. But Black Devil protected his mares with such ferocity that the Shoshones were glad to get away with the loss of only one man, whom the stallion dragged from his horse and pawed to death. Again bows and arrows proved futile. Within a few nights the black beast had stolen every mare the Shoshones possessed. They left the San Saba for their own hunting grounds.

A few years went by, and in Reconstruction days a troop of Negro cavalry was sent to Fort McKavett, on the San Saba. The depredations of the black stallion had ceased with the withdrawal of the Shoshones, but traditions of him lingered among the sparse inhabitants of the region. They were of a nature to appeal especially to Negro imagination, and "Ole Black Debble" was no joke to them.

One morning a trooper rode out alone on a mare that had been abandoned by the Apaches; at sunset he limped in afoot. Black Devil, he swore, had rushed upon him as he was rounding a hill, pulled him to the ground, and made away with the mare. Shortly afterwards two other troopers were attacked by a black stallion. Black Devil had come back.

About this time two Scotsmen set up a ranch in the San Saba hills. They lived in a dugout and built a high rock wall around a little patch of ground, which they planted in corn. They were mustangers, and after the crop was gathered, used the enclosure to hold wild horses. They had a well-bred stallion, and were putting picked mustang mares and fillies with him.

One night in their dugout the Scotsmen heard the shrieks that only stallions engaged in deadly combat make. Grabbing their six-shooters, they ran for the rock pen, and there in star-light they saw a powerful black horse fighting with their own stallion. The mares were ringed around the pair, and by the time the men got close enough to shoot without endangering their own horses, the black invader had thrown his antagonist to the ground and was chewing on him.

One of the men rushed back to the dugout for lariats. They had the far-famed Black Devil in their pen, and their one thought was to crease and tie him. Gun in hand, the first Scot crept nearer, his companion with lariat close behind. Black Devil knew the art of war. His mouth dripping blood, he lunged at his attackers. One of them fired, but the shot went wild and only tore into the horse's flank. Nevertheless, it saved the lives of the two men, for while they were madly scrambling over the fence, Black Devil stayed to bite at his wound.

But the halt was only momentary. He leaped the fence at one bound and plunged into the opening of the dugout. Though the dugout itself was roomy, the passage into it was narrow. As the powerful animal crashed downward, his hind quarters caught between the solid uprights. One of the men cut his throat. They had to butcher him into pieces before they could clear the door-way. The mustang terror of the San Saba had come to an end.

Some of the settlers said that the stallion killed by the Scots-men was not Black Devil, that Black Devil was purely a myth of the Shoshones, and that this was another horse. For a long time, at any rate, the Scotsmen used leather made from a black stallion's hide; one of them had a *cabestro* woven from his tail, and the other a girth twisted from his gleaming mane.

A story current among Apaches of New Mexico tells that horses on the Mescalero Reservation are descended from a stallion of Black Devil character.[5] Back in the raiding days, a warrior by the name of Cow Bird brought back a "big" stallion from a foray into Sonora. He named him Diablo, and named him well.

Cow Bird and Diablo carried on regular conversations with each other. The horse was not the only animal Cow Bird talked with. He was *poco loco*. The most peculiar thing about Diablo wasn't his power to talk. It was his dislike for the smell of chili. The faintest whiff of it simply set him insane. His nostrils were as sensitive as the horns of a snail. The instant they were irritated by a breath of chili, he was possessed by a raging lust for the taste of blood — the blood of the carrier of the fiery chili, human blood, even the blood of his own master.

Mexicans, with reason, feared Diablo, though they seemed not to know what infuriated him. They hated Cow Bird as leader of Apache horse thieves. They plotted to kill him and sent a knife-man to spy upon his movements and slip upon him and stab him.

One day when Cow Bird rode out alone into the mountains to make medicine with his guardian spirit, the knife-man had his chance. He followed Diablo's tracks; he knew the *tinaja* — rock hole holding water — where Cow Bird would camp. In the night he found him there. He waited far off for the hour before dawn. While he waited he ate a half-dozen chili-hot tamales. Finally, as silently as a shadow, he began crawling towards the sleeping man, not disturbing a pebble, not scraping a thorn. It was that hour when horses as well as men of the *campo* sleep deepest. Diablo was staked near Cow Bird's head, but the nostrils of wild animals do not close with their eyes.

Just as three more lengths of the creeping knife-man would have brought him to the strike, Diablo caught the maddening

[175]

smell of chili. His long, yellow teeth bared, he screamed as he sprang upon the Mexican.

As Cow Bird came instantly, but cautiously, to his senses, he heard a sound like that of a pig squealing with his head in a trough. Now in the starlight he saw Diablo champing the enemy's flesh and with angry shakes of his head flecking blood and froth to one side.

Perhaps he felt grateful at being saved from a stabbing, but he knew his horse. "Come, now, Diablo," he said in a soothing voice. "Enough for tonight."

But the black stallion was insane with fury. Normally he was most obedient to his master and in his way affectionate. Now he had no control over his lust for blood. He laid back his ears and charged. With the agility of a panther, Cow Bird side-stepped, and as the horse was wheeling for another charge sprang upon his back.

He was the best rider of whom the Apaches have any tradition. He could hang on like a tick. His instinct told him what a horse was going to do next, no matter how fast he did it. On Diablo he had the benefit of experience as well as of instinct.

Black Diablo plunged and pawed for the stars. He fence-rowed over gullies and twisted among boulders. He lunged through the chaparral with more kinks in his back than a coach-whip snake makes crawling into a rat's nest of cholla joints. He was forked lightning and dynamite in one container. Now he was showing his belly to the sky, and now streaking out like a paisano after a dodging grasshopper. He reared up on his hind legs and pitched straight down with head between his pastern joints. He flung himself to the ground, but every time he did this, the Apache stepped off and then as Diablo rose was on his back. The brute was nothing but raging energy.

Just as dawn was breaking, Diablo stumbled and fell. He knew he was whipped. Cow Bird, though victorious, was utterly whipped out. Breathing heavily and with blood running out his mouth and nostrils, he lay to one side of the no longer struggling horse. For a long time both lay in exhaustion. Finally, the black stallion managed to stand up.

"Master," he spoke, "if I could, I would kill you. Yet I love you. I have no power left within me. Now I will travel to a high mesa, where the air is pure and grass is near water. There I will regain my strength and my mind. Come not for me, Master. If you do, I will kill you. Henceforth I will be free, a free mustang as I was born. Now I say what is to be remembered: The liberty of the horse will outlast the liberty of the man."

"Horse of the Christian's Devil of Hell," the Apache replied, "I have heard you. Go where you will. You have borne me well and saved my life. My people will never disturb you. You are a mustang again as you were born."

As the sun was setting four days later, Cow Bird, lying on a blanket in his wickiup, heard a high nicker come over the breeze from the west. "Diablo is lonesome," he said. "Before another sun sets he will be lipping salt out of my hand."

It was to be days before he again had a desire to ride, but early next morning he limped out to see his sorrel mare. All he found was a pair of chewed-off hobbles. From that day to this, wild horses of Diablo's blood have ranged the slopes of Old Baldy in the Mescalero Apache Reservation, climbing where no rider can follow, their nostrils as quick to the scent of man as those of their ancestor were to the fiery effluvium of chili.

The idea of a horse's turning carnivorous, even in a legend, will appear absurd to some readers. Not to justify legend but to illustrate equine adaptability, I could adduce several instances of flesh-eating horses. One will suffice. A Montana blizzard of 1866 froze thousands of buffaloes and froze all the oxen belonging to freight trains owned by Alexander Topence and J. J. Mann. They were camped on the Quaking Asp and saved the lives of two mules by sheltering them in a tent during the worst of the blizzard. After the blizzard had spent its force, they set out to ride to Helena, five hundred miles away. They found frozen carcasses of buffaloes lying in the snow in many places. "Every night," Alexander Topence recorded in his realistic *Reminiscences*,[6] "we would take a hind quarter of buffalo meat and hang it up in a tree by means of a long pole and build a good fire under it and roast it as well as we could, and when it was done we would lay it on the ground before the mules. They would set one foot on the meat to hold it steady, and start in and tear off big chunks of hot meat and fat with their teeth and chew it just like hay. The two mules would gnaw the meat clean to the bone."

2. *Blue Streak*

In the early part of this century Blue Streak[7] lived in the arid mountains of Nevada, occasionally coming down to the sage-bush mesas. In one angle of sunlight his color was an intensified grullo (crane-colored), indicating his Spanish ancestry; in another angle, blue black, with sheen of grackle, except for white stockings and blazed face. His small hoofs were flint hard. All his flesh seemed to be deer-leg muscles, integrated by the finest steel springs. His neck had the curve of the bronze horses of Lysippus, which once stood on Nero's arch in Rome and now animate the front of St. Mark's cathedral in Venice. His back was saddle perfect.

One winter day Rube Terrill and two other ranchers of the Indian Creek country jumped him and his small band of mares on a mesa against a mountain. They were riding grain-fed horses, and while they managed two or three times to head the bunch towards rocked-up blind canyons in which other mustangs had been trapped, Blue Streak jumped over and across natural impediments that might make mountain goats hesitate. He had trained his mares to jump in the same way. He led them back into mountain roughness by ways that no rider could follow.

It was three winters before Blue Streak was seen on mesa again. That was a very hard winter, every bite of food in the high roughs under ice and snow. Fully twenty men had tried first and last to capture Blue Streak. After several runs, Rube Terrill swore off trying to capture him as he had sworn off whiskey. Then about the first of March he and two of his men went to Cock-

alorum Spring to bring in some saddle horses. As they approached the spring without being seen and against the wind, they saw the horses drinking, just beyond a barbed wire fence. Blue Streak was with them — without his mares. Perhaps in all the chasing he had become separated from them; perhaps they had been captured; perhaps in hunger and loneliness he had from mountain security seen the saddle horses and come down for company and grass. Anyhow, there he was.

Near the spring and on the edge of the meadow, was a corral with walls eight feet high that had been used as a trap for wild horses when all the springs in the country but Cockalorum went dry. The wide gate was open. Rube Terrill dismounted, went through the barbed wire, grabbed up a handful of pebbles and with a yell threw them towards the horses. Blue Streak acted as if he had no knowledge of man on his own feet. He certainly was not so fearful of him as he would have been of a horseman. He ran with the remuda into the pen.

He accepted his Waterloo with dignity. His almost docile acceptance of the saddle was disappointing. Rube Terrill left him a stallion and gave him no chance to return to the wilds.

One day he rode him to Minersville. Everybody in the country now knew Blue Streak by description and reputation if not by sight.

"Give you five hundred for him," a man yelled out.

Excited by the sight of so many people and houses, Blue Streak pranced on more magnificently while his owner yelled back, "Seven hundred fifty would not touch him."

"I guess a thousand would." The speaker was a mining magnate named Abner Temple from Salt Lake City.

He paid over the thousand and had a boxcar especially padded and bedded, supplied with grain and water and put under the care of a reliable man for transporting Blue Streak. The stallion never had shown viciousness and he traveled with an even temper.

Riding through Salt Lake City on Blue Streak, Abner Temple made the kind of sensation he had yearned for. He took pride in owning a horse that other men wanted. One night somebody tried to steal him. He put padlocks on every gate, door and window of his pen and stable. He had a blacksmith shoe Blue Streak.

Then one night the Temple household heard a tremendous pounding in the stable. By the time they arrived with a lantern, Blue Streak was gone. The wall looked as if it had been knocked out with sledge hammers. Abner Temple offered a thousand dollars for apprehension of the thief. When evidence failed to come in, he offered a thousand dollars for return of the horse and no questions asked. Newspapers ran articles describing Blue Streak and giving his history. There could not be in all Utah and Nevada another blue-black stallion with his blazed face, white stockings and spirit-lifting carriage. Even a Coca-Cola advertisement writer who had never noticed a horse would have lifted his head at sight of him.

Finally, Abner Temple received a letter from a farmer on the Utah-Nevada line. "Sur," he wrote, "I seen in the papper about your blue and black stallyern. day before yisterday I sighted an annimal of that deskripshun he was in some willers. yisterday morning there was a big hole in my plank and picket fence where he had gone throe. $5 will cover damages and oblige."

Abner Temple now got the idea that Blue Streak was managing his own escape instead of being managed. He sent for the blacksmith who had shod him. They examined the torn-out planking of the stable wall and decided that marks on it were from powerfully driven horseshoes. Abner Temple set out by automobile for Nevada. He heard that a farmer driving a team at night over the approach to a canyon bridge had been startled by hoofbeats on the wooden floor and then, while trying to control his runaways, had seen a black streak going east.

Abner Temple took the train for Minersville and from there rode to Rube Terrill's ranch. Rube Terrill had not heard the news. The reward Abner Temple offered woke him and his riders up. After riding for ten days out from the Indian Creek country and sighting various mustangs, they came upon a dead sorrel stallion, terribly mauled and lacerated.

"Blue Streak took his mares," Rube Terrill said.

That afternoon through glasses he got a sure view of the blue-black priding it over seventeen mares. He was up in the roughs, at home in his citadel.

"Maybe he'll come down this winter," Rube Terrill reported to impatient Abner Temple.

"I want him now," the mining magnate said.

"It would take five outfits of mustangers to do any good at all in those mountains," Rube Terrill explained.

"How much would six outfits of mustangers cost?" Abner Temple had checkbook in hand.

It took Rube Terrill two weeks to get the mustangers organized. Up in the mountains they guarded all waterings over a big spread of country and learned that Blue Streak could go dry for five days at a time. They located horse trails through narrow defiles and set snares, and saw that the mustangs climbed around the passes. They decided to run the manada down by relays. They ran it until Blue Streak had only six mares left. Then they lost the bunch. They went back to their homes and regular work.

One day a message came to Rube Terrill from a Paiute Indian named Roki that the blue-black stallion was in the Wind River Mountains of Nevada, a hundred miles away. Roki said he would have him in a hair rope and would deliver him for "much money." The mustangers rode for the Wind River Mountains.

One mountain of this group rises from a gulched and tumbled plain like Gibraltar above the Mediterranean. It somewhat resembles the form of a lion with tail down. The only trail up it is along the tail — not difficult at all. Whoever goes up that trail must return the same way.

And now Blue Streak and the last of his mares were climbing it. Without relenting for an hour, the Paiutes had for days been at their heels, witnessing leaps across chasms and clamberings up walls they had thought no horse could make. The Rube Terrill mustangers rode up to the mountain just in time to witness, in broken glimpses, the ascent of pursued and pursuers.

Blue Streak was in the lead, followed by four mares. Behind them rode Roki and three other Paiutes. There could be no wild rushing up the steep, narrow lion's tail of rock, defined by sheer bluff on either side. The lion's back is broader, the sheer bluffs deeper. Blue Streak led on over the back and the roughly nar-

[182]

rowed neck to the jut of the lion's head. This head has one ear, maybe a hundred yards long, hardly twenty feet wide at the point. Now the Paiutes were at the base of the ear, the mares and the stallion out on the short, narrow projection.

As the Indians paused for their horses to breathe, they took down their ropes. Head high and breathing in whistles, the blue-black faced them, came forward a few steps as if intending to rush upon them. They swung their loops. He whirled and hurled himself through the huddled mares. They followed to the granitic jags hundreds of feet below.

3. Starface

Starface [8] was a deep bay with a white star-shaped patch in his forehead and a stocking on his right forefoot. It was believed that he had Morgan blood in his veins; he might have been pure Spanish. In 1878 he was commanding a large band of mustangs that ranged between the Cimarron and Currumpa rivers in No Man's Land — the westward-pointing panhandle of Oklahoma. Every step that Starface took was a gesture of power and pride.

He would have been a marked horse anywhere, but his character made him even more noted than his carriage. He was the boldest gallant and the most magnificent thief that the Cimarron ranges had ever known. Most ranchmen in No Man's Land had horse herds as well as cattle and some raised horses altogether. Whenever Starface felt the blood stir in him, he would raid down upon these ranch horses, fight off the domestic stallions, cut out a bunch of mares with or without colts, and herd them back into his own well-trained bunch. The country was as yet unfenced, and Starface knew it all, claimed it all. He became a terror.

No man could walk him down, for Starface refused to circle. Nor could any man get near enough to crease him. Finally, the harassed ranchers organized to capture him. They took hundreds of long-distance shots at him; they cut off most of his followers; but he still ran free. Then they picked four cowboys, furnished them with the strongest and fastest horses in the country, and told them not to come back until they had killed or captured Starface. The four scouted for nearly a week before they sighted Starface's band. By keeping out of sight and riding in relays, they dogged the suspicious mustangs for three days and nights. Most of the time the cowboys kept back in the edge of the breaks on the south side of the Cimarron.

They studied the habits of mustangs as they had never studied them before. They marveled at the discipline by which the stallion kept his band in order. Now he would leave them and graze off alone, and not a mare would dare follow. Now he would round them into a knot that no yearling dared break from. Again he would course out with every animal obediently at his heels. Starface seemed to require less sleep than any other horse of the band.

It was early fall and the moon was in full quarter. Shortly after midnight on the fourth night the two cowboys on watch saw Starface leave his mares and head for the river flats. One man followed while his partner sped back to arouse their companions. A light dew on the grass made trailing easy; besides, the stallion was so intent on his quest that he seemed to pay no regard to what might be behind him. For six miles he galloped into the north.

Then, about ten miles east of the present town of Kenton, he entered a grassy canyon. Spreading out between walls of rock on either side, this canyon narrows into a chute that, in time of rains, pitches its waters off a bluff into the Cimarron River. Not far above the brink at the canyon mouth Starface passed through a narrow gateway of boulders shutting in a small valley.

Daylight was not far away when the cowboys came to the pass. They were familiar with the boxed structure of the canyon below them. They knew that Starface would before long be re-

turning with his stolen mares. They decided to wait for him.
They were sure that their opportunity had come. They were all
determined to catch Starface rather than kill him, for studying
him had changed vengeance into admiration.

In the early light they watched the bold stallion maneuvering
about a dozen mares and colts. They were untrained to his
methods, and Starface was wheeling and running in every direction, checking his captives at one point and whipping them up
at another. Like a true master, he was intent on his business —
and, for once, he was off guard.

He had worked the bunch into the pass, where the walls were
hardly a hundred feet apart, and now the mares were stringing
into discipline, when suddenly the four cowboys dashed from
behind the boulders. Pistol shots shook the morning stillness. The
wild Texas yell frenzied even the dullest of the mares. Ropes
slapped against leather leggins and sang in the air.

With a wild snort of challenge, Starface charged alone up the
steep canyon side. At first the cowboys thought he had discovered a trail out unknown to them. They stood still, watching,
not a gun drawn. As the mustang ascended into a patch of sunshine allowed by a break in the walls on the opposite side of
the canyon and they could see the sheen of light on his muscles,
one of them called out, "God, look at the King of the horse

world!" Long afterwards in describing the scene he added, "Not a man at that moment would have shot that animal for all the horses north of Red River."

But only for a brief time were they doubtful of capturing the superb stallion. They saw him leap to a bench as wide perhaps as a big corral — wide enough for a reckless cowboy to rope and manage an outlaw mustang upon. Towering above that bench was the caprock, without a seam or a slope in its face. Starface had picked the only spot at which the bench could be gained. But, like the canyon floor he had fled from, it ended in space — a sheer jump of ninety feet to the boulder-strewn bed of the Cimarron.

"Come on, we've got him," yelled one of the mustangers.

Under the excitement, the horses they were riding leaped up the way the mustang had led. Now he was racing back and forth along the bench. As the leading rider emerged to the level, he saw Starface make his last dash.

He was headed for the open end of the bench. At the brink he gathered his feet as if to vault the Cimarron itself, and then, without halting a second, he sprang into space. For a flash of time, without tumbling, he remained stretched out, terror in his streaming mane and tail, the madness of ultimate defiance in his eyes. With him it was truly "Give me Liberty or give me Death."

4. Instinct for Life

That a horse has the mentality to deliberate on whether to be or not to be is exceedingly doubtful. Instances of self-destruction by intelligent horses may seem the result of decision, but not of deliberation. Mustangs captured and ridden, but still unsubmitting, have plunged over bluffs with their riders, but the act seems always to have been done in frenzy. A big eight-year-old chestnut stallion waylaid and roped by a Shoshone in Nevada

was such a brave and sure-footed runner over rocks that the Indian rode him after other mustangs. Every time he was mounted there was a contest; on any chase he became uncontrollable. One day a band of mustangs he was following hell-bent came to the brink of a deep canyon, veered and skirted it. Refusing to be turned after them, the mad stallion went over, killing himself and rider three hundred feet below. If he "plainly preferred death to submission," the preference came while he was beside himself.[9]

Pursued deer, buffaloes, horses and perhaps other hoofed animals seem at times to lose all fear except of their pursuers. In 1912 Main Pouncey bought forty head — two manadas — of ordinary Mexican mares at five dollars around, the two stallions thrown in gratis, off the Terrazas ranch in Chihuahua and turned them loose in the Big Bend country of Texas. A year later while he was running very hard after thirteen of these mares, with colts, he saw the whole bunch vault from a canyon bluff sixty or seventy feet high, breaking necks, backs, legs on rocks below. There was no more deliberation in their act than in a brush popper's dodging a mesquite limb while running a wild cow in blinding brush.

Captured outlaw cattle and horses do seem sometimes to refuse, in a kind of phlegmatic serenity, to live longer.* A rancher in the Pecos country after dogging a bunch of twenty mustangs for days finally penned them, only to find that eighteen of them would not eat. Over a period of several days they died in their prison. They were not overheated when penned.[10]

Horse psychology is not always simple. What man calls thinking is a development — still incipient — of instinct. Instinct itself is very complex. As W. K. Shipman, of an old Texas family, told me the story,[11] in 1882 he was an eighteen-year-old cowboy on Jim Ned Creek in western Texas. He had already bossed a herd of cattle up the trail and was a mature man. Except for drift

* I have illustrated this behavior in *The Longhorns*, 297–301.

[188]

fences, the range was still open, and many mustangs ran on the prairies east of the caprock to the plains. Shipman had noted especially one band led by a blood-bay stallion with black mane and tail. He got six other cowboys to go in with him to capture this band, all agreeing that he should have the stallion if they ever got him within reach of a rope.

In the beginning, by a good deal of patience and some running, they managed to work a gentle belled mare into the wild band. The stallion adopted her, and the bell was a distinct help to the pursuers at night. After the first wide circle, they followed the mustangs in a buckboard, drawn by a pair of tough ponies, which, with driver, were changed three times every twenty-four hours. The mustangs were accustomed to watering in Jim Ned Creek, to which they had to descend down trails through rough breaks. Now they seemed afraid to enter the rough land and thus get cut off from their open running grounds, though by crossing the creek they might easily have escaped the buckboard. They kept on familiar prairie ground, circling Tecumseh Peak several times.

For three days and nights the cowboys kept so close behind them that they took no chances on going down to water and, of course, ate and slept very little. Abstinence perhaps helped them to endure; water in quantities is supposed to stiffen muscles and shorten wind. Now the mustangs were so nearly "walked down" that they could be thrown in with some manageable horses and hazed into a big cow pen.

In the pen the blood-bay stallion showed up as beautiful, as well-proportioned and as desirable as he had appeared racing away on the prairies. During the long chase he had exercised much more than the other animals of his band, often circling around them. Standing gaunt and jaded, he still showed the fire of life and looked to be as sound as a dollar. He was about four years old, an age at which any horse is still comparatively green, but his bottom had stood the test. At the age of eight he would probably have crossed Jim Ned Creek.

When roped, he struggled but did not fight. When mounted, he did not pitch. Guiding him with a hackamore and accompanied by two other men, Shipman rode out of the pen towards Jim Ned Creek, some distance off, and into water not more than eighteen inches deep. The reins of his hackamore loosened, the mustang thrust his muzzle into the water up to his eyes. Then suddenly he lay down, his muzzle still submerged. His rider quickly loosened the girth. One way to drown a horse in swimming water is to keep the girth tight. All three men struggled to force the mustang's nostrils out of the water for air. He would not submit. He drowned himself right there. No doubt he was dazed, crazy from thirst, past using clear-headed judgment. Yet, whatever psychologists may say, taking this mustang's liberty from him took also his instinct for life.

Among the thousands of wild horses grazing in the San Joaquin Valley of California in early days, a black stallion stood out as most beautiful and fleet. He and his manada ranged around Tulare Lake. Pens were built with long wings to trap him. While many other mustangs were penned here, the black never allowed himself to be hemmed in. His fame spread.

Finally two cowboys spied him feeding on the point of a long tongue of land jutting out into the lake. Loosening reatas and yelling, they rode towards him. At last they had the famous stallion cut off. He snorted and plunged into the soggy-bottomed water. When he got to where it was about half-side deep, he began floundering in the mud. The cowboys retreated to give him a chance to return to solid ground — and to come by them on his way out. The black stallion paused, seemed to consider, and then plunged farther out from the peninsula, his struggles growing more desperate. Whether or not he designed drowning rather than risking capture, he drowned.[12]

In *Ranching with Roosevelt*, a book written from civilized perspective, Lincoln A. Lang tells of two outlaw range horses, descended from mixed mustang and racing stock, that he owned. Learning that they had been rounded up at a distant ranch, he set out alone to bring them home. He found them too sullen and fierce to lead. In order to make them tractable, he clogged each with a short piece of heavy chain strapped to a front ankle. On the drive home one of the horses somehow rid himself of the clog and escaped, only to be shot. The other fought all the way to the ranch pens, where he was shut up.

"Apparently he was all in," says Lang.[18] "Should he attempt to jump out, the clog would hold him, we thought. Nevertheless, he was missing next morning. The bars were undisturbed. He had evidently jumped the fence.

"Following up the creek a short distance, I found him. Rather, I found as much of his slowly subsiding remains as still protruded above the quicksand bar in which he had terminated his existence. . . . His nose was shoved down in the sand, clear to his eyes. He could easily have held his head up. There was not the slightest indication of a struggle. But one conclusion was to be drawn. Unable to get rid of the clog after negotiating the fence, or to attain freedom as he knew it, he preferred death."

XI

CAPTIVE MUSTANGS: ORDINARY
AND EXTRAORDINARY

THE FIRST English-speaking colonists of Texas, their goods having been lost at sea, lived mainly on mustang meat through the winter of 1821–1822. They preferred it to "poor doe," and it seems to have been as plentiful. Jared Groce kept two hunters busy killing mustangs for the hundred slaves he had brought overland from Alabama until they could raise a corn crop. After carts and wagons became fairly common, the colonists used mustang tallow for axle grease, though the Mexicans preferred burro tallow. One requirement of every man who enlisted as a ranger under Captain Jack Hays was the ability to eat horse meat. For far-ranging scouts living off the country it was sometimes the only food available.[1]

On his first ride over coastal Texas, Stephen F. Austin, the colonizer, saw wild horses — inferior to those farther west — good enough to bring "from $100 to $200 in Louisiana." Some had "fine delicate heads and Arabian symmetry," but the majority were only about thirteen hands high and brought, "on the prairie," three or four dollars each.[2] The inferior ones came to be called "broomtails," though that term was often extended to all mustangs.

A New York land hunter named Fiske who disembarked at the mouth of the Brazos River in March, 1831, found a pen full of mustangs to choose from — the only means of travel. Mexican vaqueros had recently lassoed them on the prairie, bitted them with jaw-breaking iron, and mounted. If a mustang ran, the rider spurred him on until he fell from exhaustion. Then, if the mustang could "run back to the point from which he started, he had bottom enough to make a valuable horse." Fiske paid "a doubloon and four dollars" for a white with "the wild look."

His trouble began when he dismounted at the Brazos ferry. He had not been instructed to lead a mustang by a rope instead of by the bridle reins. At the first pull, the animal eyed him "with a malicious expression" and sprang at him "like lightning," clearing about "eight feet of ground." The next stop was at the house of Brit Bailey, who, before dying not a great while afterwards, stipulated that he be buried standing up, facing west, with a jug of whiskey at his feet and a rifle by his side, for, he said, "I have never looked up to any man, and after I am dead I don't want anybody saying, *Here lies old Brit Bailey*." He had just been thrown by a twenty-dollar mustang and still held the butcher knife with which he had cut the animal's throat. He pronounced mustangs in general "the most perverse, treacherous and trickish creatures in the world, destitute of all the generous traits of character found in the common horse."

When Fiske walked carelessly up to his white mustang to ride on, the animal lunged backward, pulled up the bush to which he had been tied. and took off over Bailey's Prairie, as that stretch

[193]

of land is still called. For four hours there was "racing and chasing on Cannobie Lee" until a neighboring settler roped the runaway. After traveling for miles in mud, the mustang seemed so exhausted that Fiske tarried a day in Harrisburg. Despite the rest, the pony started off in a drag but soon "began to cheer up and traveled remarkably well." Settlers said that his appearance of being played out was a mere trick.*

It was only when he saw droves of mustangs galloping over the flower-carpeted prairies that Fiske viewed them with sympathy. "They were gay and contented because they were at home on their native soil." After riding a few hundred miles, he sold his white mustang, together with bridle and saddle, for twenty dollars. He was surprised at "how little it costs to travel in Texas." [8]

Fiske's interpretation of the mustang foretells Mark Twain's "simon-pure, out-and-out, genuine damned Mexican plug, and an uncommon one at that." The satire was imitated and embroidered by Sweet and Knox in *On a Mexican Mustang through Texas*. They bought "steeds of a style and build that would suggest the possibility of offspring resulting from the union of a clothes-horse with a night-mare." On the other hand, the "active, hardy and beautifully formed little horses" native to the coastal

---

* In Texas, about 1880, "I bought for $40 a little black horse of about 14½ hands. He was handsome, quick and clever but full of tricks and as knowing as a monkey. One day while I was riding him over a flat piece of ground he got a cactus thorn in his foot and began to go very lame. I extracted the thorn, brought him slowly back to the ranch, and turned him out for a week, using meanwhile one of five or six other horses I owned. At the end of the week he was quite well and came in for a couple of days' pretty hard work. On starting out the third morning, he went dead lame. I caught another horse and turned Blackie loose. He ran off without showing the slightest lameness. The same thing happened on two or three other occasions, but I noticed that it was not always the same foot that he favored. One day after examining his foot carefully and finding nothing wrong, I continued my ride. He went very lame, first on one foot and then on another, but finally seeing that the trick was useless, gave it up, although with a very bad grace, and travelled well the rest of the day. He tried the dodge several times, till he found that it had no effect, and then gave it up for good. He had other tricks." — J. M. Pollock, *The Unvarnished West*, London, n.d., 61–62.

prairies confirmed for an English observer the Arab proverb: "The nearer the sun, the nobler the steed." He found Texas settlers capturing mustang colts and raising them on mush and milk, Indian corn and pumpkin, into horses "as gentle, obedient and affectionate as dogs," altogether trustworthy.[4]

The ownerless mustang and the saddled Spanish, or Mexican, horse must be considered as one. Josiah Gregg, who knew both well, summed them up thus: "Nothing in New Mexico has astonished me more than the little attention paid to the improvement of domestic animals. . . . The New Mexicans, so justly celebrated for skilful horsemanship, leave the propagation of their horses to chance, converting their best stallions into saddle animals. These are identical in blood with the mustangs, which are generally well-formed, with trim and clean limbs. They are quick, active and spirited, and were they not commonly so much injured in the breaking,* they would perhaps be as hardy and long-lived as any other race in existence. . . .

"Upon reaching the settlements, I experienced a delusion common to travellers on the prairies. Accustomed as we had been for months to our little mules and Mexican ponies, our sight was so adjusted to their proportions that the commonest

---

* A typical example of horsebreaking in New Mexico was described by a visitor to Lucien B. Maxwell's ranch — the famous Maxwell Grant — in 1865.

He saw Maxwell rope a wild horse out of a pen containing about 500 head. After it had been choked until it fell to the ground, it was blindfolded and saddled. Then a young Mexican mounted and a strong rope was tied around the animal's body so as to secure the rider's knees. As soon as the blindfold was removed, the horse went to pitching and within ten minutes plunged into the Cimarron River, where the water was breast high.

After cooling his sides for maybe five minutes, the horse came out of the river and in a dead run followed down it for a mile and a half. "The Mexican, instead of checking him, pushed him at the top of his speed by the free use of a whip until the horse, panting and almost exhausted, was glad enough to relax his gait, and came down to a walk. In less than an hour this horse was completely tamed; he came back as quiet as a kitten. Anyone could lead him anywhere. Young girls who had witnessed the performance of the Mexican Rory came out with blankets and umbrellas and shook them at the wild young horse but they had no more effect in frightening him than if he had been an old dray horse." — Letter from J. R. Doolittle, 1881, describing a trip through New Mexico in 1865, published in *New Mexico Historical Quarterly*, XXVI (1951), 149–158.

hackney appeared to be almost a monster. I have frequently heard exclamations of this kind from new arrivals: 'How the Missourians have improved their breed of horses!' 'What a huge gelding!' 'Did you ever see such an animal?' Frequently frontiersmen put off their meanest horses on deluded travellers [from the West] for the most enormous prices." [5]

A frontiersman riding alone in a country of Indian hostiles required a horse of not only endurance but speed, capable of outracing any enemy. He wanted a horse that shared his own tradition of domestic life. At the very time when mustangs sprinkled the prairies, an American horse of breeding, size and stamina brought a sum truly fabulous, considering the scarcity of money. Mustangs free to any taker hardly competed. In 1836 a settler near Houston offered a passer-by half a league (2220 acres) of land for his horse. In 1839 a circuit rider paid $250, about all the money he had, for a sorrel, bald-faced American horse seventeen hands high and seven years old, "well made for a race" on which there would be no bets. Even after the Civil War, on the Llano River where many good mustangs ranged, a rancher paid $100 in gold for an American horse. Looking through the eyes of a West Pointer, William H. Emory was too sweeping in his characterization of the Texas mustang, but many a frontiersman would have agreed with him on the average. "I had heard a great deal of these wild horses," he wrote, "but on examination of many hundred that had been caught, I never saw one good one. They are usually heavy in the forehand, cat-hammed, and knock-kneed." [6]

Yet the wild and free mustang always had a lure. He represented what most of the housed wanted and what some of the unhoused experienced. To rope and ride a "desert horse" was an achievement beyond the pale of commonplace living. Like the bear rug in a city doctor's office, a mustang under saddle bore testimony to prowess out in the beyond. Over the frontiers, however, his name became a commonplace synonym for saddle horse. Beside a certain wagon road through the woods of Red River County, Texas, in the year 1840 stood this sign: [7]

Geo. Antonio Dwight

KEEPS MUSTANGS AND PEOPLE, 1 ¼ LEAGUE
OFF RIGHT HAND PATH 3 TIMES

If a really good mustang was captured, the only way to keep him good was to gentle him with a care and kindness seldom practiced. Then he likely became a one-man horse. My old friend Joe McCloud, a Negro cowboy who ran horses west of the Nueces for my father, roped the finest horse he ever owned from a band of mustangs in the sand hills of northeastern New Mexico. "He was too wild to pitch," Joe McCloud said. "I tamed him gradually. He seemed to know all the other hands, but the minute a stranger rode up, he would go to snorting. He was leerier of strangers than an outlaw man on the lookout for the sheriff. I never trusted him with a stake rope but necked him to another horse at night. I sold him in Kansas for $275 to a rich man who wanted a fancy horse. I never heard whether he kept him or let him get away. If he got away, he went back to the mustangs, no matter how far he had to go. He seemed to be thinking about them all the time."

When Frémont, "the Pathfinder of the Rockies," reached Sutter's Fort in the spring of 1844, his party had only thirty-three horses and mules, all utterly depleted, out of sixty-seven with which they had started across the snows of the Sierra Nevada. Frémont's own horse had perished. After selling the Americans a hundred and thirty fresh animals, Captain Sutter presented their leader with the pride of his caballada.

This was a beautifully proportioned four-year-old iron-gray stallion with flowing white mane and tail. He had been captured by Indians as a colt from mustangs ranging the San Joaquin Valley. After he was broken and had undergone, one day, very severe riding, he swam the Sacramento River with his rider and pranced up to the ranch-fort as fresh as dew. Sacramento was from that hour his name. He was such a powerful jumper that Kit Carson predicted he would some day break his rider's neck. "Remember," Sutter added, "that he was born on the San Joaquin and will go back there some day if he has a chance."

Frémont rode him to Missouri and wintered him on the Kentucky estate of his father-in-law, Senator Thomas H. Benton, where he was bred to several fine mares. The next year, Frémont rode him back to California. In a fight with the Klamath Indians on the route, Kit Carson's rifle missed fire at a warrior about to shoot him; Frémont intervened, but his bullet went high. At this instant, perhaps touched by a spur, Sacramento hurled himself against the mounted Indian, knocking him to the ground, where a soldier speared him. "The Colonel and Sacramento saved me," Kit Carson said.

While Frémont and his men sailed for southern California, their horses were driven to Sutter's Fort for pasturage. A few months later Captain Charles Burroughs set out with them to meet Frémont at Monterey. He was riding Sacramento when near Salinas, his detachment was attacked by a superior number of Californians, among them the noted Three-Fingered Jack. As soon as this desperado's eye fell on Sacramento, he determined to have him. He shot Burroughs out of the saddle; Sacramento continued to charge the enemy. What became of him immediately after the skirmish is not known. Certainly the Americans did not recover him. Three-Fingered Jack escaped to Mexico.

When he returned to Monterey two years later, he heard the reports, well authenticated, that Sacramento was the king mustang stallion on the San Joaquin plains. He organized a party to capture him, but about this time was killed by rangers. Despite various stories, there is no proof that anybody ever captured the wise mustang. Sacramento became the chief legendary figure of California's horse world.[8]

Mustanging on the pristine prairies was like fishing in the Pacific Ocean. The mustanger never knew what he might catch — and even after he had caught he often did not know what was on his rope. In 1873 Miguel Antonio Otero was living in Granada on the Arkansas River, not far west of the Kansas-Colorado line, when a party of New Mexican buffalo hunters and *mesteñeros*, came by with a bunch of mustangs they had captured on the Kansas plains. He bought a two-year-old blue-roan stallion, castrated him and named him Kiowa. As he relates in *My Life on the Frontier*, he kept Kiowa for thirty years, until he died of old age, and in all that time never met his equal for "intelligence, speed and endurance."

One day some strangers came into Granada from the east with a big stallion that looked like a Thoroughbred. He was indeed, as Otero later learned, a race horse with a record. The strangers were eager to match him against anything in the country. Egged on by his friends, Otero put up Kiowa and a thousand dollars for a quarter-mile run, the little mustang to be allowed a handicap of fifteen feet at the finish. Every man in town turned out for the race. Side bets were plentiful not only in money but in saddles, pistols, mules, blankets, and other forms of property.

Of course there was no jockey in the frontier cow village. Barefooted and bareheaded, wearing only a white shirt and blue pants, a lithe young man rode Kiowa. All Kiowa wore was a light leather halter and a pair of horsehair reins, weighing only a little more than silk. At the pistol shot he jumped ahead of the long-legged race stallion, kept ahead, and finished twenty feet in the lead. He hadn't needed the handicap.

Kiowa's inseparable friend was a purebred English bulldog named Duke. Except in winter the horse was kept staked on an exceptionally long (125 feet) *cabestro*, or hair rope, near the Otero home. The grass was good here. There were no fences in the country, but there was a stable for winter protection and feed. Whether Kiowa was in stable or on picket rope, Duke stayed with him day and night and would allow no person other than one of the family to approach his friend. When Otero rode Kiowa, Duke went along unless kept chained in the stable.

One morning Kiowa's iron stake pin came out of the ground; it had been loosely driven in. A herd of horses bound for the Indian territory happened to pass and Kiowa followed, Duke with him. All this was discovered by the Oteros late in the afternoon. They made search but could find no trace of the horse. There was no assurance that the horse drivers had picked him up, but something prevented trailing them down. About a week later some freighters from the Canadian River country to the southeast told Otero, for he was questioning all comers, that they had seen a blue-roan horse dragging a stake rope following some distance behind a herd of horses. A bulldog was pulling at the end of the rope, they said. Otero prepared at once to take the trail. He was ready to ride when, coming yonder across the prairie, he saw Duke and Kiowa. Duke was in the lead, carrying the end of the drag rope in his mouth.

They had been gone ten days, and the evidence was that Kiowa had persisted in traveling for 150 miles before Duke succeeded in making him change his mind. But who can say what is in the mind of another, whether man, bird, or beast? Anyway, Kiowa had been traveling into the prairies of his raising. He came back home slick and full, for he had been on good grass, within reach of water. Duke was drawn, worn out. A few weeks later he was poisoned.

On an antelope hunt the following fall, Otero and five companions were making camp on Twin Butte Creek when they noticed four men riding in the distance. They decided to stand guard. Along in the night Otero and another man were sitting in silence with rifles across laps when Kiowa alerted them with a high snort. Looking in the direction in which he stood gazing with head high and ears up, they saw a man crawling towards the horses with knife in hand — to cut the picket ropes, no doubt. The man jumped up with a loud yell and ran towards the creek, which was on a rise. Some weeks later the dead body of a well-known horse thief was found down the creek.

When Kiowa was ten years old, and as frisky as ever, his master, having moved to Las Vegas, New Mexico, broke him to pull a fancy red-wheeled buggy. He delighted in pulling it at a dead run, but at a word would slow down to a trot or a dead stop. He would stand without being hitched at any place except in front of a saloon. He had had considerable experience waiting in front of saloons. If Otero went into one without tying him, he would, as soon as his master was inside the door, shake his head, go home to his stable and wait there to be unhitched and unharnessed.

Otero trained Kiowa to walk between himself and game, thus enabling the hunter to stalk up within shooting distance. At a touch he would stop and then he would not flinch when the gun went off across his back, under his neck or between his legs. "He seemed to understand everything I said to him," Otero said.

"Once a wild one always a wild one," went a saying of the range. In the summer of 1882, three T Anchor cowboys of the Texas Panhandle maneuvered three mustangs — a black, a sorrel and a paint — into a gulch and roped them. That fall after they had become fairly good cow horses, they were turned loose with a big remuda in a quarter-million-acre pasture while the outfit drove a herd of steers to Dodge City. When it got back and men went out to round up the horses, they found the three mustangs bunched to themselves. Six hands took after them. As one told later, "We ran them for fifteen miles, headed in one direction, southeast. They kept from a quarter to a mile ahead of us. When they came to the fence, they went over it without touching a wire. That was the last any of us ever saw of those mustangs." [9]

Many small mustangs became children's horses. Most of them had peculiarities. Along in the '70s the Martin Dodson family in Nueces County acquired a solid black, about thirteen hands high, with long mane and tail. He was so gentle that Mrs. Dodson rode him with sidesaddle, and he was the children's favorite horse. He always started out in a pace and would pace up with any galloping horse. He was as gentle as a dog. The hitch was in catching him. He ran with the remuda, but every time the remuda was driven towards the pen, he would break away. Even when his head was grizzled, he could outrun most horses ridden after him, his heavy black mane and tail streaming out like freedom's flag. Penning him was always a trial. Once in the pen, he was entirely submissive and under the saddle showed no particular spirit.[10]

One day in 1865 W. J. Slaughter rode up to his ranch on the Frio River in southwest Texas with a newly born mustang colt across his saddle. He was a strawberry roan from nose to heels with a spot of white in the forehead. The little round patch looked "like a button" to Mrs. Slaughter, and Button was his name. She had the trouble of raising him on cow's milk; he repaid her by giving his affection to his finder. Mary's little lamb did not follow her with more persistence than Button followed Bill Slaughter. When he grew up, he would accept no other rider. Whenever his master rode away from the house, Button had to be kept in the pen, where he would stand with head over gate watching. If the rancher stayed away two or three days, Button kept on the watch the whole time and at his return demonstrated affection by nuzzling and wild antics.

He matured into a most sagacious cow horse. Generally he would set off as gay as daffodils dancing in the breeze, but sometimes a notion struck him not to travel. Then, never pitching, he would rear and balk. A little coaxing and shifting of the saddle would generally break the spell. Once Indians stole him, but he came home within a day or two.

Not long after this experience, he absolutely refused to travel. Finally, while the cow hands waited, Bill Slaughter saddled another horse. At sight of the men riding away, Button raised his

head, gazed a minute, and then bolted after them. That day and the next he made a joyous hand in the roundup, but was so interfering that he had to be shut up. He seemed to mourn but still refused to travel under the saddle. Something seemed to have happened to him inside; yet he followed Slaughter about the ranch premises until he quit eating. He would stand for hours every day under a certain mesquite. He was thirteen years old when he died.

W. H. Hudson was born on the pampas of the Argentine in 1841. Thirty years later he left them to live in England, where he made books until he died in 1922. Whether writing about London birds, Hampshire days, deer in Richmond Park or his own Far Away and Long Ago youth, he remembered the pampas. Cristiano, the pale dun captive, alert and unceasingly remembering mustang freedom, was one of Hudson's selves. This is Hudson's account.[11]

"A gaucho of my acquaintance, when I lived on the pampas and was a very young man, owned a favorite riding horse which he had named Cristiano. To the gaucho 'Christian' is simply another word for white man: he gave it that name because one of its eyes was a pale-blue-gray almost white — a color sometimes seen in the eyes of a white man, but never in an Indian. The other eye was normal, though of a much lighter brown than usual. Cristiano, however, could see equally well out of both eyes, nor was the blue eye on one side correlated with deafness, as in a white cat. His sense of hearing was quite remarkable. His color was a fine deep fawn, with black mane and tail, and altogether he was a handsome and a good, strong, sound animal. His owner was so much attached to him that he would seldom ride any other horse, and as a rule he had him saddled every day. . . .

"Every time I was in my gaucho friend's company, when his favorite Cristiano, along with other saddle horses, was standing at the *palenque*, or row of posts set up before the door of a native rancho for visitors to fasten their horses to, my attention would be attracted to his singular behavior. His master always tied him to the *palenque* with a long *cabestro*, or lariat, to give him plenty of space to move his head and whole body about quite freely. And that was just what he was always doing. A more restless horse I had never seen. His head was always raised as high as he could raise it — like an ostrich, the gauchos would say — his gaze fixed excitedly on some far object; then presently he would wheel round and stare in another direction, pointing his ears forward to listen intently to some faint, far sound which had touched his sense. The sounds that excited him most were as a rule the alarm cries of lapwings, and the objects he gazed fixedly at with a great show of apprehension would usually turn out to be a horseman on the horizon; but the sounds and sights would for some time be inaudible and invisible to us on account of their distance. Occasionally, when the bird's alarm cries grew loud and the distant rider was found to be approaching, his excitement would increase until it would discharge itself in a resounding snort — the warning or alarm note of the wild horse.

"One day I remarked to my gaucho friend that his blue-eyed Cristiano amused me more than any other horse I knew. He was just like a child, and when tired of the monotony of standing tethered to the *palenque* he would start playing sentinel. He would imagine it was war-time or that an invasion of Indians was expected, and every cry of a lapwing or other alarm-giving bird, or the sight of a horseman in the distance would cause him to give warning. But the other horses would not join in the game; they let him keep watch and wheel about this way and that, spying or pretending to spy something, and blowing his loud trumpet, without taking any notice. They simply dozed with heads down, occasionally switching off the flies with their tails or stamping a hoof to get them off their legs, or rubbing their tongues over the bits to make a rattling sound with the little iron rollers on the bridle-bar.

[205]

"He laughed and said I was mistaken, that Cristiano was not amusing himself with a game he had invented. He was born wild and belonged to a district not many leagues away where an extensive marshy area made hunting on horseback impracticable. Here a band of wild horses, a small remnant of an immense troop that had formerly existed in that part, had been able to keep their freedom down to recent years. As they were frequently hunted in dry seasons when the ground was not so bad, they had become exceedingly alert and cunning, and the sight of men on horseback would send them flying to the most inaccessible places in the marshes, where it was impossible to follow them. Eventually plans were laid and the troop driven from their stronghold out into the open country, where the ground was firm, and most of them were captured.

"Cristiano was one of them, a colt about four or five months old, and my friend took possession of him, attracted by his blue eye and fine fawn color. In quite a short time the colt became perfectly tame, and when broken turned out an exceptionally good riding-horse. But though so young when captured, the wild alert habit was never dropped. He could never be still; when out grazing with other horses or when standing tied to the *palenque*, he was perpetually on the watch, and the cry of a plover, the sound of galloping hoofs, the sight of a horseman, would startle him and cause him to trumpet his alarm.

"It strikes me as rather curious that in spite of Cristiano's evident agitation at certain sounds and sights, it never went to the length of a panic; he never attempted to break loose and run away. He behaved just as if the plover's cry or the sound of hoofs, or the sight of mounted men had produced an illusion — that he was once more a wild, hunted horse — yet he never acted as though it was an illusion. It was apparently nothing more than a memory and a habit."

* * *

The man who gave me this true history of a horse [12] was in some ways the most interesting *hombre de campo* — man of the outdoors, master of all the ways and lore of mountains and plains — that I have ever known. He was Don Alberto Guajardo, of Coahuila, Mexico, on the frontiers of which he lived his whole life. He knew more about medicinal plants than a dozen *curanderas* (herb women), and used to export bales of them, dried, to Czechoslovakia and Italy. At his home in Piedras Negras he employed Indian weavers to make blankets — and I would not trade two of them that warm me every winter for any sold in stores. He was expert at bleating up both jaguars and deer, generally does — and in the old Indian way he was, when out for meat, no respecter of sex or season. Born about 1855, he fought Indians in boyhood and became a general in one of the Mexican revolutions. He claimed to have had a bullet wound properly treated by minnows while, after one of his battles, he lay in shallow water of the Rio Grande. He was a ranchero by breeding, and after he moved to town, his mind ranged habitually among horses on grass.

Meagerly schooled, he had in youth taught himself to read Latin, French and English; he spoke English very haltingly. He asserted that the main contributors to his education had been an old Lipan Indian and two or three Kickapoos with whom he grew up. The sense of wonder at the instincts of animals never left him. He personified the dignity of natural men. He was helpless amid machine-geared society. I loved and respected him.

About the time the Civil War was ending in the United States, vaqueros mustanging on the plains of Coahuila some fifty miles south of Eagle Pass, Texas, captured a dappled-gray, two-year-old stallion. He was led farther south by his owner, castrated, and kept from escaping by a hair rope that tied a front foot to the limb of a mesquite tree. He was very strong for his age and proved to be a fierce pitcher. He tried to bite anyone coming near him, and his owner tossed what hay or fodder he fed him from a distance. This owner disliked him and sold him at a bargain to Don Miguel Guajardo, father of the boy Alberto.

Tied up short to a hayrack, the young horse tried to bite and kick his new owner whenever he brought hay and corn. Don Miguel scolded him and calmly let him go hungry until he accepted food as a favor. Soon he was caressing and currying him and bathing him at the waterhole. He put a saddle on him, without drawing the cinch tight, and left it all day. Next he tied a piece of rawhide to his tail and left it there until the horse ceased to fear it and to twist and kick at it. The hairs growing out of the end of his tail were sparse, and when he raised it, it resembled the tail of a scorpion. Thus he received a name — Alacrán, or Scorpion.

Soon Alacrán was a different horse from the starved, abused animal that Don Miguel bought. He grew fat and sleek, was very active, and carried himself haughtily. After saddling him one day, Don Miguel told a vaquero to mount him. A few jumps and Alacrán was riderless. Don Miguel tied a bundle of hay on either side of the saddle and left him until he was accustomed to the burden. The next day he mounted the horse himself, rode him gently, and began teaching him to rein. Thereafter, no one else tried to ride him; he became Don Miguel's most trusted mount.

About this time cotton was bringing boom prices. It was freighted from Monterrey northward to Eagle Pass, thence to San Antonio and on to a Gulf port to be shipped to England. When Alacrán was four or five years old, his owner rode him to conduct a train of cotton wagons. On the route a cow-buyer headed for the Rio Grande joined the train. Danger from bandits and Indians made company desirable. One afternoon the outfit camped on a creek north of the Río Sabinas — in the very range where Alacrán had been captured as a mustang. Don Miguel staked him on the prairie by digging a hole in the ground with his knife, tying a double-knot in the end of the *cabestro* — the soft hair rope — putting the knot well down in the hole, and packing the earth back on top of it. A well-buried knot can be pulled up vertically, but it cannot be pulled up by a horse setting back or running on his rope.

The cow-buyer had come to admire Alacrán so much that during the evening he offered two hundred pesos — a very high price at the time — for him and was refused. That night during a rainstorm Alacrán broke the rope, near his neck, and left. When daylight came, though visibility was very poor on account of low heavy clouds, Don Miguel climbed on top of a load of cotton to look. In the distance he made out a moving object that he took to be Alacrán. He shelled corn into a morral (fiber nose bag), wrapped himself in his blue cape, and started off afoot.

"You had better ride one of the mules, Don Miguel," advised a driver. "Your horse is far off and the grass is very wet."

"If I ride, Alacrán will mistrust me," Don Miguel replied. "This is his country. He remembers how riders raced and caught him here."

Don Miguel walked on through the thick, wet grass and in time neared the grazing runaway. At sight of the man, Alacrán snorted and turned as if to flee. Don Miguel stopped, rattled the corn in the morral, and called the horse's name loudly in accustomed tones. The mustang snorted, took two steps forward, snorted again, then walked to put his nose in the morral, not without a final puff. Don Miguel unloosed his pistol belt and used it to lead Alacrán.

As he walked into camp, the cow-buyer said, "Don Miguel, yesterday I offered you two hundred pesos for that horse. Today I offer you three hundred."

"I do not wish to sell the horse at any price," Don Miguel replied, "but I shall have need of the money in San Antonio. I accept your offer. Before I deliver the horse to you, however, I must tell you something of his peculiarities, even defects."

[209]

"Anything you have to tell would be superfluous," the cow-buyer quickly interposed. "I too am a man of the camps. Let us count the money. The horse is mine."

The silver pesos were counted out of the owner's saddlebags. Despite the buyer's indifference to information, Don Miguel gave him these warnings: "Before mounting Alacrán you will do well to look him in the eyes: if they are inflamed and red, pacify him and wait until the wild look subsides before stepping into the stirrup. You had better uncoil the rope attached to Alacrán's neck and hold it in your hand before dismounting. He always knows whether or not he is loose. Until he becomes used to you, you had better hobble as well as stake him at night. I present you with this pair of hobbles."

The buyer rode on north, ahead of the wagon train, leaving the horse he had been riding to be delivered at the Rio Grande. It was known that he carried five hundred silver pesos, wrapped in paper, in his saddlebags.

Over the rain-soaked ground the wagons made slow progress. While the train was nooning next day, the cow-buyer dragged into camp afoot. He had been out all night and was famished. After he was revived with coffee and food, he lit a cigarette and made explanation.

"Yesterday about dark," he said, "I rode up to the camp of a goat-herder who was cooking supper in front of a well-thatched shed. He gladly gave me permission to spend the night. Like a fool, I started to dismount without taking down the rope as you advised. Just as my right foot was out of the stirrup, a dog rushed up barking. Alacrán reared back, throwing me to the ground, and ran off — with saddle and the five hundred pesos. The last I saw of him he was coming down the road in this direction. I have hunted for him all morning without seeing him or even his tracks. Don Miguel, will you help me find him?"

"I will help you hunt for him," replied Don Miguel, "but I

cannot assure you of success. A frightened horse carrying a saddle stampedes all the manadas he meets. As they run, he runs after them. Was the saddle cinched tight or loose?"

"Tight," the cow-buyer replied. "There is no danger of his getting rid of it."

"It is not that," observed Don Miguel. "If the saddle is tight, the horse will not travel far without stopping. How far from here did Alacrán break away?"

"About three leagues."

The two men saddled horses and rode forth immediately. The cow-buyer wanted to search the country on both sides of the road. Don Miguel said, "If I am to help you, you must follow me. We will ride up the road until we strike Alacrán's tracks turning out of it. Then I will trail him."

They found where Alacrán had turned out of the road not a great distance south of the goat-herder's camp.

"Was he sweaty when he broke away?" Don Miguel asked.

"The heavy ground had made sweat drip from him," the cow-buyer replied.

"Good," exclaimed Don Miguel. "That means less travel."

After the general course of the runaway was evident, Don Miguel rode in wide circles, scanning in all directions. About sundown he spied Alacrán at the foot of a range of low hills. The two rode in a roundabout way so as to approach without being seen. When they were fairly near, Don Miguel dismounted, wrapped himself in his blue cape, told the other man to remain out of sight, and started walking. He could see mud on the saddle, from the horse's having rolled on it. On account of the stinging sweat on his back and the pinching girth, Alacrán was switching his tail nervously. He was in the act of lying down to roll again when Don Miguel called his name. He pitched his head up, whinnied for pleasure, and ran to his old friend, rubbing his neck against him.

Don Miguel loosed the cinch, took the rope down from the saddle horn, and led him to where the cow-buyer was waiting. "I have left the saddle for you to remove," he said.

The cow-buyer appeared to be more concerned over his silver than over his horse. Examining the saddlebags, he found only eighty or ninety pesos left. "Somebody has robbed me," he cried.

"Impossible," said Don Miguel. "No human being on earth but myself could have approached this horse near enough to touch the saddle without either roping or shooting him. Any robber who got his hands on the silver would have taken all. It is my belief that Alacrán while wallowing broke the wrappings about the pesos and spilled them on the ground.

"Listen, my friend. To show this intelligent horse that you understand him and to win his gratitude, remove the saddle and blanket at once and then with handfuls of dry grass rub the caked mud and sweat from his sensitive skin. Later, when we arrive in camp, we will bathe him and he can rest refreshed."

It was now too late to hunt for the pesos. That night Alacrán was washed and well fed. In the morning Don Miguel mounted him and, followed by the cow-buyer, rode to the spot where he had left the wagon road. Alacrán seemed disinclined to follow his old tracks, but Don Miguel knew that he, like many other range horses, was expert at trailing himself, either forward or backward. As he was gently made to understand what was desired, he began to step in the very tracks he had made two nights and one day preceding.

"Watch for wallowing places," advised Don Miguel.

For hours, the trailers rode at a walk. Frequently Alacrán put his nose to the well-turfed ground to smell. In many places the grass pressed down by his hoofs had sprung back erect, leaving no visible trail. The trailers wound in and out and around. About midday they came to a spot where Alacrán had lain down but had not wallowed to any extent. An hour later they came to

a waterhole where he had drunk and then wallowed energeti-
cally. Pesos were shining in the sand. By dusk most of the missing money had been recovered from a half dozen or so wallowing places. Then Alacrán forsook the trail he had so patiently
followed and made for camp. He had done his duty. It was unsaddling time.

That night the cow-buyer, whose education in the management of an intelligent horse had been very much advanced, insisted, without success, on Don Miguel's accepting a considerable
amount of the recovered money. When he rode off the next
morning, he was more than owner of Alacrán; he was his understanding friend and partner.

MUSTANGER WAYS

XII

THE GAUCHOS and Indians of South America raced bareback, swinging bolas to entangle the legs of fleeing wild horses.[1] The Indians of North America, as we have seen, both snared and lassoed. California vaqueros, riding with only bridle and surcingle, to which a long reata was tied, ran and roped the fear-spurred.[2] On the "Wild Horse Desert" of Texas, vaqueros stripped everything from their mounts but bridles, tied lariats around the necks of their horses, and then, upon nearing the prey, shot forward with yells and swinging loops that maddened the blood in themselves, their mounts and the mustangs all.[3] If in the excitement a mustanger did not isolate his quarry before roping it, other horses, including those mounted, were almost

[215]

sure to run foul of his rope. The entanglement sometimes resulted in serious injury and even death.[4]

Along in the '80s, on the open, broken tableland between the Davis Mountains of west Texas and the Rio Grande, Jack Thorp and other riders came across a family of *mesteñeros* from Chihuahua who could have had few equals in wild running.

Jack Thorp was a New Mexico cowboy and cowman who had ranged over Texas and northern Mexico. In 1908 he printed at Estancia, New Mexico, a booklet of cowboy songs that preceded all other collections of the kind. John Lomax virtually incorporated it in his much better known *Cowboy Songs and Frontier Ballads*, 1910. Later Thorp published *Tales of the Chuck Wagon*. He was a cultivated gentleman and had a generous nature. About 1939, while driving from Albuquerque to Santa Fe, I stopped to visit him near a wide place in the road called Alameda. It was along in the afternoon when I arrived. At dark I hadn't begun to get through listening. We had supper and I stayed all night. We had breakfast before daylight the next morning, and I was still listening. The day was ending when I got to Santa Fe.

After Jack Thorp died, Neil McCullough Clark put his unfinished writings into a book appropriately titled *Pardner of the Wind*. This account of the *mesteñero* family, extracted from the book,* was one of the tales that Jack told me that night of golden talk.

"We saw the fast-rising dust of a band of horses approaching us at an angle," Jack Thorp wrote, "and then, as they got closer, two riders crowding them closely. One was a girl on a big white horse. As we watched, she raced alongside a sorrel that was crowding against other mustangs to get away from her. They were all going like the wind. Presently, when she got the posi-

* *Pardner of the Wind*, by N. Howard (Jack) Thorp, in collaboration with Neil M. Clark, published by the Caxton Printers, Ltd., Caldwell, Idaho, 1945. With gracious permission of the publishers, I have taken the story from pages 78–81.

tion she wanted, she reached over, grabbed the sorrel's mane, and slipped neatly from her seat onto the wild one's back. Her saddle was a sheepskin pad, held on by a surcingle to which were fastened two brass stirrups, the whole equipment weighing hardly more than three pounds.

"All she took with her when she made the glide was a hair rope about ten feet long. As the sorrel raced on at full speed, she threw a little loop over his head, tightened it, and then threw upward two half hitches around his nose. With only this *bozal* (nose band) to guide the runaway, she passed from sight, veering out from the mustang bunch.

"Immediately after she changed horses, her companion caught the reins of the white mount and led him over to where we had halted in astonishment.

" 'How's that girl going to stop her horse?' I asked in Spanish. 'He's liable to run into the Gulf of Mexico, no?'

" 'She'll be back pretty soon,' he replied. He was her brother, as we learned.

"In about half an hour she was back on the sorrel, now well winded. Using the hair rope as a rein on the *bozal*, she had checked him, gradually brought him around, and was now guiding him. She was maybe fourteen years old, small and wiry, weighing about seventy pounds. Pony express riders used to change horses with spectacular rapidity, but theirs were broken. This bit of a girl was skimming onto the backs of mustangs that had never felt human hand or rope."

Jack Thorp went to the camp of these people. There were six in the family. The father had caught wild horses in the way his daughter was catching them now, but at different times had broken both arms and both legs. He was still light and active. The mother had been a *mesteñera* too. The son had once mounted wild horses on the run, but had grown too heavy for the acrobatic feat, also for his horse to race up beside the wild ones. Two daughters, mere children, were herding about twenty head of horses that their older sister had caught within the month and were eagerly looking forward to the time when they could be genuine *mesteñeras*. The captured mustangs were either hobbled, side-lined, or necked together in pairs to prevent their running away.

The family had a snug camp, shaded by a brush *ramada* and convenient to water. They were well supplied with wild meat and baked their bread in a little round *horno* (oven) made of mud. When they moved, all their goods were loaded into a *carreta* of two high wheels, drawn by three big burros. They had been making annual expeditions to this range after mustangs, which were better, the head of the family said, than most of those south of the Rio Grande. After they had caught fifty head, they were going back to Chihuahua to spend the winter, selling their catch on the route or after they reached their own *ranchito*. Their running horses were fine animals, about sixteen hands high and weighing perhaps eleven hundred pounds each. Sometimes, the girl said, she had to race the *mesteñas* two or three miles before she could attempt a leap.

They had a corral built against a rock bluff, three sides of it made of limbs and brush packed down between pairs of well-planted posts, about two feet apart, that were lashed together at the top with rawhide. It was bull-proof and horse-high.

The mustangs were penned at night. In the morning the son roped a big sorrel mare to break. He put a blinder on her before saddling and mounting. Meanwhile the little *mesteñera* held a hair rope tied around one of the mare's front ankles, while her father held one tied around the other. When the blinder was pulled off, the mare started bucking. Simultaneous pulls on the hair ropes brought her to her knees. She had to be pulled down six times before she quit trying to pitch. The rider said that her knees would be swollen for only a few days, that she was probably cured of bucking, and that if she bucked again, all that

[218]

would be necessary to make her give up the idea would be to tie a short piece of hair rope around each ankle.

Racing and roping — not to speak of the flying leap — was a wild and glorious sport. It belonged to youthful vigor that had never been leashed by attempts to think against complex civilization; it belonged to a turf that, unscarred by man-activated erosion, was in its prime. As long as any mustangs remained, whether on dog-holed prairie, on rocky mesa, in prickly pear thicket, or in mountains where only the panther could be casual-footed, riders dared death to experience the zenith of life in this sport. It was freedom even while quelling freedom.

"You must know," recorded Robert Beverley in his *History and Present State of Virginia* (1705), "they have many horses foaled in the Woods of the Uplands that never were in hand and are as shy as any Savage Creature. These, having no mark upon them, belong to him that first takes them. However, the Captor commonly purchases these Horses very dear, by spoiling better in the pursuit. . . . The wild Horses are so swift that 'tis difficult to catch them; and when they are taken, 'tis odds but their Grease is melted, or else being old, they are so sullen that they can't be tamed. . . . The young People take great delight in the Sport of pursuing them, some times with Dogs and some times without." [5]

In the range of the Spanish mustangs I have come across only two or three instances of chasing them with dogs. One was in the Old South part of Texas. About 1843 a man living on Leon Prairie east of the Navasota River had a pack of bloodhounds trained to round up wild horses, which he shot for their food. [6]

Creasing, too, was a kind of sport — without sportsmanship. If a rifleman wanted to kill a horse, he did not aim to crease it; if he aimed to crease, he frequently killed. Only the most expert marksman at close range could win a live horse. If the bullet barely grazed the spinal nerve along the top of the neck, the animal would be stunned temporarily, during which time it could be tied. Most bullets either missed or killed. Some men aimed at a spot close to the withers, some "about a foot" behind the ears.[7] A good shot — who had no hesitancy in talking about his marksmanship — told me that in New Mexico he became so expert in grazing one of the vertebrae a little forward of the hips that he stunned twenty out of twenty-five wild horses at which he shot. In 1807 Indians brought into Natchitoches, for a reward, "a small bay American horse" captured among mustangs on the Sabine River in east Texas. He had a hole through the neck near the windpipe made by a rifle ball that had been aimed at his crest.[8] A horse, like a man, can survive wounds in many parts of the body, but talk about creasing a horse by shooting him in the belly [9] is absurd.

Amateur mustangers tried all sorts of dodges to get a sure crease shot. One was to stake a mare near a concealed man to lure up a stallion. Three frontiersmen who had failed in running down a beautiful black stallion dug a hole, large enough to hide a waylayer, out in the prairie grass where he and his band frequently used. They carried the dirt away so that it would not arouse horse suspicion. The pit was invisible except to eyes almost over it. Morning after morning two of the men rode to it; one would get down in it with his rifle to wait all day for a shot, and the other would lead his horse out of sight, returning only at nightfall. The mustangs would come within sight of the waiting man but not within shot. One day his partners hazed them a little nearer. The bullet paralyzed the beautiful black stallion all right — permanently.[10] Pits modeled on those for trapping bears were easily avoided by wild horses.[11]

Creasing seems to have been brought west from the Old South. After the earthquake in Missouri in 1811–1812, many settlers left the country, abandoning their horses and cattle to the wilderness. Woodsmen learned that the solution from a rain-soaked sack of salt hung in a tree would bring wild horses as well as deer to lick the ground beneath. A man would secrete himself near one of these prepared salt licks to kill deer and crease horses. One ambusher, a Frenchman, knocked a horse down, ran with halter, fastened it on the victim's head, tied the rope to the tree under the salt sack, waited for the horse to rise, and then discovered that he had broken its neck.[12]

The snaring of wild animals goes back to the dawn of history. Before 1750 wild horses were being snared at salt licks in Mississippi. A man would lay the noose of a long rope on the ground near the lick, hide himself, holding the rope end, and when a horse stepped into the noose draw it up and fell him.[13] A strong, active mustang would be very difficult for a lone snarer to throw down unless both front feet were caught in the noose. A horse rises on his forefeet and so is roped by the forefeet to throw him off balance and bring him to the ground; a cow rises on hind feet, and so is *pialed* (roped by the hind feet) for a "busting."

The most successful snares — though men who made mustanging a business seldom wasted time on them — were set at trail passages through brush or woods. If wild horses were rushed at such a place, some might run their heads into loops cunningly suspended from branches. Unless the rope was tied to a limb that would give, a snared horse was likely to choke himself to death before the snarer arrived. Twelve snares set in the Nueces River country in 1869 caught three mustangs out of thirty. One broke his neck; one broke the rope and got away; only one was captured alive.[14] It was hard to hide a noose so that an undisturbed mustang would not detect it.

Better in theory than in practice was a man's climbing a tree under which he had tied a mare, fixing himself for free casting of a reata, and dropping the loop over the head of an interested stallion.[15] It was snaring from a tree that gave Mustang Gray his name.

Mayberry B. Gray of South Carolina, called Mabry by the Texians whom he joined when nineteen years old, fought in the battle of San Jacinto, led raiders after Mexican cattle and horses, captained a company of rangers in the Mexican War, shortly thereafter died in the arms of a señorita on the Rio Grande, and then for many years had his life prolonged in a song that Texas cowboys carried all the way to Montana.[16]

> There was a gallant Texian,
>   They called him Mustang Gray,
> When quite a youth, he left his home,
>   Went ranging far away.
>
> He ne'er would sleep within a tent,
>   No comforts would he know,
> But like a brave old Texian,
>   A-ranging he would go.

Not long after coming to Texas, he was a-ranging after buffalo, far away from the settlements, when his horse fell, throwing him to the ground. He held to the reins, but the charge of a buffalo mortally shot so frightened the horse that he jerked away and ran out of sight. After trailing him for a long time and finding his tracks mingled with those of wild horses, Gray came back to the slain buffalo for a meal. He took some of the meat to a pond near by, built a fire, and cooked it.

Tracks and freshly topped mounds of manure told him that mustangs were watering here. If he but had a rope, he might catch one. He climbed a tree over the main horse trail for a look. Before long he saw a band of mustangs galloping to water. Some of them, including a heavy-set stallion, passed beneath him. The smell from a man, or any other animal, in a tree does not generally float groundward.

After the mustangs had watered and left, Gray came down from the tree with a plan. If he attempted to walk back to the settlements, he would certainly suffer from thirst. Walking was against his principles, anyhow. He went to the dead buffalo, skinned it, and pegged the hide out to dry. Hot sun and dry wind

did their work quickly. He trimmed the hide into an oval and, beginning on the outside, cut a thong, maybe two fingers wide, around and around, until it was about thirty-five feet long. He wet it, tied one end to a bush, twisted it until it was cylindrical, worked it to make it pliable. The whole process occupied him for about three days.* In the end he had a reata strong enough to hold a buffalo bull. He made, also, a hackamore, or halter, working buffalo tallow into the hide to soften it. Meantime he kept out of sight and smell of the mustangs and lived well on buffalo ribs.

Animals have regular hours for watering, and when the time approached on the fourth day for the mustangs to come to the pond, Gray was ready for them. Having tied one end of the reata

---

* Two of his contemporaries worked with more celerity. "Captain Mathew Caldwell caught a mustang stallion the other day, & held him until his fellow hunter shot an other, & skinned a larriette to tie him, & they have him here now, an exploit not surpassed by Gen. Putnam's wolf story." — J. W. Robinson to Lamar, Feb. 24, 1839, *The Papers of Mirabeau Buonaparte Lamar*, Austin, Texas, 1922, II, 468.

to a low, stout branch, he took the other up the tree to an open space immediately over the trail and made it into a loop. He knew that he would have but one throw at one mustang. He wanted the heavy-set stallion. He did not miss.

The stallion jerked himself flat, but got up. For hours he plunged, ran, jerked, snorted, but gradually as the man talked to him in low tones and moved gently, he calmed down. It was the next day before he tremblingly allowed a hand on his neck and then the hackamore on his head. Gray was six feet and one inch tall and as active as a wild bull. He leaped on the mustang's back and leaped free when the mustang hit the end of the reata, without, however, jerking himself down. The taming process went on until Gray was sufficiently master to untie the reata from the tree and secure it to the hackamore. He was determined to take his rifle, but the only way he could manage was to strap it to his own back. That made mounting difficult, but by using his bandana as a blind he got the stallion to stand until he was firmly seated. Then, headed towards the settlements, he pulled the bandana free. For many miles the prairie was open. The mustang ran until he was completely exhausted. That evening Gray watered him and hobbled him short. The next morning he had comparatively little trouble keeping him under control. Riding bareback, he came to the camp of men who knew him. They dubbed him Mustang Gray, a name still attached to a place as well as to legend and song.

Colt-catching entailed chores beyond the pale of wild rider and roper ambition, but until about the time of the Civil War it was the main source of horses for many Texas settlers.[17] Riders chased the mares until their young foals dropped behind; then the tired little trusting creatures would usually follow home the horses ridden by their chasers.[18] Sweetened water delighted them, and cow's milk agreed with them as well as mare's milk. Ben Corder of the Frio, in the brush country, with a hand to help him, used to run a manada into a prickly pear thicket, where the colts, unable to leap the thorns, would be left behind by their mothers. They would snuggle against the sides of the mounted horses and after following them to the ranch drink milk, diluted with water, out of a trough. Raised gently, a mustang colt often became vexatiously domestic.

Mexicans gave a picturesqueness to colt-catching, as they give to whatever they touch. *Mesteñeros* from New Mexico caught thousands of colts on the plains. One encountered by Texas surveyors in 1878 had a wagon, two cows and calves and about thirty captured colts. A hair rope tied the tail of each colt to a front ankle. They were limping along, utterly dejected and skinny, the insides of their thighs and fetlock joints worn bloody by the tight hair rope. Looking at them, O. W. Williams understood why many mustangs he had seen under saddle lacked the "beauty of contour" remarkable in all free mustangs.[19]

Frank Collinson came to know some of these *mesteñeros* well.[20] Two brothers, Pedro and Celedón Trujillo, raised enough corn on *ranchitos* on the Pecos River above Fort Sumner to have their roping horses in prime condition when the time came for mustang mares to foal. Then they would load women and children and other possessions into wagons, string out all their burros and cattle, mostly milch cows, and, accompanied by several light riders and more dogs, head for the plains. They moved camp frequently. Their *modo* was to locate, unseen, a manada coming to water. After it had drunk, bareback riders, with reatas tied to the necks of their horses, would try to run the mustangs towards other riders, so as to close in on them from both sides. The riders carried extra tie-ropes, and if the colts were very young, one man often caught two or three on a single run. It took but a minute for a practiced hand to rope and tie a colt and be after another.

After the run was over, the colts were picked up and carried to camp. The women made the milch burros adopt colts. Other captives were fed a little cow milk. Some died. The cows gave mighty little milk. Some years the Trujillos took as many as a hundred colts back to New Mexico. Meanwhile they had spent a season living the kind of life they wanted to live. As Somerset Maugham sums up: "The beauty of life is nothing but this, that each should act in conformity with his nature and his business."

As the plains afforded no wood, these *mesteñeros* had no pens. Not all confined their captures to colts; some out for colts captured grown animals also. In the spring of 1878 eight men with twenty saddle horses came from San Miguel in southern New Mexico to the Casa Amarilla country to capture brood mares. For four days they dogged by relays a manada of eighty-odd animals, letting the old, the unhardy and young colts drop out. Some mares they wanted got so tired that they lay down and had to be whipped up. Finally the manada was stopped at a lake, where the exhausted ones were allowed to lie while the remainder were walked about all night. The next morning there on the prairie vaqueros roped out thirty-five picked mares and fillies, threw them, branded them with irons heated in a fire of buffalo chips, and "kneed" them, severing the knee ligament and letting the joint water out.* The crippled things could now be herded by one man at the margin of the lake. After they and other mares thus secured had rested and grazed a few days, they were started on their slow four-hundred-mile limp to the lower Rio Grande in New Mexico. They would never be able to run, but they could raise colts.[21]

Like other techniques of the open range, that of penning wild horses came from Mexico. The earliest account of this kind of

* Something like kneeing seems to have been practiced by aboriginal Americans before horses were introduced to them. In 1540 De Soto's Spaniards, who were enslaving Indians themselves, came among a tribe possessing many captives from "other provinces." In order to prevent these slaves from fleeing, the Indian owners "had perpetually and inhumanly fettered each one by cutting the tendons of one foot above where the instep joins the leg, or above the heel." — *The Florida of the Inca*, by Garcilaso de la Vega, translated by John and Jeannette Varner, University of Texas Press, Austin, 1951, 329-330.

mustanging that I have found is by a German Jesuit who went to Sonora in 1756, at which time the practice seems to have been well established. Apache raiding had reduced the number of branded horses and mules to hardly a fourth of what it had been. Agriculture had been abandoned except under communal protection; herdsmen shrank from tending to livestock. Meanwhile, as a result of neglect, the numbers of wild burros, horses and mules had greatly increased.

In early June, when only a few springs and puddles afforded water, sturdy corrals were built, or repaired, at the watering places. To prevent the wild animals from dashing themselves to death against the walls at corners, the corrals were circular; they were five or six times larger than those in which horses and mules were driven around and around to thresh wheat. Leading from a wide gate, lines of freshly cut branches and shrubs flared outward. Running wild horses would crowd against each other to avoid touching these sham lane fences — which any running coyote would dodge into at first chance.

The men were divided into companies, some afoot, some mounted. Riders hidden in brush or gullies near the entrance to "the green lane" waited for a wild herd coming to water; footmen were stationed along the wings, on the outside so as not to be seen. At the approach of horses and mules, the riders burst forth from their rear, shouting, hurrying them forward, the footmen adding to the bedlam as they rushed down the funnel. As soon as they passed through the gate, it was barred.

"If the catch is successful," the German Jesuit wrote, "vaqueros enter the corral afoot with reatas. One lassos an animal around the neck, and while it is struggling, another ropes it by the front feet — the *mangana* — and it falls. Then the *sarprima* is fixed by tying one end of a short rope around the fetlock joint and the other around the lower neck, thus pulling the foreleg up so that the animal can only hop along. After the whole caballada has been laced up in this way, it is driven away from the corral so that another catch can be made. After the captives have been kept under herd three or four weeks, the *sarprima* is removed, they are necked to tame horses and mules, and driven to the ranches. Well worn-down now, they become tame to the saddle after having been ridden only two or three times. Yet they must be watched carefully for a year lest, remembering their former freedom, they escape to their place of birth." [22]

The process of corralling developed with time and varied according to typography and tradition. South of the lower reaches of the Rio Grande, the *corridas* (runs) were ordinarily made in November and December after fall rains had put out water and brought weeds up in the mesquite flats. From a hundred to two hundred vaqueros over a big range would join together in fiesta mood, taking plenty of saddle horses, *pinole* (ground corn, sweetened) and *tasajo* (jerked beef). Groups of from half a dozen to a dozen would scatter over the range repairing old corrals, making new ones, disguising the wings to corral gates with freshly cut brush. Then somewhat larger groups would drive the wild horses into the pens, trying to allow them to drink just before the final *susto* (scare). [23]

One problem was preventing too many horses from rushing into a corral. Two or three hundred were a desirable number. More were likely to trample each other to death, break down the fences and leave only carcasses that would, in Zebulon Pike's phrase, raise "an insupportable stench," rendering the corral unusable for a long time. [24] Mustangs that escaped would remember the place and could hardly be driven to it a second time. Some of the captives would die, anyway, of *despecho* — indignation, wrath, nervous intensity. Imprisoned animals were kept "without food or drink for six days." Then they could be herded with gentle mares to controlled ranges. [25]

By 1870, hundreds of mustang pens, many old ones by that time rotted to the ground, had been built by Mexicans between the Nueces and the Rio Grande. They were of two kinds. The

simpler and less laborious to construct was the *corral de espiar* —
a spy, or catch, pen, sometimes called night pen. It enclosed water
and the gate was left open except when a hidden watcher shut it,
usually at night, on wild horses accustomed to drinking there.
When water was abundant over the country, this kind of pen
was of little value. The big catches were made in corrals with
wings. This kind was usually spiral in form and was called *caracol*
(snail) or *sordo* (deaf — perhaps from the fact that wild horses
were deaf to its silent warning until they found themselves enclosed). There was a Rancho Sordo on Padre Island and another
in the Hebbronville country. Sometimes the pen was built in the
shape of a double gourd, or the figure 8, to prevent the wild runners from doubling back, as they could in a lane or in a pen
merely circular.[26]

Every corral in the Mexican country had a name signifying
something; on occasion it could be altered. A certain don of the
18th century who came with his men from Mexico to take possession of a grant of land camped beside a corral at a *charco*, or pool,
on a dry creek. Inside the corral were scattered the bleaching
bones of two or three men and several horses — victims of an
Indian attack. That night the campers imagined they heard the
groans of dying men and the shrieks of agonized horses. Known
before this time as Corral de las Comas, from a motte of coma
trees near by, the pen was renamed Las Ánimas, or Lost Souls.
El Rancho de las Ánimas, which includes the site of this mustang
pen, long vanished, still exists.

The location of a corral was strategic. The bank of a creek at
a used crossing was strategic. Brushy hollows and canyons were
usual locations. Running horses raise so much dust that in some
localities where the prevailing wind is from the south the corral
opening was made on the south side; flying dust would precede
the runners and hide the pen until they were almost at it.[27] After
a manada had been virtually run down and driven up to a pen
gate, it would sometimes refuse to enter. The ordinary cow pen,

around which a clearing is desirable, would not serve for trapping mustangs. One band of mustangers hazed a tamed-down manada for many miles to a big, strong cow pen on the plains and after reaching it had to walk the mustangs around it for two days before getting them inside. The stallion, a big pinto, cut off alone, was chased fifteen miles and then escaped.[28]

On the plains furrows were sometimes plowed out for half a mile or so from the gate opening to serve as sham wings. Wild horses feared a black line of unsodded earth more than they feared, until many had been cut, the thin lines of barbed wire. If, however, the wires were hung with white rags, the sight would deter them. Like some herds of cattle, they would refuse to cross a railroad track. A wornout saddle blanket hung up at a watering would, for a time, keep them scared away, forcing them to go many miles to another watering where waylayers waited. A mustanger of modern times in Nevada devised corral and corral wings out of bolts of canvas eight feet wide, fastened to pickets. Not being able to see through the canvas, the wild horses regarded it as impregnable. It had the advantage of being readily portable.[29]

A few mustangers used decoy horses, but they were not of much use until the mustangs had been tired down; then the decoys had a steadying effect on the drive to a pen. The best decoy was a belled mare. If the wild stallion adopted her, and he generally did, she seemed to have a psychological effect on the whole band, making them adhere to her, or perhaps to her bell, as she led the way to imprisonment.[30]

An odd character on the plains had two mares, and no other horses at all, that he used to attract mustangs and then to betray them. His chief reliance was an old mare he called Topsy. She was so well trained that she would lie down at his command and remain on her side until he gave word to rise. During cold storms, he used her as a windshield, making his bed against her. When she was loose with mustangs, she would obey the sound of his voice or whistle or the wave of his hat, guiding the wild bunch for days until her master brought them to a pen.[31]

The most fantastic method of tiring down mustangs that I have heard of was to catch a mustang, somehow, while he still had plenty of life in him, fix "an imitation man" on his back, and then turn him loose. He would run for his accustomed associates. As soon as they caught sight of him, they would flee, setting every manada on the prairies into a grand stampede that did not end until the stampeders were exhausted, in which state cowboys would pen at least some of them.[32] Few runs of this kind were planned.

The most reliable and by far the most practiced method was to "walk" the mustangs down. As the operation will be detailed in narratives to follow, little need be told of it here. Usually two or more men relieved each other in dogging a band of wild horses until they became too tired, sore and sleepy to resist. A solitary man persisting after them could master them in time. Steadiness of gait and direct traveling kept a horse burdened with saddle and man from tiring like the wild horses that dashed away sporadically, covering much more ground than the pursuer. Wear on their nerves contributed to exhaustion. Lack of water and grass was not so subduing as lack of sleep.*

The fun of penning turned to trouble in taming. Most of the pens were without water. There was no feed to give the captives while they were taught submission. There were no small pastures

---

* This walking-down process seems to have originated with American frontiersmen and not to have been a Spanish-Mexican method, as most range techniques were. The Plains Indians enjoyed running and roping too much to "walk" after mustangs, though some walked elk into traps. Four Dakota Sioux followed a herd for two nights and a day and into the second day without eating or resting, heading them towards the tribal camp, near which the elk were slaughtered. The two swiftest and most enduring of the four runners flanked the herd, one on either side, and, when the animals tried to veer from a direct course, turned them by barking like wolves, "it being a peculiarity of the elk to walk slowly in the opposite direction from the howl or bark of the wolf." — *Iron Face, the Adventures of Jack Frazer*, recorded by "Walker-in-the-Pines" (Henry H. Sibley), The Caxton Club, Chicago, 1950, 72–74.

in which to hold them. They were a bear by the tail: You have him; what are you going to do with him?

In addition to methods of hindering movement already described, there were numerous others. One was to girth the horse's body with a rawhide thong and strap a front foot, at the ankle, to it. Walking slowly, the animal could bear a little weight on the foot, but upon trying to run would fall as if he had a broken leg. A few falls would make him give up trying to run.

Sometimes a rawhide strap about four inches wide and six feet long was tied to a front ankle. Taking care to avoid being tripped by his own hind feet and by the feet of other horses, the mustang could travel slowly, but in a run would go down. A drag chain or a drag log served the same purpose and was more unmerciful.

Clogs, or togs, commonly used, were of two designs. One was a forked stick fixed to a front ankle, the prongs lashed together in front of the ankle. At a gait faster than a walk, a hind foot would "interfere" with the shank of the stick and result in tripping as well as skinning the ankle. A block of wood about eighteen inches long with a groove cut in the middle for fitting against an ankle and with notches for a binding thong served the same purpose. Some mustangers tied a block of wood to the mustang's foretop. Then the head would be knocked bloody from running.

Individual mustangs could be ridden away from the place of captivity, but management of a herd was difficult and generally brutal. Often, after a period of starvation and thirst, a few mustangs at a time were let out of an inner pen to mingle with gentle horses in another pen, the mixed bunch then being driven away and the process repeated until the entire catch had been disposed of. Any stallion that showed fight was shot. Paiute Indians are said to have sewn up the nostrils of captives, cutting off the breath required for exertion. Californians blindfolded captives and drove them with gentle horses, to which in their helplessness they would try to keep close.[33] Burros made good neck animals for wild horses as well as for wild cattle. A burro stands for no foolishness from an animal tied to his neck. He decides when to drink, when to graze. He gets his burden home to be freed from it. The first thing any mustanger wanted to do with captives was to take them out of the country and sell them.

The earliest Anglo-American mustanger of record was Philip Nolan — prototype for Edward Everett Hale's romance of patriotism, *The Man Without a Country*. Between 1790 and 1800 Nolan made four expeditions from Louisiana into Texas. On the first he lived with the Comanches off and on for two years and captured fifty mustangs. From the second he brought back 250 horses, which he sold at Natchez and Frankfort, Kentucky. His "dexterity in taking wild horses" had given him such wide fame that on June 24, 1798, Thomas Jefferson, always hungry for knowledge, wrote Nolan requesting information on the wild horses of the West. Nolan had gone on his third expedition when the letter arrived, but an associate, Daniel Clark, Jr., responded from New Orleans promising an account, when he should return, of wild horse numbers and habits that would "stagger" the President's belief. In subsequent letters Clark wrote Jefferson that Nolan had returned with 1000 horses, most of which had been purchased in the mountains of Tamaulipas, and was taking some to Virginia, where he would present one "remarkable for Colour" to Jefferson. Whether Nolan ever gave horse and facts to Jefferson is not known.

In March, 1801, he caught his last mustang. On this last expedition he had no permit to enter Spanish territory. He went well provided with goods to trade, leather for saddles and "cotton to put in horses' ears." He had with him 18 Americans, 7 Spaniards, and 2 Negro slaves. They built corrals on a branch, which took Nolan's name, of the Brazos River in the high prairie country of what is now Hill County. They had a fortified camp at which they broke wild horses and lived principally on horse meat. Taking only the best animals corralled, and releasing others to breed, they had captured several hundred when a strong Spanish force attacked them. The captain cut off Nolan's ears to show as proof of his death; his men were taken as prisoners to Mexico.

Nolan seems to have done his mustanging on what came to be known as the Grand Prairie, of central Texas. Among horses he captured or bought, as records show, were duns, roans, grays, whites, blacks, sorrels, bays, browns and paints. Some bore brands from mission ranches on the San Antonio River; some had been earmarked by Indians. Mules mixed with the mustangs brought higher prices than horses.[34]

XIII

AS THE MUSTANGERS TOLD IT

1. The Mustanger Who Turned Mustang

THE MOST ORIGINAL mustanger I ever met, either in person or through hearsay, was an ex-slave named Bob Lemmons. He was not a pure-blooded Negro. The mixture probably came from Southern chivalry, but he had an Indian look. He was eighty-four years old when I talked with him on his little ranch out from Carrizo Springs, west of the Nueces, in 1931.[1] He had grown up with the mustangs; until he was mature he had known no other life than that of range and trail; after people and fences came, he lived alone in the brush.

"I acted like I was a mustang," he said. "I made the mustangs think I was one of them. Maybe I was in them days. After I stayed with a bunch long enough they'd foller me instid of me having to foller them. Show them you're the boss. That's the secret."

He always mustanged alone. It was never his aim to "dry out" a band — starve it for water — or to tire it down. He rode a horse with a good bottom but seldom struck a run. After starting a bunch he made no effort to keep up with it; he followed tracks. He trailed one bunch for five days without seeing it. In a country of many wild horses he knew how many were in the bunch he was after, and he could distinguish the tracks made by two or three of these animals from all other tracks. About the second day, droppings from traveling horses will be dry in contrast to the moister and softer droppings of horses undisturbed on their range.

After he began following a manada, he changed neither horse nor clothing until he led it into a pen. Any help until he was ready to pen would have been a hindrance. If a rider from the outfit for which he worked wanted to tell him where to find a supply of provisions, he was not allowed to approach nearer than a hundred yards. The provisions were in a morral hung on a tree. When Bob Lemmons rode up to it, he took out the contents and put them in his own morral, to the smell of which the wild horses had grown accustomed. His bedding was a Mexican blanket that served also as slicker.

Within a week the band he was after would usually allow him to direct their course. His purpose was to get them to accept him as their leader. Towards the end of the second week he was supplanting the stallion as commander. At this stage he would begin working them away from the range over which they had been circling, for on strange ground they would surrender more readily than at home.

By long and patient observation, he had come to know not only wild horse habits but preferences as to water, grass, trave

ways and bed ground. When he led them to a watering, he considered direction of wind and the lay of the ground so that they would feel free of attack. He let them see him smelling for danger. Sometimes, to show his power, he would not allow them to drink. When he was ready, he would ride into the water with them.

He would not allow them to come too near his horse, though they were curious and eager to associate with him more intimately. If the stallion had a chance, he might fight the horse or run him off. At night he unsaddled in front of the mustangs and picketed his horse at his head. When the mustangs saw him afoot, they kept their distance, though when mounted he could move very near, even among, them.

He was a light sleeper. Many a night he was awakened by a nicker, telling him that stallion or mare wanted to leave and was calling the other mustangs to come along. Certain mares, after they were fairly mastered, would not want to leave. They had given, in the manner of females, their allegiance and were not willing to turn from the horseback leader. When he was awakened by a restless nicker, he would saddle, round

[237]

up the manada in the manner of a stallion, and leave with it.

If he saw a man riding a long way off, he would gaze at him with a demonstration of alertness and distrust — just as if he were a wild horse — and then lead in flight. If his band came to a wagon road, he would snort his suspicion and run away. Fresh panther sign made him as wary as a mare that had lost her colt to a panther. Once when he saw where a "leopard cat" (ocelot) had killed a colt, he led the stampede. If he saw an unusual piece of brush or a chunk of wood in a trail through a thicket, he made his horse "climb the mesquites" getting around it.

If for any reason he left his mustangs, he would upon return-ing come with the wind so that they would smell him and not be alarmed. Thus day and night, for week following week, across prairies and through thickets, huddled in rain, spread out on the ground in sunshine, listening in starlight to the encircling coyote concerts, lingering for the grazers as unhurried as the shadow of a circling buzzard, this lone man in primeval silence and space lived with the mustangs and, except in not eating grass and in having the long, long thoughts that only a human being can have, lived as one of them.*

He was not invariably successful. One band that he started out of the Anacacho Hills, near Spofford, never submitted to his direction. After veering around considerably, these mustangs coursed southeast until they came into the great Randado horse

---

* "Pedro Cuje, who died last year on the Tejon Ranch, was riding herd at one hundred and three. He had a miraculous power over young colts. Driving young colts is like trying to drive young turkeys; they are all over the place at once. Old Pedro drove them alone. He would work no other way — always alone. When it came time to move the colt herd, the old man climbed into his ancient saddle, gave a low whistle to the colts, and set off across the fields like the Pied Piper of Hamelin. He never looked back or paid the slightest attention to them. The colts would run away from the column, kicking and playing, but, after their scamper, they would always come back to follow him. I asked him how he did it. 'No stranger knows my children,' he said. 'They are good chil-dren.'" — Harry Carr, *The West Is Still Wild*, Boston, 1932, 219–220. Quoted by permission of the Estate of Harry Carr, Balboa, California.

ranch, about 180 miles by direct line from the starting point. When he got among the manadas of the Randado, he gave up the chase, for it was not ethical to disturb them. He figured that the stallion or the lead mare had been raised on this ranch, though neither bore a brand. The conduct of these horses occupied his mind for years. He concluded that some smell from his morral made them averse to him.

Another manada he started was led by a big bay stallion that was branded, as were three of the mares. He could not get close enough to them to make out the brands, but after they left their range and began coursing southeast, they allowed him to keep fairly near. On the third day of this direct traveling they crossed several wagon roads and Bob Lemmons glimpsed a few ranch houses and "lots of people" — perhaps a dozen. The bay stallion did not shy from these signs of man. He coursed straight and finally led his mares into a corral behind a ranch house. A man came out and asked Bob Lemmons what he meant by driving those horses. They were his, in his brand, though he had not seen them for three years. His supposition was that Indians or other horse thieves had driven them away and lost them up the Nueces, where they had taken up with the mustangs and the stallion had added wild mares to his bunch. The ranch where Bob Lemmons now found himself was in Live Oak County. He rode home with a note from the rancher to his employer explaining why he was not bringing in the band of mustangs.

Habitually, after he got a band under control, he led them homeward, taking plenty of time. One day he would see a rider on the lookout. Giving the mustangs to understand that they were to remain behind, he would ride to within easy shouting distance. Then he would stop and ask what day of the week it was. He would set the day and hour for penning, provided the wind was right. Procedure of the ranch hands near the pen was understood. On the appointed day Bob Lemmons would increase his speed gradually as he led the mustangs towards the opening between the wings of the pen. When their position was right for the waylaying ranch hands to crowd them from the rear, he would break into a dead run, the wild horses at his heels. After he entered the gate, he would dash across the big corral and be let out at a small gate kept in readiness by a man placed there for the purpose. This man and one or two others would suddenly appear before the now terrorized horses, waving blankets and shouting in order to get them milling and prevent their dashing into the fence. Meanwhile the wide entrance to the pen had been strongly barred. After the horses had milled until they were tired, ropers would enter and catch and clog them.

There are men whom bees will not sting. There are men whom a fierce yard dog will not bark at, much less bite. What is it inside some individuals that makes horses untamable by others submit to them gently? I am not talking about fake horse-whisperers, though I think there have been some who were not fakes. Back in the days of open range and long trails, when remuda men for months at a stretch guarded, grazed, watered and moved over an unpeopled world with the saddle horses of isolated cow outfits, one now and then led instead of driving his remuda. The horses would follow him like mules magnetized by a bell mare. I myself have known of only two such *remuderos*: one was a Mexican and one a Negro — primitives with primitive instincts not worn slick by the machinery of society. No Indian medicine man, mounted on a white horse, bleating like a buffalo calf, maneuvering at precise distances and gaits, and employing other ruses, showed more primordial skill — magic, some have called it — in leading a herd of buffaloes by moonlight to the *pis' kun*, or slaughter pen, than Bob Lemmons sustained until he actually became the leader of a band of wild horses that followed him into a pen as fresh as they had been when he first sighted them.

2. On the Nueces in the '50s

The one man who left a record of mustanging with Mexicans on the great wild horse range between the Nueces and the Rio Grande while Indians were still adding to the *mesteñas* was J. W. Moses.[2] His fellow *mesteñeros* came mostly from along the Rio Grande, many from the Mexican side, between Laredo and Matamoros, and from settlements as far east as Goliad. Many made their living by catching mustang cattle as well as mustang horses. They operated in companies under captains, at times as many as a hundred in one company. Few of them were well armed and ammunition was always scarce. The wild cattle and javelinas on which they depended for meat were nearly all roped. Coffee and *piloncillos* (brown sugar moulded into cones) were luxuries with them. They made their own lariats of rawhide and wove their girths, bridle reins and hackamores of manes and tails roached from wild mares. Their Saltillo blankets turned water but were not wide enough to shut out freezing northers. They knew no law confining mustanging to certain seasons, and no representative of the law knew them.

One of the ablest *mesteñeros* among them was a Laredo man named Roque who for many years had been a captive among the Comanches. He was more effective with bow and arrow than most of his fellows were with firearms. His brother Romano was a noted captain of mustangers. Both could follow trails invisible to other eyes. No wild animal had an instinct for the *campo* keener than theirs.

However primitive and lawless these *mesteñeros* might be, they operated with a ceremonialism unknown to the Plains and the Northwest. No corral they constructed was considered finished until it had been dedicated to a saint and a cross — usually of ax-hewn mesquite — had been put up at the entrance. Then after mustangs had been run into the corral, there must be the *lazo de las ánimas* — horses lassoed for the benefit of the souls of *meste-ñeros* who had been killed. The money these horses brought was paid to a priest to say masses. If the mustang catch numbered a hundred animals or more, a whole *lazo* (two horses) was dedicated; if it was under a hundred head, only half a *lazo* (one animal) was required. Every captain was duty bound to see that the *lazo de las ánimas* was not neglected. The rite was observed with more devotion when Indian sign was fresh than when everything was *pacífico*.

Once while J. W. Moses and ten other *mesteñeros* were out, Indian sign caused them to throw in with another party under Don Clemente Zapata. The combined force of twenty-five men had hardly a dozen serviceable rifles, but they felt secure. Having sighted many wild horses in the vicinity of the corrals named Los Patricios, they made camp at a waterhole, protected by brush and trees, not far off. The next morning while the *aventadores*, or starters, were galloping forth to head the wild horses into the V-shaped corral wings, they saw a large drove running in the direction they wanted them to run. Dust raised by the runners prevented their seeing about fifty Comanches crowding them from the rear.

Whether the Comanches intended to pen the mustangs or not, at sight of the *mesteñeros*, they veered for them. They killed two before the *mesteñeros* could concentrate for defence in the timber about their camp. After trying all day to dislodge them, the Comanches left. They had killed four men, wounded three more severely, and taken and killed half the saddle horses. Several of the unarmed Mexicans now pulled out for their homes, but the remainder combined with a third *partido* of wild-horse hunters, raising the number of armed men to thirty, and captured a big caballada.

During a dry time years later, one of these men had just taken his stand near the gate of a catch pen at a waterhole amidst a thicket on Amargoso Creek, when he saw ten Indians riding down the trail. They had scared off the mustangs and were coming for water. As the catch pen was new, they were unaware of its existence. The spy rushed to alarm the *mesteñeros* in camp, and some of them crept around behind the Indians, killed one and by yelling and shooting stampeded the others into the corral. Finding themselves trapped there, they abandoned their horses and clambered over the pickets to safety. The *mesteñeros* gained ten good horses.

Luck could be on either side. Adversity could come in various forms. In March, 1850, the J. W. Moses outfit found so many and such large droves of wild horses west of Agua Dulce Creek that they felt sure of a full catch. Their first run was towards a corral at the base of a natural pass between hills. So many manadas joined in the run that after the pen was full the *encerrador* (encloser), whose business it was to bar the gap, could not halt the stream pouring in behind the leaders. He waved his blanket and yelled; the *cortador*, his helper, tried to *cortar* (cut back) the oncoming flood. The wild runners only became more frantic. Lunging forward, they trampled over the backs of the tightly packed animals and broke down the pickets. Everything except the dead and maimed escaped back to freedom. More than a hundred mares and colts were left dead. Their carcasses raised such a stench that the corral thereafter bore the name of Hediondo — Stinking.

The mustangers went on to another pen, caught all the mares they could manage, and were on their way back to San Patricio, when they fell in with Captain John J. Dix, a noted surveyor, leading a fine mustang stallion just captured. The captain had the lead rope tied fast to his saddle horn; his high-strung mount and the high-strung stallion were frenzying each other. While they were following a narrow trail lined on both sides with prickly pear, the stallion set back with all his strength. The jerk broke the girth, and the mustang plunged away, dragging the saddle with Captain Dix still in it. By the time two vaqueros roped the runaway, Dix had a thousand thorns in his body. A pair of tweezers was a part of the equipment of any outfit working in the brush country, and by sundown the brush men had pretty well unthorned the sufferer.

For the general run of captured animals the mustangers got five dollars around, releasing many that were unsalable. In some seasons the catches oversupplied demand and the price went down to a dollar. Moses, however, always got good prices for picked horses after they were broken. He refused fifty dollars repeatedly for a dark bay that had been castrated and named Dormidor (Sleeper) on account of his drowsy looks when not excited. No horse could outlast him on a chase.

A *bayo naranjado,* a bright orange dun with white mane and tail, drew Moses on one of his most memorable hunts. A paint mule for which the owner had offered a good reward was in his manada. Moses wanted the dun and his friend Romaldo Longoria wanted the mule. They proposed to rope both, and they set out with only a *mozo,* or servant, to tend camp and their extra mounts.

After reaching the dun's range they rode for three days, during which time they roped two branded horses that had taken up with mustangs, before they located him. His mane, snow white, was "so heavy that it bent his neck over to one side when he grazed. He was close-coupled, clean-limbed, with a small head and a white stripe down his face." Moses at once named him Gavilán — Hawk.

The ropers pitched camp, saddled fresh horses, lightened equipment to the minimum, and then waited for the mustangs to drink before starting after them.

"I knew," Moses wrote, "that I could overhaul Gavilán in a league or two. Dashing into the water-logged manada, Don Romaldo cut off the paint mule and I got behind the stallion. He bore up country through some scrubby brush towards Monte Redondo [Round Thicket]. I was gaining on him, but after we got clear of the brush, I had to hold back on account of gopher holes in the light soil. Finally, however, I got within roping distance. Just as I was about to throw the reata, my horse fell.

"When I recovered my senses, the sun was going down. I must have lain unconscious for two hours or more. The bridle reins were still in my hands, but when I tried to stand I could not bear weight on my right leg. The knee was alarmingly swollen. I managed to pull up into the saddle, but was too muddled from thirst and pain to have any sense of direction. I gave my horse his head, and in time he brought me to the waterhole where we had jumped the mustangs. I crawled off, drank of the muddy water and bathed my knee in it for a good while. Then I dragged myself into the saddle again and rode to camp.

"Don Romaldo had roped the paint mule. He and the *mozo* were about to start out to hunt me. Days passed before I could walk. In the end I bought Galiván from another mustanger. I had the pleasure of gentling him. He remained beautiful but was not fast."

Many a mustanger came to John Young's conclusion. As his story goes in my book *A Vaquero of the Brush Country*, after running a manada for ten days he was so sure of it that he sent in his helper (a Negro cowhand named Bill Nunn), with the camp outfit to get two or three vaqueros to help with the penning and roping. On the eleventh day, however, the mustangs were utterly demoralized by a mule hanger-on, and John Young rode his horse to death twenty-five miles away from the pen. When, on a crazy mount borrowed from a sheep rancher, he finally got there he made Bill Nunn "a present of all the mustangs left in Texas."

3. The Ghost of the Llano Estacado

In the spring of 1879 Frank Collinson [3] set out on a hunt for strays to the west of the Tongue River range he was managing in Motley County, Texas. Cowmen were taking over the Staked Plains, just released from Indians and buffaloes, but had barely started killing off mustangs. After Collinson got above the cap-rock he began seeing carcasses of horses, along with those of lobos and coyotes. Late in the day he rode into the camp of Bob Payne, a friend of buffalo-skinning days. With only a few scattering remnants of buffaloes left to shoot, Payne had turned to poisoning wolves for their pelts and had been shooting mustangs for bait.

That night he was full of talk about a three-year-old white stallion running on Black Water Draw. Two winters back he had singled him out as a yearling following his mother, a flea-bitten gray, in a big band of mustangs. If the band ran, the mare led it, usually keeping a little to one side. In time she and her yearling stud cut off from it. She was no ordinary broomtail. She looked like a Thoroughbred — thin mane and tail, trim legs, good feet, a little under fifteen hands in height. Her son had all her marks, except that he was pure white.

Two or three months before Frank Collinson came along, Bob Payne spotted the two again, a paint yearling filly now following the mare. The white stallion had grown taller than his mammy. The three were keeping to themselves. Payne tried to get them to take up with his horses, but he might as well have tried his dodges on antelopes. He had heard that a horse might be creased by shooting it through the thick of the ham, and thought that if he crippled the mare this way he might neck her to one of his horses and gradually work the white stallion and paint filly in with her. He was a good shot. One day he got up within close range, rested his rifle on the cross-sticks which all buffalo hunters used, aimed and fired. The mare fell. When he got to her she was bleeding to death, her thigh bone crushed to pieces. He went back to the carcass the next day and saw the stallion and filly near it. The stallion ran but the filly stood. He shot for a neck crease and broke her neck. The day following he saw the stallion disappearing about a mile off. Now he was pulling out for Dodge City with his last load of buffalo hides, filled out with wolf pelts.

A year later, in May of 1880, Frank Collinson rode to Fort Sumner on the Pecos to inspect some high-grade bulls. On the way back he found Celedón and Pedro Trujillo and their outfit camped at Los Portales — the portals to the Staked Plains on the New Mexico side. The Trujillos were the most noted *mesteñeros* of the Plains, and they had made a full catch of colts around Spring Lake and on Black Water Draw.

"Did you see or hear anything of a white stallion, about five years old?" Collinson asked.

Pedro Trujillo laughed. "Every *mesteñero* on the Pecos has tried to catch him," he said. "I saw him, but that's all. Some call him the Ghost of the Llano Estacado."

Right there Collinson and the Trujillos agreed to hunt the stallion down in partnership, but no time was set for the hunt. Another year went by, and then the Matador Land and Cattle Company bought out the Tongue River cattle and range. Collinson set up a ranch of his own, in partnership with two other men, on Duck Creek in Dickens County. Grass could not have been finer anywhere on earth than it was that year all over the plains. When fall came, with all stock contented and thriving, Collinson set out for the Pecos to arrange with the Trujillos for the white stallion hunt.

It was agreed that the meeting place should be on Black Water Draw the coming March. The Trujillos would be on their annual hunt for mustang colts and mares. They would have several riders and grain-fed horses. On the appointed day, in 1882 now, Frank Collinson and a cowboy named Dick Lane, equipped with extra mounts and with grain, grub, and bedding on pack horses, found the Trujillos camped on Black Water Draw. They had already located the Ghost with a big band of mares.

Most of the mares were near foaling time. The Trujillos were to have whatever mares and younger stock they wanted; Collinson was to have the stallion, paying half the price he was mutually valued at — after he was caught. The plan was to walk the starch out of the Ghost and his band without trying to run them down. As they would eventually circle back to the starting point, after any chase, there was no need for more than one man to follow them. Pedro Trujillo was to make the first run; the other riders were to keep on the lookout, and the first man to see him when he returned was to take his place.

Early on a fine, crisp morning all hands rode for the Ghost's range and soon sighted him. Before long his band was disappearing, Pedro following at a more moderate speed. His brother Celedón had brought a long slim pole with a piece of red cloth tied to one end. The pole was stuck up near the spot where the mustangs were grazing when they took alarm. The red flag would serve as a marker for the area to be watched.

No more was seen of Pedro or the mustangs that day. By daybreak next morning the other mustangers were scattered for ten miles around the starting point. Collinson and Dick Lane, riding together, saw the dust raised by the returning manada and then the mustangs. Pedro reported that they had run straight north at least twenty miles before turning west and then kept that direction until after dark, when they headed back south. He had managed to course them through the night and about daylight found them grazing. Then, after resting his horse a while, he had started them off again. He estimated his ride at about seventy miles.

Dick Lane kept behind the Ghost and his mares all the second day. After dark he left them halted near Spring Lake and rode to camp.

Frank Collinson was to be the next runner. He was off before daylight on a bay horse that a cattle-buyer claimed to have ridden from Fort Worth to Brownwood without unsaddling — a hundred and thirty miles. He was sixteen hands high and bull strong.

Riding out with him to locate the bunch, the Trujillos took along two vaqueros and a half-breed Apache who did most of their roping. He was light in weight and rode bareback except for a tanned rawhide surcingle girted tight, with a loop of rawhide laced to each side for stirrups. He stuck only his big toes in these loops. A piece of inch rope, padded with a strip of old blanket, was tied around his horse's neck. To this collar one end of his reata was tied. The other end was ready to use. The rig had proved effective with colts and broomtails, and the Apache was eager to try it out on the big white stallion.

On this third morning, the Trujillos were expecting to catch mares too stiff and sore to run, but none started off in that condition. Collinson followed them off alone. He did not crowd them for the first few miles, but after his bay had warmed up and pretty well emptied himself, he struck a long lope and kept them moving. They held a course almost due north until they came to Tule Draw about noon, and then they went west. They did not mix with any of several bands of mustangs sighted along the run. Once in a while they would slack down, trot a way, and then make another run. Along in the afternoon some of the mares began to fall out. The stallion made no effort to punish them, showed no fight towards his man enemy.

An hour before sundown he turned south, keeping up his speed. By dusk only eight or ten mares remained with him. The stars and a moon in its second quarter made a good light. About nine o'clock, seeing that the band wanted to stop, Collinson halted, unsaddled, and staked his horse. He had been following the mustangs for fourteen hours and estimated that he had covered eighty miles.

At daybreak the mares were all lying down, but the Ghost was on his feet. Down Black Water Draw he led them, mostly in a long trot. Two hours later they came in sight of camp. The stallion then took a southeast course, only three mares remaining with him. Collinson ate breakfast, changed horses, and with the other hands struck south for Yellow House Lake. Near noon they saw the Ghost coming straight west again, alone, the last mare having dropped away. Celedón was a half mile behind him.

Spreading out, the mustangers turned the Ghost south, towards Yellow House Lake. The Apache, now on the bare back of the fastest horse the Trujillos owned, was racing over his tracks. Pedro was running on the west flank and another runner was on the left flank. Yellow House Lake was one of the big alkali sinks, or basins, on the Staked Plains. Nothing would drink its water. It was usually only a few inches deep and was as white as snow. Under this white surface lay a black, bottomless bog. After a rain nothing heavier than a coyote could cross these alkali lakes. Broken ridges jutted out into Yellow House Lake, the bog coming up to their bases.

The stallion took down one of the ridges. No doubt desperation had confused him. After nearly four days of constant travel, he was still ahead of fresh horses. Surely he would turn back when he sensed the big alkali bog hole, but, no, on he went, the Apache ready to make a catch whenever he checked.

He came to the bluff, the white bog in front and on each side. He did not check one step or veer a fraction from his direction. He made one tremendous leap, striking the bog at least twenty-five feet out from the foot of the bluff, which was not less than twenty feet high. Frank Collinson was close enough to hear the splash. When he looked over the bluff a few seconds later, the stallion was nearly out of sight. His head and neck were still clear, but every flounder he made the deeper he sank, and the foul mud was filling his nostrils. He shook his head and coughed a few times and then sank from sight.

By now all hands were on the bluff. "I guess," Frank Collinson said, "that none of us felt very proud of our work. I never saw a range horse out of an Arabian, Steel Dust or any other highbred stallion that came up to this wild horse in looks or performance. He had been foaled on the best short grass that ever grew, in an invigorating climate. He had grown bigger and stronger than any other mustang I ever saw. We took after him at the time of year when range horses are at their weakest. After having been run for towards three hundred miles by successive relays of grain-fed horses, he could, at the time of his fatal jump into Yellow House Lake, have easily run away from any horse chasing him."

4. The Houlding of Black Kettle *

Late on a June evening of 1867 a band of Cheyenne warriors under Chief Black Kettle swooped down upon a Mormon wagon train camped on the Smoky Hill River trail, about a day's journey east of Fort Wallace, and ran off all their horses. Among them were several Kentucky Thoroughbreds intended for breeding in Utah. A year-old black stud of this stock escaped the Indians and joined the wild horses. Thus Cheyenne tradition explains the origin of the most noted mustang ever chased upon the plains of Kansas. The facts of his adult career are well authenticated.

Men in the region of Fort Wallace began calling him Black Kettle. As he developed, Indians tried repeatedly to capture him. Until he was thirteen years old, his range was mostly in Sherman County, surrounding the present town of Goodland. During

* The narrative that follows is a condensation, into third-person narrative, of a forty-page pamphlet entitled *Black Kettle*, by Frank M. Lockard, published, but not copyrighted, by R. G. Wolfe at Goodland, Kansas, about 1924. A less skilled condensation was published in *Mustangs and Cow Horses*, issued by the Texas Folklore Society in 1940. This, without acknowledgment, was lifted, in a somewhat sawed-off form, into *Great Horse Stories*, selected by Page Cooper, Doubleday & Co., Garden City, New York, 1946.

Francis Marion Lockard was born in Ohio, 1855, moved to Kansas in 1874, taught school two years, became a horse trader, mustanged for a spell, went to Monterrey, Mexico, in 1884 and bought a herd of horses, which he trailed to Kansas. Later he drove three herds of Texas cattle up the trail. He was elected to the Kansas senate in 1888. He wrote a history of Norton County, Kansas, besides numerous newspaper articles. He died in 1928.

these years the Custer Road, laid off by the army, ran straight through Black Kettle's range and on north to the Republican River. Soldiers, buffalo hunters and other travelers over the road saw him, and by the time he was five or six years old he was famous. In grace, speed, and endurance he excelled every other wild horse in western Kansas; no other was chased by so many men.

Black Kettle's raven coat glistened like burnished metal. When he stood still, his tail reached to the ground; when he ran, especially against the wind, it streamed so far out behind that, from a distance, it made him appear to be about twenty feet long. His foretop reached to the tip of his nose, and on the run he continually tossed his head, throwing the mane back over his ears so that he could see. This action and the long mane made him look a foot taller than he actually was.

The exceedingly long mane and tail were contrary to Thoroughbred characteristics. Moreover, most of the other stallions dominating bands of mares in Black Kettle's country were black. Roan stallions were more numerous, but most of them were without mares, hundreds roaming about alone or by twos and threes. The local name for these outcasts was "dog soldiers." The majority of mares were red roans, occasional blue roans among them looking black from a distance. Maybe one in ten was really black. Any bay, gray or white mustang was supposed to have escaped from movers or cattlemen.*

One night Captain Homer W. Wheeler of Fort Wallace led out a troop of cavalry and spaced the riders around a stretch of prairie about the size of a township in which Black Kettle was known to be ranging. The plan was to hold him inside the cor-

* By 1880 many of the wild horses on the plains were marked by American blood. Some weighed up to 1400 pounds. One captured in 1878 weighed 1700 pounds. Such could be run down within a day's time. — "Wild Horses in Kansas," Ellis (Kansas) *Weekly Headlight*, May 8, 1880; "Pioneering," by L. S. Scott, Bazine (Kansas) *Advocate*, July 9, 1937; "Wild Horses," *The Chronoscope*, Larned, Kansas, June 19, 1879.

don and chase him by relays until he was tired down sufficiently for a cowboy to rope. At daylight a few cavalrymen got a fine look at Black Kettle, but he broke through the line before the run was well started.

Later while Ame Cole was in Robidoux's store at Fort Wallace, Captain Wheeler came in and announced that he would give two hundred dollars to anybody who delivered Black Kettle in sound condition on the end of a rope.

"By God, Captain," Ame Cole spoke up, "I can walk the tail off that God-damned horse in five days."

"I consider the tail the most valuable part of the horse," Captain Wheeler replied, "and would not give much for him without it."

Ame Cole was a character. He belonged to Black Kettle's range and in a way to the Black Kettle story — for it is the story of a dream shared by many men who were not mustangers as well as by men who were. Ame Cole had come to Kansas in 1866 to hunt buffaloes. He usually hunted alone. After the buffaloes were killed off, he homesteaded the ground where he had made his first camp, built a cabin, part dugout and part log, and lived in it alone for fifty years. It was a museum of Indian skulls picked up on battlegrounds. He used them for candlesticks and when lonesome burned candles the night through to drive away evil spirits. He also set the skulls up for targets and gradually shot them to pieces. He claimed that a footlog across the creek near his cabin was charmed and that any Indian who started across it dropped off into the surging waters to rise no more. The water was about a foot deep. A tree beside the cabin was full of lead that he had shot at an imaginary Indian he called Blazeface. Old Blazeface was always spying on him from that tree. If another man's talk did not interest Ame Cole, he would say, "Oh, pitch it to hell." Profanity began his greeting and ended his good-by. Drouths confirmed him in the belief that western Kansas had been created by God for Indians and buffaloes; so he sat in his cabin and waited for the settlers to leave and the buffaloes to return.

One time while he and a partner named Grant were skinning buffaloes, a roan outcast stallion stole his four wagon mules. The only way to recover them was to shoot the stallion. Cole started after them on foot, expecting to kill the thief within an hour. "I think I walked one thousand miles in the next two weeks," he would tell, "trying to get a shot at that damned stud, but whenever he was within reach he always kept a mule between him and me." Finally he killed him. After that he shot every "dog soldier" within range of his buffalo rifle. Other hunters and then the stockmen and settlers did the same.

When Ame Cole left Fort Wallace on the day he heard Captain Wheeler offer two hundred dollars for Black Kettle, he expected to return within a week leading the stallion. Relying on his walking powers and marksmanship, he planned to crease the horse. His realistic partner, Grant, was against turning from buffalo hides to wild horses, but Cole had his head set.

On the level plains a man rarely got closer than a mile to a wild horse. While he was trying to creep up to one, other wild horses would see him and by their actions notify the whole country of danger. Black Kettle had been chased so much that he would sometimes run twenty miles in a straight line when badly scared. He had two main watering places, one in Wild Horse Draw, near the Smoky, and the other at the head of the Beaver. These waterings were about twenty miles apart. Black Kettle was no nomad, but settled in habits.

Cole located the band on a high prairie. They ran northwest and in the course of an hour passed out of sight. Cole followed, walking and trotting, until he felt sure he had gone as far as Black Kettle would go in that direction. Far away on the horizon, in all directions, he could see horses, but as he had no field glasses, he was uncertain which was his bunch. After following one until late in the afternoon, he found Black Kettle was not in it. Thirst drove him to camp. Starting out early next morning, he tramped all day up and down the Smoky, watching for Black Kettle to come down for water, but at dark had not seen him. That night Grant said, "Tomorrow we leave for the Republican," and Cole reluctantly gave in. The next afternoon near the Beaver they saw Black Kettle. Cole wanted to try after him again but Grant would not stop. For years Cole intended to come back and catch the horse, but never found time when he was in the mood.

Another character who tried for Black Kettle was W. D. Street. He had fought with Custer and pegged down buffalo hides. Then, dressed in buckskin and moccasins, his auburn hair curled down to his shoulders, he graduated into the Kansas legislature. He liked to express himself and about 1878 published a long article on Black Kettle in the Decatur County weekly newspaper.

Frank Lockard read it, clipped it, put it in his vest pocket, and kept it until it was worn out. He was twenty-two and, fresh from books, was trading horses in partnership with William Simpson at Norton, Kansas. He took the mustang fever and communicated it to his partner. For Lockard, Black Kettle became the fire that will not burn down, the lode of lost gold to be found, the lure of fleeting beauty to be grasped. The village of Norton was on the edge of things. Southward the country was filling up with settlers requiring horses. Westward, still unoccupied, stretched the plains of free land, free grass, free wild horses, and the freedom of life that illumines the storybook of the West. Fort Wallace was a name about 125 miles southwest. Whenever a buffalo hunter came in, the two young horse traders asked if he had seen Black Kettle. Success in managing the broncs they bought and sold made them confident that they could capture and tame any wild horse on the prairies. They heard of two wild roan mares running between the Solomon and Saline rivers and spent two days following them without getting nearer than a mile. To capture Black Kettle, all they asked was sight of his trail.

About the middle of December in 1879, after traveling for three days without water, Lockard and Simpson made camp near the headwaters of the north prong of Smoky Hill River. They knew nothing of the lay of the land. The weather was cloudy and foggy. They did not recognize the Custer Road when they came to it, though it was later to be a very useful landmark across the markless plains. The first day in camp, Simpson killed a buffalo out of a small bunch in a draw. They now had a full supply of meat and were to learn that the draw was called, as it still is, Wild Horse Draw.

The next morning they rode to a point overlooking the plains of the Smoky. Through field glasses Lockard counted more than fifty bands of wild horses. They named this place Point Lookout and planted a post flying a red undershirt that could be picked out with glasses on prairies to the north fifteen miles away. During months to follow a signal fire from buffalo chips on this point guided Simpson or Lockard to camp many a dark night.

On their first day's ride they started up between two and three hundred wild horses. Every black herd stallion that came into view was taken for Black Kettle until he himself was sighted. Thenceforward there could be no mistake about his identity. A white horse splotched with carnation red would not be more distinguishable in a pen of browns than Black Kettle was from all other stallions on the range. His vitality and carriage as well as his long mane and tail set him apart. He had twenty-nine mares — the largest band that Lockard saw during all his time in wild-horse country.

The hunters had located Black Kettle — but they did not know of a pen within a hundred miles. They rode strong mounts and had grain for them in their wagon, but they had no idea of being able to run onto Black Kettle and rope him. In a hazy sort of way they expected to drive him and a great herd of other wild horses back to the home corral in Norton.

At daylight the morning after their discovery, Frank Lockard was in the saddle. He was twenty-four years old and weighed a hundred and forty pounds. He and his horse were ready for a hundred miles of chasing. Simpson was to haul a load of buffalo chips to Point Lookout and have a signal fire burning if his partner did not show up by dark. About two hours after leaving camp Lockard sighted Black Kettle and took after him at a lope, making about ten miles an hour. He kept up that pace for the next ten hours. He was expecting to have Black Kettle headed in the direction of camp before sundown, then to ride on in, eat, sleep and resume the chase the next morning on a fresh horse. During the day he crossed the Custer Road two or three times, but was ignorant of its lay.

To lighten weight he rode without carrying his overcoat. The weather had been consistently mild. Before dark a stiff north wind was bringing flurries of snow. Lockard halted to feed his horse corn from the saddle pockets and to chew on cold biscuits, walking about at the same time to warm his stiff legs. When he mounted to ride on, he realized that he did not know in what direction to head. He was too green to trust his horse to know. Deciding to stay where he was till daylight, he unsaddled and wrapped himself in the saddle blanket for sleep, but within a brief time the sweat-moistened blanket was frozen stiff. He resaddled and walked away, leading the horse — toward camp, he hoped. He had to walk to keep warm. Within a short mile he came to a shallow ravine. Supposing it to be a branch of the Smoky, he took down it. All night long he walked with constant expectation of coming upon camp.

In the first light of dawn he saw that he was going down a broad valley drained by a dry creek. He mounted and kept riding down it, mostly in a trot. About sundown he came to a ranch on the Sappa. The rancher told him he was fifty miles from camp and oriented him with respect to the Custer Road. The next morning he started back west, hit the Custer Road before dark, turned south on it and after traveling all night dragged into camp on the Smoky about daylight.

Simpson was just coming in from Point Lookout. He had spent most of the three days and nights of Lockard's absence watching and keeping a signal fire going. They decided that a pocket compass was necessary for horse-hunting on the plains.

"We'll get that compass before you start out again," Simpson said.

"Black Kettle has some of the starch walked out of him now," Lockard countered. "I want to keep on after him."

"I have located a good corral about three miles from here," Simpson said. "We'll go after the compass, come back, and corral Black Kettle."

The two headed back for Norton a hundred and twenty-five miles away for a pocket compass. As they learned later, the corral had been built by the **X Y** cattle outfit, which was no longer in the country. The 10th of January, 1880, found them camped in a dugout at the corral, near a waterhole in the Smoky River. In addition to the pocket compass, they had six strong saddle horses, a wagon load of corn pulled by four other horses, and Ed Maple as driver and cook. They were fully prepared — except in the knowledge that comes from experience.

For one thing, they were ignorant of the fact that a tired mustang does not mean a tamed mustang. They had learned of a man named Wild Horse Johnson ranching on west, and they rode to his ranch for education. About fifty captured wild horses were grazing near his corral.

"I never try to run a wild horse down," Wild Horse Johnson said. "If one is run until he can't go any farther, he is ruined for life. If the leader of a band plays out so that he can no longer command, the others scatter. I follow a bunch in a buckboard until they are sore-footed and then corral them. Then I rope them and tie a clog to a front foot. After they wear clogs a few days, stay shut up in the pen at night and learn to graze under herd, they can be driven anywhere."

Wild Horse Johnson drove his captives into the pen for inspection. They did not look nearly so large as the wild horses running in freedom.

"Have you ever seen Black Kettle?" Lockard asked.

"I chased him once for two days," Wild Horse Johnson replied, "and then lost him. He has been run so much that he is more cunning than the serpent in the Bible. Don't bother with Black Kettle. There are hundreds of horses on the plains as good as he is. He weighs about 800 pounds and is getting old. There is nothing to him but his mane and tail."

On the way back to camp, Lockard and Simpson decided that Wild Horse Johnson wanted Black Kettle for himself. They were not going to be thrown off his trail by talk. They killed a buffalo and two antelopes, enough meat for weeks.

The next morning they rode out together. Simpson carried a half bushel of corn for the horses and a supply of biscuits. When they found Black Kettle, Lockard was to do the running, Simpson keeping watch from high ground and following slowly across angles. After an hour of riding, they sighted Black Kettle and his roan mares grazing about two miles off. Taking advantage of a fold in the ground, they managed to approach within a mile before the band took off, northward.

Although Lockard followed at a stiff gallop, the runners gained on him. At noon he came to a waterhole on the Beaver where they had drunk and then turned west. About mid-afternoon he sighted them and Simpson at the same time. Simpson was cold from inaction. Within a short time they were both cold. A blizzard of snow and ice was upon them. They took refuge in a dry lagoon, not much protection. Although they managed to gather about a bushel of buffalo chips, they could not keep a fire going. They were wearing the high-heeled boots prescribed by cowboy stylists, without the overshoes required by Alaskan weather. The wind whipped their cowboy hats about so that in order to keep from losing them they jammed them into saddle pockets and wrapped their heads in strips cut from saddle-blankets. During the long night, saying hardly a word, they just sat and shifted. With daylight, the fury of the storm increased.

A fire they managed to start lasted only a few minutes. Simpson stood in the ashes. He was not so strong as he looked. His feet were freezing. He wanted to stay where he was, but Lockard started off, leading the horses, breaking a trail through the snow, in the direction the wind was blowing. After following a short distance, Simpson cried, "Stop!" He sat down. The soles of both his boots were gone, burned out. Lockard wore overalls over corduroy pants. He took them off, split them, and tied them around Simpson's feet. Then he took a double blanket from under his saddle, laid it over Simpson's saddle, got him on his horse and wrapped him as best he could. By the time they reached camp, he had a high fever. As soon as the storm died down, the cook and Lockard put him in the wagon and drove for Norton. Black Kettle was still free.

It was May before Frank Lockard set out again on the chase. This time he had a buckboard in which to carry water, coffee pot, skillet, bed roll, provisions, and feed for a team. He had four good teams and a saddle horse. The wagon, driven by Ed Maple, was loaded with enough corn and groceries to last sixty days. At a roundup in the Pawnee Grove country five cowboys asked to join the wild-horse hunt. What they really wanted was to shoot a buffalo. Not far from the **X Y** corral, Lockard's headquarters henceforth, they saw two old bulls and during an hour's run filled them with lead.

Camp had hardly been made before Ed Maple left to help drive a trail herd, of which he had accidentally learned, about to leave Fort Wallace. At the same time, the cowboys decided to go back to their outfits. By one of them Lockard sent for Billy Rogers to keep camp. During the week before his arrival, he relocated Black Kettle.

On June 2 he drove out in the buckboard to begin the chase. He found Black Kettle about where he expected to find him. His method now was to jog along and not rush. For the first three days the band ran at sight of the buckboard. By nightfall the man was as ready to camp as the wild horses were. Whenever they drifted within convenient reach of headquarters, he drove in, changed teams, and ate Billy Rogers's sourdough bread. On the fourth day several mares began limping and at times Black Kettle was not more than half a mile off. That night it hailed and rained.

The lagoons and draws were all full of water and the prairie was splashy. It was late in the afternoon before Lockard located Black Kettle about fifteen miles northwest of camp. The soft ground was easy to the feet of his band and they quit limping. Water to drink stood everywhere. Lockard followed them for five days without returning to camp. They moved back and forth between the Beaver and the Smoky, going about fifteen miles east or west before circling back and never getting nearer than ten miles to the corral. As the ground dried, they began to limp again.

Before he actually turned, Black Kettle habitually gave notice of his intention. He would stop and loiter a considerable distance behind the mares. His movements indicated on which side, right or left, he intended to make the turn. Lockard learned to favor his desires instead of opposing them.

How he communicated his orders to the leader remained uncertain, though he seemed to signal with his ears. The leader was a beautiful blue roan mare about twelve years old that Simpson had named Aunt Susan. She reminded him of an old lady by that name. Except when Black Kettle ran ahead to drive off a "dog soldier" or to regard some other possible danger, he stayed behind his bunch, keeping between them and the enemy. He increased or lowered their speed by a slight movement of the head hardly perceptible even to a close watcher. The lead mare kept an eye on him, but the other mares seemed to have no responsibility beyond following her. If one dropped out of place even for a few steps, the stallion moved at once to put her back in place.

On the morning of the fifth day after the rain, Lockard found that the band had gone around him during the night but were not a mile away, some lying down, the others standing tired instead of grazing. As he started after them, they moved on west, at first in a walk and then, as he drew nearer, in a trot. But they did not appear to be excited or afraid.

The morning seemed to be in everything that breathed it. The atmosphere was so clear that from the higher levels one could see every detail on the prairies stretching to the horizon. Wild flowers in bright colors and new grass everywhere filled the air with fragrance. As Lockard leisurely followed the wild horses, enjoying the spring in himself, he suddenly heard something like the roar of distant thunder and felt the earth tremble. Then he became aware of wild horses by the hundreds converging upon him at full speed from all directions. Black Kettle broke into a wild run, other bands rushing alongside his. The buckboard team wanted to run, and Lockard let them out at full speed. The flying wild horses ahead kept increasing in numbers, hundreds abreast of each other. Every herd stallion was busy preventing his band from mixing with others and keeping the "dog soldiers" from joining it. In this grand mass flight, each band kept its identity and seemed to have a certain space reserved for itself. Antelopes by the hundreds joined in the run.

Just after the great collection of wild horses crossed the Custer Road, about fifty buffaloes joined them on the right flank, running parallel. Then a dozen or so joined the run on the left flank.

[262]

They soon dropped behind the horses and crossed over to the larger bunch — the last buffaloes ever to be seen on this part of their native range.

Black Kettle was about the middle of the running line, a half mile wide on each side of him. He was watching every movement of his band. Presently a colt dropped behind, and when its mother tried to turn back to it, Black Kettle forced her to go on, leaving it. Other colts were dropping behind, but the stallions by laying ears back and shaking their heads at the mother mares kept them racing forward. Lockard's team began to weaken, but by applying the whip he kept them running.

Meanwhile, the strangest mirage of his experience was changing the appearance of everything within view. At times the wild horses looked to be fifty feet high, and then a golden mist would hide them completely. On low ground the mist lifted so as to leave only their legs visible, and the legs looked to be as long as telegraph poles. In a flash the mist would blot out this view, and on beyond the blur in which the wild horses were running would rise towers and spires as of a great city.

When the mirage dissolved, Lockard saw that the horse bands had separated and were diverging from each other, still running, some southwest and some northwest. Black Kettle had been hemmed in by the horses flanking him on both sides. He could not run fast enough to cut around them, and he dared not drop back towards the man ever crowding his rear. However weary, he had kept his place at the front. The breakup found him many miles away from his accustomed range.

The buckboard team stopped in utter exhaustion. They had run thirty miles. They were worth more than a hundred wild horses, and they were ruined for life. After giving them time to blow, Lockard turned campward, traveling in a weary walk. He began meeting many little colts. Whether the stallions permitted the mother mares to come back to hunt them, he never knew.

After he had driven about ten miles, he discovered a horse standing on the prairie with two colts beside him. Coming closer, he saw that the horse wore harness, iron trace chains looped over the hames. The cause of the great stampede was explained. The runaway horse had followed it until he came to the colts and had stopped with them. He walked up to the buckboard team and Lockard hitched him to the near horse and drove on. One colt followed for several miles and then turned back.

"If I don't catch Black Kettle," Lockard said to himself, "I have found a pretty fair horse to help pay expenses."

Late in the afternoon he met a man riding bareback — the only stranger sighted by Lockard during his months in the Smoky country.

"Call me Bony Joe," he said. "That is all the name I have out here."

He was gathering buffalo bones for the market. The preceding night he had camped at a waterhole only four or five miles from

Lockard's camp. That morning he had put the harness on his horses before breakfast, tied one, and left the other free to graze while he ate. Presently he looked up to see the loose horse making for a wild bunch crossing the draw below camp. The rattle of the harness stampeded them, the harnessed horror following with all his might.

Bony Joe said, "I knew if those old trace chains stayed on him I'd get him again, for no wild horse would allow him near."

The morning after the big run, Lockard, driving a fresh team, met Black Kettle and his band returning to their home range. They ran for two miles or so before slowing down to a trot that they kept up all day, circling as usual on familiar ground. That night it rained, the soreness in their feet disappeared, and the next day they were nearly as wild as they had been on the first day of the chase. For a week it rained every night and their tender feet kept improving.

Soon after the prairie dried off, they showed sore feet and Lockard was able to direct them — up to a certain point. He had followed them more than twenty days, and they now permitted him to keep within a hundred yards of them and even closer at times. Each evening he would drive them near camp, where he spent the night. Each morning he expected to corral them that day. He would get them in sight of the corral, and then they would break away, run a mile or so, and wait until he caught up with them. He rode after them only in the buckboard. His best team was no longer usable; the other teams were worn down. The only help Billy Rogers gave was in cooking antelope steaks and other camp work. The contest between mustangs and mustanger seemed about a draw.

In hope of a gradual push, Lockard tried herding them near the corral. They would graze a little and rest uneasily, but they had a deadline about two hundred yards from the gate.

One morning Billy Rogers said, "This makes thirty straight days you have been after Black Kettle. If you don't pen him today, you had better quit him and try another bunch."

"I'll pen him before dark," Lockard said, and drove away.

When he got out on high ground, he saw the bunch going up the slope on the south side of the river. He had never seen them on that side before, although he had tried to put them there several times. They were moving at a slow walk, Black Kettle in the lead, a little ahead of Aunt Susan. Fifteen minutes later Lockard was in front of them, trying to turn them toward the corral. In the stupor of weariness they merely walked around him, some on one side and some on the other. He rode close enough to touch them with his whip. They trotted around him and moved on in a walk. Black Kettle had lost all interest. His feet were so sore that every once in a while, when a part of the bunch stopped, acting as if they did not intend to follow any farther, he would halt and hold up one foot. Lockard's only recourse was to keep the bunch moving as a unit, away from their stamping grounds. If they separated, they were lost. Slowly, painfully, Black Kettle and Aunt Susan kept on southward. They and their followers had become indifferent to everything but the desire to rest.

That day several old mares and yearlings dropped out. Lockard felt sure that he could have held them had not his team been so drag-footed. He was now in a range unknown to him and the horses alike. Late in the afternoon he came to a deserted one-room house and a pole corral.

After a few trials he got the horses into the corral, just as the sun was going down. There were seventeen head out of the original twenty-nine. He had not eaten a bite since breakfast, and was about as tired as his team and the wild horses, but he "felt like singing the national anthem and did sing it." He unhitched and fed his team and went into the shanty. The grub box was bare, but a bed with mattress and blankets stood in one corner. With hardly a thought of the food in the buckboard, he lay down and was instantly asleep. Along in the night he was aroused

[266]

by a man's getting into the bed with him. As he began to apologize, the stranger said, "Sleep here as long as you want to." At daylight he awoke to find himself alone.

His first act was to look into the corral. He saw Black Kettle and the other horses standing close together in one corner resting. While he broke a twenty-four-hour fast on a pot of black coffee and sourdough biscuits he considered the next move. Camp and Billy Rogers were twenty miles away. To rope, hobble and manage the whole bunch of wild horses alone would be impossible. He decided to tie Black Kettle and come back for him with help, but to turn the others out now and drive them to the **X Y** corral. They would naturally want to go in that direction.

He was not an expert roper, but caught Black Kettle the first throw. The stallion made a lunge at the fence and landed on top with head and front feet on the outside. After struggling for an instant, he got over free and started north, dragging the forty-foot lariat.

Lockard hitched his team to the buckboard as quickly as possible and turned the bunch out. They soon caught up with Black Kettle. Aunt Susan led them straight north. They seemed at peace with themselves as they walked slowly towards the Smoky. One would have supposed that the drag rope on Black Kettle would have kept them excited but, except when it touched one of them, they paid no attention to it. With Aunt Susan in the lead and Black Kettle bringing up the rear, they seldom noticed the rope at all. They reached the Smoky about noon and turned upstream towards the **X Y** corral. Lockard had difficulty at times in keeping them headed right, but a little before sundown drove them through the gate into the big corral. They had surrendered.

In the words of their conqueror, "At the end of the 31st day I had them safe. I called Billy to bring the saddle. Although I was very tired and hungry, I wanted to ride Black Kettle that night. We both got hold of the rope and snubbed him to a post and saddled him. I got on and rode him for a few minutes inside the corral. We left the saddle on him for the night and went to camp. The next morning we caught and hobbled a few of the mares and turned the bunch out to graze. We staked Black Kettle near camp. Within a week all the animals were tame."

Black Kettle ate corn from the start and after two days of handling was as gentle as a plow horse. Billy Rogers cut horseshoes from a piece of rawhide and nailed them on his feet with shingle nails. They were a great relief to his soreness, but he took the Texas itch from a saddle blanket that had been used on a horse afflicted with that disease. His hair began to slip, and nearly all of it, including his famous mane and tail, came off. He was a sorry-looking specimen. No one who had seen him in his glory could have recognized him now. Bacon grease stopped the itch, but the new mane and tail never grew long. All the new hair was coarser than the original. An expert at plaiting rawhide and weaving horsehair, Billy made a fine headstall and bridle reins out of the mane and tail.

After resting two days, Lockard set out to capture another bunch of wild horses. During the next two months he penned six bunches, of from ten to fifteen head each. A dry prairie, favorable weather and knowledge gained from experience enabled him to pen a bunch within seven or eight days after starting it.

A black stallion among the captives made a good mate for Black Kettle. Lockard named him Black Hawk, but Billy called him Black Pot. After the two were broken to harness, Lockard called them Hawk and Kettle, but Billy insisted on Pot and Kettle. The public, later on, stood with him.

Late in October Lockard started east with his captives. There were seventy-six head. He valued Black Kettle above the other seventy-five, not that he would bring more money. His value lay beyond that of dollars. There was but one Black Kettle in the whole plains world. To his captor he represented something of a dream fulfilled. As a trophy he would in the eyes of plainsmen elevate his winner.

He led better under the saddle than without it. Billy Rogers drove the wagon, trailed by the buckboard, and, tied by a long rope, Black Kettle followed it. Lockard on horseback guided the herd. On the evening of the second day's travel, a settler's dog ran out barking. Black Kettle lunged, broke his halter and started back west in a long run. This was the first time he had been loose in four months. As Lockard saddled a fresh horse to follow, he doubted whether he should ever ride his prize again, but when he overtook him about five miles back, Black Kettle stopped. He stood while his master dismounted and walked up to him.

During days that followed, several horses became too tenderfooted to travel and had to be left behind. On the election day that brought James A. Garfield to the presidency, the outfit reached Norton with Black Kettle and fifty-four other captured wild horses.

Lockard began selling them off at once. Most of the prairie farming at that time was done with small horses — ordinary range stock. A man named William Case who lived on the Kansas-Nebraska line was planning a visit to his old home in New York state and wanted to take back a pair of wild horses for show. He bought Aunt Susan and a younger mare that looked very much like her and was probably her daughter. He broke them to the buggy and with his wife drove them to Little Valley, New York. There he sold them for a fancy price, just because of their history.

W. D. Street, whose newspaper article had introduced Lockard to Black Kettle, and Ame Cole, who was going to "walk his tail off" in five days, both came to see the famous captive. They claimed to recognize him even without the magnificent mane and tail, but were disappointed in his size.

Most dreams for most men fade. Frank Lockard did not know

it, but the marvelous mirage, through which he ran after Black Kettle and the hundreds of other wild horses on that freshest of all spring mornings in his memory, was a symbol. While his dream was fading and the struggle to keep up with the American standard of living was increasing, he sold Black Kettle and Black Hawk to a man who drove them to a milk wagon. Then Jim McGinnis bought them and for several years farmed with them. They were equally willing to pull a plow or a wagon. After passing through other hands, they came to a farmer named Harlen Day and remained his until they died at the age of about thirty years. They were close comrades and died within a few days of each other.

XIV

UNDER THE SADDLE

NOT for Plains Indians alone did the Age of Horse Culture exist. The Spaniards who saddled their horses on the sands of Vera Cruz Bay and beside the muddy banks of La Plata and rode until they had mapped the continents from the Horn to Montana belonged to that age. The padres who rode with them and made every mission a horse ranch belonged also. The earliest American explorers and trappers of the Plains and the Rockies won and lost by their horses. A pack train of mules driven by men on horseback beat out the Santa Fe Trail. The first fast post across the continent was Pony all through. The frontiersmen and cavalrymen who conquered the horsed Indians were equally horsed. It has been said that "civilization follows the plow." West of the Missouri and of a line running from its mouth to the Gulf of Mexico, the plow was in most places preceded by a cowboy, maybe half civilized, certainly half horse. Booted rangers and sheriffs expressed the Age of Horse Culture while bringing law to the frontiers; the long-riders, often outriding the law, could be no better than their horses. All these men on horseback, irrespective of how they differed on God or Gain, believed in horses.

A horse's performance under the saddle tells what he is. The stories that follow are, in a way, the finality on the mustang breed. They belong to the times when "a man on foot was no man at all," when a man's horse was his "best friend," and a horseman unhorsed was *sin pies* — without feet. They express or imply the cooperation between carrier and the carried, flesh conforming to flesh, spirit blending with spirit, intelligence recognizing intelligence.

One day during the years while Apaches harassed all the trails of Chihuahua, Colonel Richard I. Dodge saw on the plaza in El Paso a Spanish pony, hardly fourteen hands high, that took his fancy. He offered the owner, an American, what he considered a high price, $40. "I would not take less than $600," was the reply. Every week for the past six months the pony had been carrying his owner between El Paso and Chihuahua, traveling only by night, remaining hidden by day, covering the distance in three nights. As the crow flies, it is fully 200 miles from El Paso to Chihuahua City; as the trails wound, it was much farther. The rider was carrying dispatches; he went south one week and came back the next, getting a hundred dollars for each round trip. "Six months of this work had not diminished the fire or flesh of that wonderful pony." [1]

Many and many a pony of the ranges was just as durable but went unnoticed by any enduring record. Only by accident, for instance, is a white stallion out of a California manada remembered. His body was round and well-ribbed, his legs flat, his black hoofs as hard as flint. A man weighing 180 pounds was riding him daily to reconnoiter for a big surveying party in rough country of Alameda County.

About dark one evening word came to headquarters on the ranch being surveyed that several hundred range horses had gotten through the fence separating upland pastures from a great grainfield cultivated by squatters. All hands turned out to bring back the horse stock, already widely scattered. A heavy man rode the stallion until 2:30 A.M. At daylight, a vaquero saddled him to go after horses overlooked in the darkness and rode until noon. This riding after horses was fast and continuous. At the end of it the stallion had been under saddle for about 12 hours and had probably covered 120 miles. A young ranchero now mounted him to go to a town 15 miles away, where he tied the stallion up while he made fiesta. He got back to the ranch before daylight and then the man with the surveyors rode the stallion out on his regular work. The horse had gone fully 150 miles during the past 36 hours and was not sagging in the least.[2]

Many years ago a little old cowman named W. B. Slaughter who had once owned great herds but who, then broke, was coming to the end of his life in San Antonio, told me this story. "Early in 1873, before grass had started, my brother J. B. Slaughter and I came down from north Texas to Mason County and contracted for 1500 head of big steers at $16 around, spring delivery. I was twenty-three years old and had already bossed two herds up the trail to Kansas. My brother was just nineteen. From the day we signed the contract, cattle prices began going up. By the date agreed on for delivery, the middle of April, those steers were worth ten dollars a head more than the contract price. When we got to Mason with our outfit to receive the steers and start up the trail, we found a downhearted, sullen set of cowmen. If they could break the contract, they would make $15,000, and they were the kind of men to break a contract if they could.

" 'Have you got the cash?' they asked.

[273]

"We showed them a letter of credit from a Dallas bank for $50,000. They laughed at it. That was not money. There was a little private bank in the town of Mason. We took the letter of credit there. It didn't have more than a thousand dollars in the vault. The banker couldn't help us. The stage for San Antonio had just driven into town. I took it. We had three or four days left to produce the cash.

"Colonel Breckenridge was the main banker in San Antonio. He told me what kind of money belt to buy. Then he helped me pack $25,000 in ten- and twenty-dollar gold pieces into it. When the gold was all packed away, the belt weighed 104 pounds. I weighed around 135. I went to a second-hand store and bought the sorriest-looking hat and the most run-down pair of boots in stock. I went to one of the horse pens and picked out a pony that to some people would look disgraceful. He was a dunnish roan, tough and wiry. I paid $15 for him. I saddled him with an old hull that cost $5.

"Towards sundown I set out. The rough Llano River country across Mason County was at that time the hide-out place for as hard a set of outlaws as Texas ever had. There were so many of them and they were so bold that two years later the rangers rounded up every human male of that section into a stockade and cut the sheep out from the goats, just as you would cut cattle. The good men had nothing to fear and were glad to be rid of the others. On the straightest possible road, it is about 115 miles from San Antonio to Mason. My route was across the open range west of the stage road. It must have covered over 130 miles. If I met any stranger I was to pass as a green youth from Gonzales looking for a job with a trail herd. My purpose was not to meet anybody, especially men on the watch — for I was expected with the cash.

"By daylight I had covered something less than half the distance. I stopped close to water and staked my horse in a little opening enclosed by brush. Then I crawled into the brush and slept. Of course I had a sixshooter. At dark I saddled up and rode on north. About every two hours I'd unsaddle and let my horse graze. He wallowed once or twice. Lots of the time he traveled in a lope. By sunup I was getting close to Mason. Instead of riding straight into town, I circled it and came in from the north. I learned later that the stage from San Antonio had been carefully looked over by some strange men several miles down the road.

"Well, when we planked down the gold, those ranchers had to take it. The Mason banker didn't want it, and I guess the ranchers got it to San Antonio all right. Nobody in that country wanted any money about his premises. I threw that little yellow-roan pony in with our remuda and just north of Red River we sold him and the other cow horses along with the steers at $28 around. The ride was not particularly hard; the pony was not outstanding. He was straight Spanish."

To appreciate Ellie Newman's ride, once the talk of southwest Texas, one must consider his belief in dreams. During the earlier part of his life he had been considerably on the dodge. Once while he was dodging, he went to his uncle's ranch to spend the night. The house was in a small clearing. He staked his horse near by and went to sleep on a pallet on the front gallery. Along in the night he awoke with a start, arousing his uncle, who was sleeping on the same quilt.

"What's the matter?" muttered the uncle.

"I've had a dream I don't like," Ellie Newman replied. "I dreamt I heard dogs barking and saw horsemen riding on a clearing."

"Aw," growled the uncle, "all the matter with you is you ate too many frijoles for supper. Turn over on your belly and go to sleep."

Ellie turned over, but within half an hour he leaped bolt upright out of the pallet.

[275]

"What the devil is the matter this time?" swore the uncle.

"By God," answered Ellie — and his voice was steady — "I've dreamt three times now I heard dogs barking and saw horsemen riding on a clearing. I'm riding. Adios."

By the time he had done speaking he had on his boots, from which the spurs were never unstrapped. He walked with a low whistle to where his horse was grazing, for it was still too early in the night for horses to sleep. The moon was bright, and in ten minutes he was riding out of the clearing on which the little ranch house stood and was entering the mesquite fringe of a hollow to the west.

"Just as I got into the brush," so he used to tell the story, "I heard the dogs at the house open up. I stopped my horse and bent around so I could look back. I saw seven men riding up to the front gallery. They were Texas Rangers."

Thereafter Ellie believed more strongly than ever in his dreams. He always claimed that a dream of a stampede or of catfish was a sure sign that some of his people needed him badly. Then, no matter where he was, he would get up from his bed and head for home. Once he had started up the trail with a herd of steers and was a week's drive to the north when he dreamed of a stampede. He awoke to find the cook grinding coffee. By the time it was boiling he had his night horse saddled. Then after two hot cups he headed south.

The time that he made his famed ride from above Kerrville, he was with the Schreiner outfit on a big roundup. Schreiner was putting up a string of 3000 steers for a Northwestern contractor and they were about ready for delivery. Then one night Ellie dreamed of a stampede and a catfish together — a combination of omens as direful as a preacher and a gray mare on board a Mississippi steamboat at the same time. In the dream he was pointing the herd into the Llano River. Just as the lead steer, a big rangy brindle, got his feet in the water and was snuffing it, an immense catfish flopped to the surface and splashed water all over the brindle's head. The steer let out a bellow that woke up the drag cattle a half mile away. The stampede that followed, as Ellie always narrated the dream, "shook rocks out of them Llano mountains." With such a stampede and such a catfish in one dream, Ellie absolutely had to ride.

His horse was nothing extra, in a way, just a good Spanish cow horse. He crawled on him in rocky country, followed trails partly rocky for seventy-five miles, passed through San Antonio, got into heavy sand, and before he pulled the saddle off at the Butler ranch in Karnes County had ridden 150 miles without stopping to graze.

Ellie was the kind of rider that cow-horse people have always liked to discuss — not because he would "ride anything that grows hair or feathers" — he would — but because he could "get out of a horse all that the horse had in him." A good rider is more than a horse *breaker*, and many a modern rodeo star couldn't stay long enough to unroll his blankets on a ranch where horses are friends to be cared for and not antagonists for a mere spectacle. Ellie Newman could "ride a horse from hell to break-fast and the horse would never know the difference." A cowman for whom he worked said he could "straddle a played-out horse and get more out of him than most other hands could get out of a mount fresh roped from the remuda."

Ellie rode as if he were "growed to the animal." He sat erect, never lounging to one side or the other. The only give in his frame was in the lower six inches of the spine. In that part of his back moved a kind of rhythm with the horse's movement, whether the horse fox-trotted, galloped "like uncoupling freight cars," or "swallowed his head" and pawed at the horns of the moon. Ellie liked to talk of horsemanship and frequently remarked: "If them last six inches of a man's backbone don't give and take, he'll never be a sure 'nough rider. A heavy man can

[277]

ease his horse with that spring, and without it a light man can kill the best buckskin that ever went up the trail."

No ride on picked Spanish horses has been more celebrated than that of Colonel John C. Frémont, who would rather have been president than right. He was carrying a message to Garcia less important here than how he carried it. At dawn, March 22, 1847, he set out from the village of Los Angeles for Monterey, over a road up the coast that was merely a trail through mountains and forests. With him were his ranchero friend, Don Jesús Pico, and his colored servant, Jacob Dodson, as skillful with rope as in the saddle. The three drove six loose horses, all unshod. About every two hours, at intervals of twenty miles, they halted and changed mounts. When not galloping they rode in a hard trot.

The first day they made 120 rough miles. The second day, on the spurs of the Santa Barbara Mountains, they passed the skeletons of fifty horses that had died in a storm. By nine o'clock that night they were at San Luis Obispo, in Don Jesús Pico's home, 135 miles north of their last sleeping grounds. A breakfast banquet detained them until eleven o'clock in the morning, when they set out with eight fresh horses, two of them presents to Frémont. They were a pair of *canelos* — cinnamons, or red roans. The third night they camped in the valley of the Salinas. Prowling grizzly bears stampeded the horses, but the bears were put to flight by yells and the horses were secured. A great fire kept the bears at a distance until dawn. At three o'clock in the afternoon of the fourth day, after a ninety-mile sprint, they galloped into Monterey. They had covered 420 miles in less than four days.

They tarried a day and then headed back south. Don Jesús Pico insisted that Frémont now put one of the *canelos*, the older of the pair, to the test. Frémont rode him for 40 miles and, after camping for the night, resaddled him and rode him for 90 miles. They were now only 30 miles from San Luis Obispo. The *canelo* showed no fatigue and Don Jesús wanted his friend to continue the ride on him, but Frémont changed to the younger *canelo*, perhaps for his own sake, for nothing rests a rider like a change of mounts. The released *canelo* led the remuda to San Luis Obispo, "neighing with exultation" upon approaching, at a swift gallop, his native pasture. Meanwhile, the younger *canelo* under Frémont was pulling at the bit.

Nine days after having set out from Los Angeles the three riders returned. They had spent 76 hours in the saddle, used 17 horses, and traversed 840 miles. The only feed for the horses, except for a few quarts of barley at Monterey, had been grass.[3]

The significant horses in Frémont's ride were *canelos*. *Canelos* carried other riders to celebrity on the Pacific slope.[4] The color was so outstanding in California that it became almost a generic term, like buckskin in other regions. Writing from Monterey in 1849, Bayard Taylor said: "I have more than once bestrode a *canelo* and run races with the wind." [5] The California *canelo* was in direct line from the "Barbary Roan" that King Richard II (1367–1400) "loved as an only son." An old saying of the Southwest, often applied to people, expresses popular esteem for the type: "To hear him talk you'd think they were all red roans and natural pacers."

For sustained endurance, speed and distance, I rank a ride made by François Xavier Aubry as supreme in the whole riding tradition of the West.[6] "Little Aubry," they called him. He was small, only five feet and two inches tall, weighing hardly more than a hundred pounds. Every ounce of his body was distilled energy. He was quiet and modest; he loved fame and adventure. He led wherever he went.

A French-Canadian by birth (in 1824), he came to St. Louis at eighteen and went to clerking in a big store of general merchandise. He heard talk of bull trains and pack outfits. He sold goods consigned to Independence, the jumping-off place for the

West, up the Missouri River. The stuff in his body was not compounded of clerkly tameness. He bought goods on credit from his employers, went to Independence, and joined one of the freight trains setting out for Santa Fe. He prospered as a trader and soon had extensive interests.

The year of his great rides was 1848. It generally took three or four weeks to ride the 800 miles between Santa Fe and Independence. The schedule of the military mail was thirty days; ox wagons required from two to three months. Early in January, Aubry arrived in Independence after having been on the road only fourteen days. Five men who started with him had dropped out. Mexican robbers, Indians and a blizzard had delayed him; he had killed three mules and covered the last 300 miles in three days. The *Daily Missouri Republican* (published in St. Louis) declared the ride "unprecedented in Prairie life."

For Aubry it was merely a warming-up exercise. As soon as the first weeds of spring were greening for oxen to graze upon, he loaded his wagons for Santa Fe. By the time they reached their destination the whole country was on a boom; the United States had defeated Mexico in a war of conquest and taken from her an immense territory that included New Mexico. Aubry sold his goods at 100 per cent profit and determined to return to Missouri and bring out a second cargo the same season. This procedure was "unprecedented." The freight outfits in Santa Fe could not get back in time to haul for him, but there were always oxen and bull whackers on the Missouri.

He announced that he would make the ride in eight days — and bets ran high. Before he had gone 300 miles, six men who set out with him had fallen behind. The remainder of the trip Aubry performed alone. He killed three horses and two mules. Indians took his baggage, his food, even letters he was carrying; but he contrived to slip away from them. He walked forty miles, went three days without a bite to eat, slept — off his horse — only four or five hours on the whole route. It took him eight days and ten hours to make the trip; but, counting out the time lost to Indians and on the walk they made him take, his actual traveling time was about seven days.

When Aubry got back to Santa Fe in late summer, the plaza was buzzing over his record. "I can do better," he said. "I'll bet $1000 that I can make the ride within six days." The money was covered. Aubry at once began making preparations. He sent men ahead to have horses in readiness at Fort Mann on the Arkansas, Council Grove and another point or two. Over certain stretches of the route he would drive extra mounts, California style. It was to be a lone ride over an empty land.

Before dawn on September 12 he left Santa Fe in a swinging gallop, and he ate only six meals on the ground, stopped only once to sleep — for two hours — before he reined up his final horse, heaving and atremble, at Independence on the Missouri. On the way he killed six horses and broke down six others. Several of these he had purchased from wagon trains encountered on the road. He ate a little while riding, and after the first day and night out tied himself to the saddle so that he could doze without danger of falling off. So long as he kept steady in the saddle, a good horse would keep the gait. It was the rainy season of the year; for a whole day and night rain fell on him continuously, and high winds were blowing most of the time. Streams were swimming deep.

Picture Little Aubry as he makes his ride! In the yellow morning sun and under the slant rays of autumn noon he races down the mountains past the village of San Miguel, where he changes horses, and on to another change at the Rio Gallinas, now the site of Las Vegas. For hours and miles and for miles and hours, in twilight and then in darkness, he listens to hoofbeats. In the dead of night he comes to the camp of a Mexican pack train; the boss knows him and lets him have a grullo that has never been tired. The Morning Star is still shining when, nearing Point of Rocks, he gives the long-drawn-out "coyote yell" of the West and the man whom he sent out a week ago stirs the coals around a pot of coffee and draws in the stake rope of a fresh mount.

The mount is "a yellow mare" — without doubt a Spanish dun — named Dolly. One deduces that all the mounts Aubry sent out from Santa Fe were native New Mexican horses.

"I'd kill every horse on the Santa Fe Trail before I'd lose that thousand dollar bet," he says to his man, "but it's not the money I care about. I'm riding to prove that I can get more out of a horse and last longer myself than any other man in the West."

The man by the fire of buffalo chips does not have time to answer. The saddle has been changed, Aubry has gulped down a quart of simmering coffee and sprung onto Dolly's back with a roasted buffalo rib in his hand.

"Adios!"

He rides on. The high, dry country recedes behind him and a chill autumn drizzle hides the sun. He cannot see Rabbit Ear Mounds, but he knows where they mark an edge of the wide, flat plains. At Rabbit Ear Creek he passes Alexander Majors's wagon train "at a full gallop without asking a single question as to the danger of Indians ahead." At roaring Willow Bar he takes off the bridle for a blow and a drink.

But where are the relay horses that were to be here, over one hundred miles from Point of Rocks? Indians? A dead man's scalped head answers. Beautiful Dolly must go on. On, on, until she has carried Little Aubry one hundred and fifty, two hundred, miles in twenty-six hours. So far as I know, this is the world's record for one horse in one day and night, plus two hours, of galloping.

The yellow mare bears him lightly across the Cimarron of the quicksands and somewhere beyond he delivers her for safekeeping to a wagon-master who knows him and gives him the best horse he can spare. Hidden in timber above the ford on the Arkansas, three fresh horses await him. He mounts one and cracks his whip over the others. The old church at Santa Fe is still less than four hundred miles behind. He is not quite half way to Independence. He cannot spare horseflesh now. He wears the first of the relays down in ten miles, the second in about the same distance; the third unexpectedly drags his feet. In a minute Aubry has unsaddled, hidden his saddle and blanket in the grass, and, silver-plated bridle in hand, is trotting on east afoot. For twenty-four miles he does not see a human soul. Then he walks into Fort Mann, where he finds one of his own freight trains and has to spend a long while tending to business. Here he lies down for two hours and sleeps while a certain horse is being brought in.

Refreshed now, he skims the ground past Coon Creek and past Pawnee Rock, where so many good men have bit the dust. To detail all the changes of horses would betray Aubry's swiftness. At Council Grove he pauses long enough for coffee to boil, ties himself on a fresh horse, rides on. It is a hundred and fifty miles to Independence yet. He hardly notices the beautiful trees and hills to which the plains have given away; he does not hear the cawing of the crows in the valleys. It takes a full twenty-four hours, most of it in rain, to make that last lap. At Big John Springs, by paying heavy boot, he swaps with a trapper for one of the best mounts on the journey.

At ten o'clock on the night of September 17 he halts in front of the Noland House, called also the Merchant's Hotel. It is bright with lights. Men rush out from the bar and "lift" him from his saddle. It is "caked with blood." The few words he breathes out are in a thin whisper. He has won his bet. He bolts ham, eggs and coffee and tells the proprietor to wake him in three hours. The proprietor waits six hours before rousing him. He bounds up "rather wrathy" at the misjudged kindness. "I like to take my food and rest in broken doses," he says. He is up in time, however, to catch a steamboat just leaving the dock for St. Louis.

The next summer in Santa Fe, Captain R. B. Marcy met Aubry at a supper being paid as a debt to the great rider. At Marcy's request Aubry wrote down and signed a short account of his ride. "I made the trip," he said, "travelling time only counted, in 4 days and 12 hours, though the time spent between Santa Fe and Independence was 5 days and 16 hours. I made a portion of the trip at the rate of 250 miles to the 24 hours; made 200 miles on my yellow mare in 26 hours."

In 1852 the California gold boom drew Aubry on west, pioneering a new route across deserts and mountains. He rode the yellow mare out of Santa Fe, followed by ten big wagons loaded with goods, a herd of 3500 sheep, and over 100 surplus mules and horses. When he got back to Santa Fe the next year he gathered up 14,000 sheep to drive to the booming market, and other men followed his trail with three times that many. He kept diaries of these trips. On August 3, 1853, west of the Little Colorado River in Arizona, he recorded: "Indians shooting arrows around us all day wounded some of our mules and my famous mare Dolly, who has so often rescued me from danger by her speed and capacity of endurance." There is "no suffering like the suffering from thirst," he added. On August 16, held back by weaker men, all living on half rations of horse meat, he himself having been wounded eight times, he entered these words: "I have the misfortune to know that the flesh we are eating is that of my inestimable mare Dolly who has so often saved me from death at the hands of Indians. She gave out on account of her wound."

A year later a newspaper bully in Santa Fe stabbed Little Aubry to death, aged thirty. The newest and fastest steamboat on the Missouri River had just been christened the *F. X. Aubry*. Between her smokestacks she had the carved figure of a light rider on a yellow mare. This was fame. Later the Santa Fe Railroad followed, between Albuquerque, New Mexico, and Bakersfield, California, the routes he had pioneered and recommended. Long ago the *F. X. Aubry* with her emblem of horse and horseman was turned to dust and rust. Nevertheless, so long as a few people know the length of a mile measured by the legs of horses

[284]

and men and multiplied by hundreds, Aubry will live. The legends of the Tartars and Scythians do not recall his equal.*

Alexander Majors, whose firm did the biggest overland freighting business that has ever been done in America and also enterprised the Pony Express, knew Aubry well, knew horses, knew the land. He wrote: "Perhaps not one man in a million could have lived to finish" the ride made by Aubry. Perhaps not one in a million had such elasticity and endurance. Buffalo Bill knew whereof he was speaking when he declared that "fifteen miles an hour on horseback will in a short time shake any man all to pieces." Aubry was made of animated rawhide.

Buffalo Bill is credited with a ride, as Pony Expressman, exceeding Aubry's record as to distance covered within a limited time: 322 miles in 24 hours and 40 minutes. On that ride, however, he had a score of station men to help him along, and used 21 horses in relays. A fresh horse freshens the rider. No two horses have the same gait. Jaded cowboys on jaded ponies sometimes swap with each other to the relief of both man and mount.

The Pony Express schedule called for delivery of mail between St. Joseph, Missouri, and Sacramento, California — 1966 miles — within ten days. One trip was made in less than eight days. Over most of the route relay stations were maintained at intervals of about ten miles; over some stretches they were twice that far apart, and once in a while one of them was rubbed out. No rider of the system ever made a single-handed ride comparable to Aubry's, and no horse on the route was ever put to the test that Aubry's yellow mare stood. A majority of the horses, all selected for speed and endurance, were of Spanish blood, many

---

* In his *Revolt of the Tartars*, De Quincey narrates the escape of a Russian prisoner and three Kalmucks from the Khan on "wild horses of a docile and beautiful breed" which abounded for hundreds of miles out from the Torgau River and which they had captured. Each "led six or seven horses besides the one he rode; and by shifting from one to the other (like the ancient Desultors of the Roman circus), so as to never burden the same horse for more than half an hour at a time, they continued to advance at the rate of 200 miles in the twenty-four hours for three days consecutively."

"California mustangs" among them, but some were of American breeding.[7]

Although machinery has reduced miles to minute decimals, it has not reduced the *sense of speed* felt by a horseman and shared by his horse. A running team of mustangs hitched to a buckboard will give the driver more *sense of motion* than the fastest automobile on a straight concrete road. A powerful horse galloping over prairie or through low brush, leaping gullies and dodging boulders, his heart drumming against the rider's legs, his vitality passing into the rider's body, communicates an exhilaration unfelt by the housed pilot of a jet plane outrunning its own sound.

Kamal is out with twenty men to raise the Border-side,
And he has lifted the Colonel's mare that is the Colonel's pride. . . .

The Colonel's son has taken a horse, and a raw rough dun was he,
With a mouth of a bell and the heart of Hell, and the head of the
    gallows-tree. . . .

It's up and over the Tongue of Jagai, as blown dust-devils go;
The dun he fled like a stag of ten, but the mare like a barren doe.

The dun he leaned against the bit and slugged his head above,
But the red mare played with the snaffle-bars, as a maiden plays with
    a glove. . . .

They have ridden the low moon out of the sky, their hoofs drum up
    the dawn;
The dun he went like a wounded bull, but the mare like a new-
    roused fawn.

The dun he fell at a water-course — in a woeful heap fell he,
And Kamal has turned the red mare back, and pulled the rider
    free. . . .

In 1886, Lucky Baldwin, the California plunger, and Richard K. Fox, owner of the *Police Gazette*, offered a prize of $3000 for the best rider and horse to start from Galveston, Texas, and finish at Rutland, Vermont, 1799 miles away. On September 6 of that year fifty-six riders headed north from Galveston, among them cowboys, ex-cavalrymen and professional horse trainers. The rules stipulated that no man should ride more than ten hours a day. Judges were kept informed by cards that the riders were required to present for punching at designated stations along the route.

Frank T. Hopkins rode a dun stallion seven years old, with the dark line down his back, black mane and tail and black hoofs, weighing about 800 pounds. He had been caught by Buffalo Jones in a band of wild Indian ponies ranging in the Shoshone Valley of Wyoming. After horsebreakers gave him up as an untamable outlaw, Buffalo Jones gave him to Hopkins. "In two months' time of careful handling," wrote Hopkins, "I rode him after buffalo. He never seemed to tire. He was the only horse I ever saw that after finishing a run with one herd of buffaloes was ready to take on another. I called him Joe. . . .

"I never was a sprinter, but I knew a thing or two about long distance riding. I did not press Joe at first. The other riders all passed me. Then I began passing them, one by one. I rode for thirty-one days, and then waited in Rutland, Vermont, two weeks before the second man rode in, and we two waited together for several days before the next rider got in. We three were the only riders who finished — three out of fifty-six. My daily average on the ride was 58 miles." [8]

It was not speed that swirled in the consciousness of Gregorio Cortez as he fled on a little brown mare. What he remembered best long after the ride was the mare herself — her fidelity, her staying power, her generosity.

On June 13, 1901, Gregorio Cortez killed Brack Morris, sheriff of Karnes County, Texas. Morris had shot Gregorio's brother. Instead of making for the other side of the Rio Grande, Gregorio fled east. In Gonzales County he killed Sheriff Dick Glover and a deputy. Then he struck southwest for that muddy line which for so many generations has meant life or death to men straining from both sides to cross it.

Gregorio Cortez was afoot. In Atascosa County he stole a brown Spanish mare, not much over thirteen hands high, and a saddle. By now a company of rangers, a dozen sheriffs, posses of citizens, and Manuel Tom, the best trailer in southwest Texas since Bigfoot Wallace, were after him. The chase consumed many days. Two sheriffs rode six horses to death. To go 100 miles, Gregorio Cortez twisted and doubled over 300 miles, through brush, barbed wire fences, and prickly pear, over dry arroyos and into caliche hills. He was captured asleep about twenty-five miles from Laredo on the Rio Grande. . . . The jury cleared him on one murder charge and sent him to the penitentiary for fifty years on the other two. He could talk a little English, and there in the penitentiary he told the story of his ride this way.[9]

"When I find the brown mare I am tired, very tired. For seven day and night I already been in brush, sometimes with horse and sometimes on my feets and no sleep. I find the mare in the night and pick out one star that I know is by the Rio Grande and I ride to that star. When I come to one fence, I cut the top wires with a file, and the leetle mare she jump the bottom wire easy and high. Then by one gate I find some cattles and I ope the gate, drive cattles tru, and then drive 'um back so they cover up my track.

"After while when I come to fence and cut the wire, my leetle mare drag her hind feets on the bottom wire and cut herself. She cannot jump high and easy now. But she go on. I am so tired and sleep that I stop by one fence and roll me one leetle cigarette. I lean back against a post and smoke just one breath and then I am sleep. I feel the reins jerk in my hand. I wake up and that leetle mare is looking back. I can hear the brush break way back there in the dark. We go on.

[288]

"We twist roun' in the chaparral and I am so sleep that I near fall off. I stop by one mesquite tree and make 'nother cigarette. My head he will not stand up and I fall down on that tree. Then I feel the reins jerk and when I wake up I see the ears of that leetle mare pointing where she is looking back. Far away I hear brush break and a dog bark. We go on. We cross rock hills and leave no trail, but mens are everywhere. In the day times I watch, watch and the leetle mare she is watch too. We slip tru more brush.

"But the time is come when that leetle mare can go no more. I take the saddle off her and hide it in a *mesquital*, and I turn her loose and I pat her on the side and I say to her: 'You are one good leetle mare. Adios, my frien'.' She is too tired to move, but she look at me with kind eyes.

"Then I walk maybe so three mile more. I do not see one other horse I can catch. I cannot walk more. I find ole house and no-body there. I fall on floor and I am sleep when I hear, 'Hands up.' Now I am here for feefty year for keel man that I do not keel."

It may be added that Gregorio Cortez did not remain in the penitentiary at Huntsville for "feefty year." A governor pardoned him. He became a horse thief and was killed out near El Paso. Along the border a song is still sung about —

> Gregorio Cortez y su yeguita trigueña.
> (Gregorio Cortez and his little brown mare.)

Chester Evans was seventy-eight years old and was running the weekly newspaper at Lebo on the plains of western Kansas when he told me the main story out of his life. This was in 1940.[10]

Sixty-six years before that, back in Iowa, he had bought the colt he named Prince for eighteen dollars. The colt's mother was a Sioux mare of unmixed Spanish blood; his sire was a French-Canadian stallion, with a touch of Spanish. Chester was only a colt himself, his mother dead, his father always busy at his print-

[289]

ing office. They lived in a boarding house. Prince and Chester grew up together, keeping steady company with each other. The colt would come at the boy's call and follow him wherever permitted. He delighted in carrots and lumps of sugar. He was a strawberry roan with blazed face and white stockings on front feet.

Chester wanted to be a cowboy. After he nearly died from lung fever in the winter of '77–'78 and continued to be frail, his father said he might go west to the Smoky Hill Pool northwest of Dodge City. An uncle worked on this range. Riding Prince, the boy set out with a man driving a team of big sorrel horses to a wagon. While they were still hundreds of miles from Dodge City, and the country was getting wilder all the time, one of the sorrels took colic and died. The owner sold the other to a government horse buyer, and Chester went with him. He was delivering a bunch of horses to Fort Riley. From there Chester trailed a troop of cavalry to Dodge City. Herds of Longhorns were coming up from Texas. The town was alive with young men who wore spurs that rang. Within a few days the uncle came in and took Chester out to the Smoky Hill Pool headquarters, seventy miles away on Cheyenne Creek.

Now Prince was four years old and weighed around 1000 pounds. He had extra heavy mane and tail, and he carried his neck arched and his tail curved. Chester was twelve years old and went at once to riding the line. "I'm not saying how good I was," he said, "but in time Prince got to be as good a roping horse as a cowboy ever swung a loop from, and, without a finger touching the bridle reins, he could cut out any cow that dodged and doubled in a herd."

In the fall word came from the south that Chief Dull Knife was stirring up the Cheyennes in the Indian Territory. Two years before they had been herded down there from their Montana range. On the morning of September 27, 1878, the valley of Cheyenne Creek looked to be full of Indians. Somebody had to notify Fort Monument on Smoky Hill River eighteen miles away. Because Chester was light weight he was selected to make the dash.

He led Prince up the canyon a way, mounted, and hit the flat a-running. Fifteen Cheyennes dashed to cut him off. Prince ran several miles before they got in shooting distance. Then an arrow stuck in his shoulder. Chester pulled it out and the blood spurted so that he held his thumb in the wound. Next Chester got an arrow in his right leg. To pull it out he had to shift his hand from Prince's shoulder, and then he noticed that the blood had stopped flowing. When he yanked on the shaft, it came free but left the arrowhead in his leg. Three more arrows clipped him, and Prince got one in the rump. A sergeant at the fort, there being no doctor, cut out the arrows. Prince never liked Indians after this experience. He could smell them as far as he could smell water. Twenty years after this run, some Oklahoma Indians stopped at a blacksmith shop in Lebo half a mile away from the little pasture in which Prince grazed. He snorted like a buck deer that's heard something he can't wind and he pawed the ground like a wild bull.

In the spring of 1880 Chester was hunting antelope about twelve miles south of the ranch when the wind changed in both direction and intensity and he found himself facing a raging prairie fire. He did not have a match with which to start a back fire. Prince seemed to understand that he must run for the lives of both. When they reached a big buffalo wallow with about a foot of water in it, Chester thought of trying to save himself there. But what of Prince? Instantly the decision was made: "If one of us has to die, we will die together." Prince spurted up his speed, but the fire was gaining. It was racing literally faster than the wind, for the heat brought the cooler air rushing to the blazing waves. By the time boy and horse reached a plowed fire guard, the cinders were falling thick on them and the air was stifling. That fire guard saved them.

The next spring it rained. In turning a steer, Prince fell on the slick grass. He got up, but his rider could not stand. His leg was broken. The two were alone. In the words of Chester Evans, "I called Prince and he was at my side. I hate to think of the pain and the struggles to get into the saddle. Prince seemed to try to help me. He took me nine miles to the ranch. Nobody was there except the hired girl. I lay down on the floor and braced my good leg against the door jamb while she pulled on the other. She couldn't pull it into place, and I told her to tie the bridle reins around my foot and to set back on them. She did, twisting around a lot, and the break finally slipped into place. We splintered it. She left me on a pallet, got on Prince and rode him to Wakeeney, forty-four miles away, for the nearest doctor. All he did when he got to the ranch was to put on more and better splints. The leg healed first rate."

A year later Chester rode Prince to a ranch south of Amarillo in Texas and helped trail a herd of cows back to Kansas. On range and trail he rode other horses, but Prince remained to him "the only horse I ever really knew. I could camp anywhere with him and he would never leave me. With his keen senses he was a sentinel for game, wild cattle and horses by day and for anything prowling by night. He would grab an outlaw horse trying to leave the bunch by the neck and bring him to his milk."

You can look at the map of Kansas north and west of Dodge City and see that few people live there to this day. Fewer were there when the big blizzard of '87 hit. That was the winter Charlie Russell painted "The Last of the Five Thousand" and struck the trail for fame.

Before daylight on the morning of January 7, Chester's uncle awoke him and told him to ride for the doctor at Wakeeney. His wife was about to give birth. He bade Chester tell the doctor to come at once but said to put Prince in the livery stable and let him rest four hours before starting back. It was dusk when Chester headed for home, and the wind was rising. Prince seemed

as eager as ever. Before long the mist had turned to snow and sleet and the wind was like knives.

"I guess I made a mistake in not turning directions over entirely to Prince," Chester Evans said. "I kept quartering the wind when I should have headed into it. It was more west than north. There was no real road, and the snow blotted out all trace of whatever trail there was. A man, like any other animal, has an instinct to turn his back to a blizzard. Then he will veer and try to course against the wind, only to dodge it later. Daylight came and I didn't know where we were. If Prince knew he couldn't tell. I got down and he put his muzzle close to me and seemed to say we had better keep going. That day wore on. We didn't strike even a lobo track. All cattle had drifted south. A lot of them were no doubt already dead. It was slow, slow work breaking through the drifts of snow. Sometimes I got rid of the freezing numbness by walking. At the deepest drifts I would help break through.

"There were times when we couldn't see anything for the driving snow. There was no shelter, just plains of snow and ice, on and on, no canyons, no breaks. Dark came early. I knew Prince was hungry. Several times that night while I was stumbling along I tried to sit in the snow. Each time Prince would nuzzle me, and if the nuzzling didn't stir me he would paw me — not hard, just enough to make me move. He never would have left me.

"The second day came and some time that morning Prince brought me to a standstill at the Steele ranch on Beaver Creek. It was away south of the home ranch. We had missed the head of Cheyenne Creek, to the east. The creek would have told me where we were. We got something to eat. The blizzard had broken. Mr. Steele got on his horse and rode home with me. The doctor had arrived in time to help bring a baby boy into the world. Prince did not seem any worse off for the experiences, but it was several days before I was able to leave the house. Thirty-eight men died in western Kansas in that blizzard. The Smoky Hill Pool started into the winter with 6,000 head of cattle. The next spring we gathered 181."

After this breakup in the ranch business, Chester Evans and Prince moved to Lebo. The only person in town who thought the young man better looking than his horse was the girl he married. When the Cherokee Strip was opened for settlement in 1889 and thousands of people lined up to wait for the pistol shot that was to start the race for land, Evans rode Prince. He staked out his quarter section, lived on it two years, and then hitched Prince and "a five-year-old Know-Nothing" to a spring wagon and headed for California. Before long he and his family, in which he included Prince, were in a boxcar rolling back to Lebo to settle down for good.

In telling this story of his horse, Chester Evans seemed to have no thought of any other person and only of himself in association with Prince. At the very end his voice choked so that he had to pause for words.

"I bought a little pasture," he said, "joining the townsite and built a good shed on it to shelter my friend. He would bring the milk cows in from the pasture of an evening. I would hitch him to a spring wagon and turn him loose and he would go to the feed store, where somebody would load the wagon, and then bring the load back to the barn. He enjoyed grazing on the grass and enjoyed being with me, especially when I talked to him. My children and their playmates learned to ride on him.

"The center pole of this shed I built was set on a big flat rock. The feed box was attached to it. As the years went by, Prince's teeth wore down until they were of little service. He took to pawing while he ate. This pawing, without my giving proper attention to the matter, loosened the dirt under the big rock. One day in the fall of 1912 a telephone lineman hurried to my office with word that Prince was trapped under the fallen shed. The rock had settled to one side, causing the center pole to slip. Prince was pinned to the ground by timbers across his back. He had attracted the lineman's attention by whinnying to him. We raised the timbers and Prince tried to get up but could not make it. He seemed paralyzed in the hind quarters. We got a board under him, helped raise him, and supported him to the spring.

"Here he took a good drink and stepped off a little distance and lay down on a nice bed of bluegrass. I stayed with him all that day and all that night. Two or three times he kind of lipped my hand like he used to do on the range. Maybe he was remembering back. I don't know. The next morning I went to breakfast. When I came back to him, he was dead. He was thirty-eight years old. He had been my constant companion and my friend during his whole life. No man could have had a more congenial companion or a truer friend."

[295]

XV

THE COYOTE DUN AND OTHER COW HORSES

"HE IS of the race that dies before tiring," the vaquero people still say of the coyote dun. Another saying goes, "If you would lead the riders, pick the coyote dun." Considering bay as the emblem of refined breeding, a horsemaster who had ridden on all the continents wrote: "The bay dies while the dun will thrive wherever there is grass, from the fierce dry heat of the Gobi Desert to the utmost rigors of Siberian cold. The dun keeps cool amid difficulties that set the bay into a panic." [1]

All the virtues ascribed to the dun have been ascribed, just as deservedly, to the sorrel and other colors. The dun came to represent the best qualities of the breed. What counts, of course, is not the color itself but the *brío escondido* — the hidden vigor — beneath. Spanish-speakers began the tradition of the dun; it was old and widespread before English-speaking ranch people of the Southwest took it up. A dun pony that Charles Augustus Murray saw among the Pawnee Indians in 1835 had, he wrote, the "long mane and frontlock, wild fiery eye, and light active form" marking horses native to the "Western wilderness." [2] Primitive toughness and instincts had never been bred out of the dun's ancestors. While centuries of wild and half-wild life in the Americas reverted the type towards the primordial, it strengthened the hardihood of Arabian-Barb breeding.*

The dark line running down the horse's back gave him his name: *bayo coyote* (coyote dun), also *bayo lobo* (lobo dun), the fur of both coyote and gray wolf being shaded along the spine. In South America the color is called *gateado* — brindled like a cat; it is the most representative color of horses of Spanish blood being preserved in the Argentine. The dark line is usually accompanied by black mane, tail and hoofs, and often by horizontal streaks around the lower legs; sometimes by a transverse stripe over the shoulders.

That dorsal line is the sign of the primordial: on the striped skunk going its you-be-damned way after insects in grass roots; on the wild ass and Grevy's zebra of Africa; on the onager and kiang of Asia, along with the gaur of black-tipped horns and ridged backbone in the Malay Peninsula. The rich brownish gray of the blacktailed deer becomes dark along the back. No buck was ever wilder, no buffalo bull fiercer, than the line-backed, mealy-nosed "mustang" bull descended from the *ganado prieto* (black stock) introduced by Spaniards into California and Texas. As these cattle of the fighting bull strain reverted to the primi-

* "I feel bound to emphasize the suggestion that the excellent points of the South American Criollo and of the Mustang are due to the hardiness acquired by four hundred years of natural selection, quite as much as to the inheritance of Arabian and Barb blood." — Thornton Chard in *The Journal of Heredity*, Vol. 21 (September, 1930), 454.

tive, their colors became more various and stripes of white, yellow, black, blue, and brown ran down their muscled spines. German scientists attempting to revive the extinct wild aurochs by selective breeding picked specimens of back-striped, nose-ringed cattle surviving on the island of Corsica.

In his *Tropical South Africa*, Sir Francis Galton wrote: "No more conspicuous animal can well be conceived, according to common idea, than a zebra; but on a bright starlight night the breathing of one may be heard close by you, and yet you will be positively unable to see the animal. If the black stripes were more numerous, he would be seen as a black mass; if the white, as a white one; their proportion is such as exactly to match the pale tint which arid ground possesses when seen by moonlight." Primal tawniness is the most protective shade of nature; rings and stripes add to the camouflage. The line-backed dun tarpan of the steppes was hunted by the striped and tawny tiger; the dun horse of pampa and plain was waylaid by the dun puma.

Any breeder of Arabian horses will assert that duns never exist among them. The color is assigned to Barbs. To Major-General Tweedie's admission of an occasional Arabian dun, they would reply that the animal could not be purebred. Yet among the finest Arabian horses one may see not only black points and black manes and tails but the relic, perhaps only a shadowy suggestion, of the primitive dorsal stripe — a relic that prolonged feral existence would accentuate. In the large Arabian stud maintained by Lynn W. Van Vleet on his ranch near Nederland, Colorado, I observed a light-brown mare with the dark line down her back running into darker mane and tail. An Arabian horse named Akbar that made a record on the Calcutta race track in the last century had a pronounced stripe along his spine. Like many other Arabians, his withers were lower than his loins — a common fault of the Spanish pony. "Blazing red," a beautiful chestnut color much prized by the Arabs, is characterized by "very dark mane, tail and legs, black rims to ears and eyes, and often a black dorsal stripe." ' Only by persistence was the dun suppressed in the Thoroughbred line. The first volume of the Thoroughbred Studbook, dating back to 1738, shows that the color was initially frequent. Striped or unstriped, the dun color is not necessarily a denial of Arabian blood. After it has been bred away and the dorsal line has faded, the terminals of that line linger and its shadow can still be seen between mane and tail.

Darwin concluded that all domestic breeds of horses stem from a single wild species "of a dun color and more or less striped," to which modern descendants "occasionally revert." All the known primitive horses had, or have, the dorsal stripe, most of them being dunnish. The eel-backed dun of Norway, which once pawed in defense against bears and which continues to paw through snow and ice for forage and slides on haunches down mountain slopes, goes back to times antedating the earliest Scandinavian history. The Kattywar breed of northwestern India, the line-backed duns of ancient Prussia, Hungary, and Spain, and the duns of Java, Sumatra and other islands all incarnate the original ancestor.

The dun and the stripe are always waiting to come back. All colors but gray and roan are, in biological language, recessive to dun.[4] I cannot draw up tables of dates and numbers, but to me it is evident that for three and a half centuries, say from 1520 to 1880, dun was progressively emerging over the American continents among descendants of horses marked sparsely by that color when Spaniards planted them. Before that time selective breeding had driven the dun color into hiding; feral life brought it back.

In 1928, Mr. Robert T. McCready, of Pittsburgh, Pennsylvania, began writing me about a stallion named Kit Carson. Living among what used to be called the peon class of Mexicans, I have often thought that cultivation is not necessary to a gentleman, but as I read now the file of letters from Mr. McCready, I realize that among people of property only cultivation of mind and taste can make a fine gentleman. He was an attorney-at-law and raised a line of "gold" saddle horses. He could trace them back, through an unbroken line of golden color, with black points, manes and tails, and of endurance, grace and spirit, to a mustang stallion, "noted for the swiftness of his pace," captured, according to tradition, on the Canadian River in the Texas Panhandle about 1846 and taken to the vicinity of Mexico, Missouri.

From one or two old horsemen in Missouri who preserved traditions, this was about all Mr. McCready could learn concerning Kit Carson. Some called him a dun, others "golden sand" color; some, seemingly influenced by the legend of the Pacing White Steed, said he had white mane and tail. The unvarying black points and black mane and tail of his progeny disproved this.

One of his descendants, Rex Rysdyk, ridden by Mr. McCready in a three-hundred-mile endurance test conducted by the U. S. Cavalry in Vermont in 1925, carried 225 pounds, crossed and recrossed sixty miles of mountains in nine hours, and made a perfect record. Standing or moving, he had "the look of the eagle" and was unflaggingly vigilant. In 1931, Mr. McCready wrote that Jonquil, sister of Rex Rysdyk, had been shipped to the Anacacho Ranch, out from Spofford, Texas, on the border, to be bred to Edna May's King. I went to see her. When I regarded her golden color, her black mane and tail and the suggestion of dark line down her spine, I knew that I was looking at a descendant — a descendant through generations of scientific breeding — of a true Spanish mustang — the coyote dun.

Buckskin and claybank are other names for dun. On the northern plains, buckskin was the usual term, and many a horse called Buck owed his name to color rather than to deer-like fleetness. The buckskins are always showing up in the chronicles of the West. Once on a chase after Indians, Buffalo Bill's fine horse was outrun by a Pawnee scout's. Giving the Pawnee some tobacco and trinkets as boot, Buffalo Bill swapped — and Buckskin Joe rose with him to fame. "He was rather a sorry-looking animal," but one time Buffalo Bill killed (he said) thirty-six buffaloes from his back on a single run and another time (he said) ran him for eighty miles on a desperate stretch. When, as guide for the Grand Duke Alexis on a grand hunt, Buffalo Bill mounted the conductor of the Duke's wagon train on Buckskin Joe, the teamsters took him for "the king." For them the grandeur demanded a king and no man titled lower than a king could be riding Buckskin Joe.[5]

Ranchers and planters on the Brazos River at the time of the Texas Republic held that the best-bottomed of all horses were "yellows" from Mexico with long, heavy whiskers.[6] Some men can still remember those Spanish horses with mustaches, the hair as coarse as tail hair and parted on the upper lip.*

In the early part of this century, cowmen of lower Texas, who had generally quit raising their own mounts, had a strong preference for horses out of the rough country of Tamaulipas — away from the coast. Their feet were small and of durable hardness. A great many were line-backed: *bayos blancos* (light duns), *bayos azafranados* (saffron hued, between dun and sorrel), *bayos naranjados* (orange duns), *bayos tigres* (tiger-like stripes circling legs and running over shoulders, another name for *gateados*), *bayos cebrunos* (dun shading into smoky color). Grullos were numerous and were outstanding as cow horses. The color has a resemblance to that of the *grulla* (sandhill crane) and is often translated as slate- or mouse-colored; there are many shades of grullos, but the most characteristic runs into a kind of blue. Nearly all grullos, along with many faded bays, had barred legs and the dorsal stripe, a line over the shoulders often making the *cruz* of the Christ-marked burro.

---

* While the Texas expedition to conquer New Mexico was outfitting at Austin in 1841, its chief chronicler rode "a little, rough-looking Mexican mountain pony wearing a huge pair of *mustaches* on his upper lip. He was as tough as wrought iron, and although one hour's riding would bring on a lazy fit, ten would not tire him." — George Wilkins Kendall, *Narrative of the Texan Santa Fe Expedition*, New York, 1847, I, 30.

The bays, browns, blues and grullos that came up from Mexico were every bit as good as the duns. These horses were not jug-headed; they were neither Roman-nosed nor dish-faced. Their faces, inclining to flatness, were wide, especially between the eyes. Short, sensitive ears topped well-set heads. They were barrel-bellied, had thick shoulders and hind quarters.

The toughest cow horse I have known was a rusty black with the map of Mexico on his left thigh. We called him Hippy, for he had a hip knocked down. He had a stubborn disposition. After days of hard riding, he always stepped free, head up. He was the kind of horse that range men of southwest Texas rode on cow works before remudas and chuck wagons came into use: one horse to one man for maybe a week of "running cattle," a sack of biscuits, a cut of salt bacon, coffee and coffee can in a morral on the saddle horn.

Eccentricities, the mark of individualism, were common in the breed. Asa Jones, who has handled thousands, had a zebra dun that no man could endure long enough to ride down — at reasonable gaits — but that could be bridled only after a great deal of managing. For this reason, although preferring him to any other horse in the remuda either for running or cutting cattle, Asa Jones turned him over to a cowboy named Zeno. Zeno could not bridle him without hobbling him. Even then he would sometimes exhaust himself and turn blue around the gills before getting the bit into Dun's mouth. One day, by chance, he saddled the horse before trying to bridle him. To his surprise, Dun accepted the bit as easily as a pet filly accepts an apple. After that, the regular procedure was to saddle him before bridling. Maybe he had been broken that way.

The two Spanish cow horses remembered in cowboy song are the Zebra Dun and the Strawberry Roan, both pitching outlaws. The first was the more celebrated. The song begins with the arrival in camp of a mouthy stranger who used big words and "talked about foreign kings and queens." Finally, after he had showed how green he was, he wanted to borrow a nice, fat, gentle horse to ride on to the **7 D** ranch. With glee the boss roped him out the horse nobody could ride.

Old Dunny was a rocky outlaw that had grown so awful wild
He could paw the white out of the moon every jump for a mile.

When the stranger hit the saddle, Old Dunny quit the earth
And traveled right straight up for all that he was worth,
A-pitching and a-squealing, a-having wall-eyed fits,
His hind feet perpendicular, his front ones in the bits.

We could see the tops of the mountains under Dunny every jump,
But the stranger he was growed there, just like the camel's hump;
The stranger sat upon him and curled his black mustache,
Just like a summer boarder waiting for his hash.

An old cow hand named John Custer who faded out in San Antonio told me that about 1880 he saw the horse and the ride that inspired the song. He said the "greenhorn" made a cow horse out of the outlaw dun. "That dun could *stay* until the flames of hell turned into icicles."

The head of many a big bucking horse seen in modern rodeos indicates lack of intelligence, but the most intelligent *potro* — unbroken horse — can be turned into an outlaw. An old stove-up cow hand named Cole whom I encountered in Austin in 1922 told me this story.

"One day the man I was working for got in two new horses to break. I roped out one; he was a big sorrel. A Negro he roped the other, a barrel-built dun. When we saddled up, my sorrel didn't do a thing but stand as if he had been saddled every day for a year. The dun he pitched all over the pen with the saddle. The Negro was afraid to ride him and so we swapped. Well, sir, that sorrel horse nearly killed the Negro, and the dun never even humped his back after I got on him. Lots of times a horse that pitches with the saddle won't do a thing when a man crawls on him.

"I rode the dun for two months or so on cow work. He was plumb gentle and had lots of cow sense. He was getting to be the best kind of cow horse. Then one day while I was on herd, resting easy in the saddle under a shade tree, the boss and a couple of hands rode up to talk. Just to be fooling, the boss gave my horse a light lick with his quirt across the back. That dun struck out pitching right through the middle of the herd. He pitched for half a mile right and left, backwards and forwards. There was no getting his motion. He pitched till we were both broke down and I was bleeding at nose, mouth, and ears. I never saw such pitching in all my born days.

"After that it was the same thing every time the dun was saddled. Nobody but me could ride him and before long I wouldn't ride him. He got to be a regular outlaw. He went plumb crazy from that quirt lick across his back, and it was a crazy thing for the boss to make it. Finally he was traded off, and the last I heard of him he was just running free, nobody ever even roping him."

Pitching seems to be unknown to horses in Arabia; I have met with no account of pitching among Barbs or among horses in Spain. Occasional European horses have from time immemorial been vicious or have buck-jumped and reared, but the bronc with "belly full of bedsprings," pawing for the moon, breaking in two half way up, sunfishing on the way down, and then hitting the earth hard enough to crack open his rider's liver, was a development of the Western Hemisphere. Spain had no word to express something unknown in horse conduct. To denote the act of pitching, Mexico gave to the verb *reparar* a new meaning. In Spain a *potro* is a colt; in Mexico and the Southwest, *potro* came to mean an unbroken horse with a disposition to down his head and try to jump out of his skin. The Spaniards came to the Americas riding Moorish style, "English style," as it is called in the West, with short stirrups. As their horses grew wild and pitched when mounted, riders found that short stirrups prevented their getting a quick seat and clasping legs against a complexly squirming horse. They lengthened their stirrups to make range riding more effective, also more comfortable.[7] Indians frequently used no stirrups at all.

Nobody says just when descendants of the original Spanish horses acquired their disposition for "promptitude," but from the pampas of Patagonia to the plains of Alberta, range men came to believe that they got it from practice in pitching off panthers.[8] Transmission of acquired characteristics is contrary to biological law. The old-time range way of allowing horses to run untouched by human hands, except when they were castrated and branded, for three or four years before the process of gentling was undertaken, whereas in Europe and the Near East colts grew up gentle, no doubt contributed to the pitching habit. The brutal process of breaking — the word *gentling* being foreign to the vocabulary of the open range — must have been another contributor. Perhaps, also, some substance in grass or water affected equine temperament. Anyhow, a range horse "without a little life in him" came to be distrusted. One Texan is supposed to have said, "Any mustang that outgrows a hankering to elevate is guilty of treason to the grand old State of Texas." Pioneer Australians ascribed the pitching of their range horses to dams imported from South America.

Owing to endless iteration of the cowboy myth and to exhibition riding, the popular conception of cow horses is a distortion of reality. The cow horse was — and remains — a work horse. Good work on horseback could never come except through harmony between man and horse. In times when most cow horses were Spanish and cowboys lived and worked with them in complete isolation — and in entire ignorance of the ideal subsequently enjoined by film and pulp print — comparatively few maintained the habit of pitching. They were valued for reliability and intelligence as much as for energy and endurance. The young pitchers, which generally settled down in maturity, bore

[305]

slight resemblance in either form or sense to the jug-headed, Percheron-shaped outlaws of modern rodeos.

All the old-time range men of validity whom I have known remembered horses with affection and respect as a part of the best of themselves. After their knees begin to stiffen, most men realize that they have been disappointed in themselves, in other men, in achievement, in love, in whatever they expected out of life; but a man who has had a good horse in his life — a horse beyond the play world — will remember him as a certitude, like a calm mother, a lovely lake, or a gracious tree, amid all the flickering vanishments. I remember Buck.

He was raised on our ranch and was about half Spanish. He was a bright bay with a blaze in his face and stockings on his forefeet. He could hardly have weighed when fat over 850 pounds and was about 14 hands high. A Mexican broke him when he was three years old, but I don't think he pitched much. From then on nobody but me rode him, even after I left for college. He had a fine barrel and chest and was very fast for short distances but did not have the endurance of some other horses, straight Spaniards, in our remuda. What he lacked in toughness, he made up in intelligence, especially cow sense, loyalty, understanding, and generosity.

As a colt he had been bitten by a rattlesnake on the right ankle just above the hoof; a hard, hairless scab marked the place as long as he lived. He traveled through the world listening for the warning rattle. A kind of weed in the Southwest bears seed that when ripe rattle in their pods a good deal like the sound made by a rattlesnake. Many a time when my spur or stirrup set these seeds a-rattling Buck's suddenness in jumping all but left me seated in the air. I don't recall his smelling rattlesnakes, but he could smell afar off the rotten flesh of a yearling or any other cow brute afflicted with screw worms. He understood that I was hunting these animals in order to drive them to a pen and doctor them. In hot weather they take refuge in high weeds and thick brush. When he smelled one, he would point to it with his ears and turn towards it. A dog trained for hunting out wormy cases could not have been more helpful.

Once a sullen cow that had been roped raked him in the breast with the tip of a sharp horn. After that experience, he was wariness personified around anything roped, but he never, like some horses that have been hooked, shied away from an animal he was after. He knew and loved his business too well for that. He did not love it when at the rate of less than a mile an hour he was driving the thirsty, hot, tired, slobbering drag end of a herd, animals stopping behind every bush or without any bush, turning aside the moment they were free of a driver. When sufficiently exasperated, Buck would go for a halting cow with mouth open and grab her just forward of the tail bone if she did not move on. Work like this may be humiliating to a gallant young cowboy and an eager cow horse; it is never pictured as a part of the romance of the range, but it is very necessary. It helps a cowboy to graduate into a cowman. A too high-strung horse without cow sense, which includes cow patience, will go to pieces at it just as he will go to pieces in running cattle or in cutting a herd.

Buck had the rein to make the proverbial "turn on a two-bit piece and give back fifteen cents in change." One hot summer while we were gathering steers on leased grass about twelve miles from home, I galled his side with a tight cinch. I hated to keep on riding him with the galled side, but was obliged to on account of shortage in horses. As I saddled up in camp one day after dinner, I left the cinch so loose that a hand might have been laid between it and Buck's belly. We had to ride about a mile before going through a wire gap into the pasture where some snaky steers ran. As we rode along, a vaquero called my attention to the loose cinch.

"I will tighten it when we get to the gap," I said.

"*Cuidado* (have care) and don't forget," he said.

[307]

At the gap, which he got down to open, I saw him look at me. I decided to wait until we struck something before tightening the girth. Two minutes later my father yelled and we saw a little bunch of steers high-tailing it through scattered mesquites for a thicket along a creek beyond. I forgot all about the cinch. Buck was easily the fastest horse ridden by the four or five men in our "cow crowd." He left like a cry of joy to get around the steers.

As we headed them, they turned to the left at an acute angle, and Buck turned at an angle considerably more acute. Sometimes he turned so quickly that the *tapadera* (toe-fender) of my stirrup raked the ground on the inside of the turn. This time when he doubled back, running full speed, the loose saddle naturally turned on him. As my left hip hit the ground, I saw stars. One foot was still in a stirrup and the saddle was under Buck's belly. I suppose that I instinctively pulled on the reins, but I believe that Buck would have stopped had he not been bridled. His stop was instantaneous; he did not drag me on the ground at all. He had provocation to go on, too, for in coming over his side and back the spur on my right foot had raked him. He never needed spurs. I wore them on him just to be in fashion.

Sometimes in running through brush, Buck seemed to read my mind — or maybe I was reading his. He was better in the brush than I was. In brush work, man and horse must dodge, turn, go over bushes and pear and under limbs, absolutely in accord, rider yielding to the instinct and judgment of the horse as much as horse yields to his.

Buck did not have to be staked. If I left a drag rope on him, he would stay close to camp, at noon or through the night. He was no paragon. Many men have ridden and remembered hardier horses. He was not proud, but he carried himself in a trim manner. He did the best he could, willingly and generously, and he had a good heart. His chemistry mixed with mine. He was good company. I loved to hear him drink water, he was so hearty in

swallowing, and then after he was full, to watch him lip the water's surface and drip big drops back into it.

Sometimes after we had watered and, passing on, came to good grass near shade, I'd unsaddle and turn him loose to graze. Then I'd lie down on the saddle and while the blanket dried, listen to his energetic cropping and watch the buzzards sail and the Gulf clouds float. Buck would blow out his breath once in a while, presumably to clear his nostrils but also, it seemed, to express contentment. He never asked me to stop, unless to stale, and never, like some gentle saddle horses, interrupted his step to grab a mouthful of grass; but if I stopped with slackened rein to watch cattle, or maybe just to gaze over the flow of hills to the horizon, he'd reach down and begin cutting grass. He knew that was all right with me, though a person's seat on a grazing horse is not nearly so comfortable as on one with upright head. Occasionally I washed the sweat off his back and favored him in other ways, but nobody in our part of the country pampered cow horses with sugar or other delicacy.

While riding in boyhood and early youth, I fell in love with four or five girls but told only one. She was right in considering the matter a joke and thereby did me one of the biggest favors of my life. All those rose-lipt maidens and all the light-foot lads with whom I ran in those days have receded until they have little meaning. They never had much in comparison with numerous people I have known since.* Buck, however, always in association with the plot of earth over which I rode him, increases in meaning. To remember him is a joy and a tonic.

Men who herded over wide ranges and up the trails picked the most trustworthy horses for night horses. They valued them above the cutting horses, about which so much has been said. Often the night horse had to do the cowboy's seeing and

* A man who calls boyhood the richest part of his life is either lying according to sentimental tradition or has remained puerile-minded.

hearing; on dark and stormy nights he kept his rider from getting lost. No matter if a herd drifted or ran miles from camp, a good night horse, given his head, would travel straight back for the chuck wagon. He knew, as well as a plow mule knows when noon comes, the hour at which the guard should change. On a ranch of the lower Texas plains was a brown Spanish horse branded **C I D** and called Sid. He was used only as a night horse, and having Sid in his string marked a cowboy as favored. When the time came to change guard, Sid might by main strength and awkwardness be persuaded to make two or three more rounds of the herd. He would concede that much to the possibility of error in his estimation of time. Then he would take the bit in his teeth and head for the chuck wagon. His rider, of course, generally agreed with him.

Soon after the Civil War ended, Uel Livingston of Hamilton County, Texas, went up the trail with a herd of Longhorns. One night while he was on guard the cattle were so quiet and he was so sleepy that he decided to take a nap. He rode a little to one side, dismounted, and was immediately dead asleep. A rumble and vibrations of the earth against his ear awakened him to a stampede. As he started to rise he saw that his horse was standing over him, front feet on one side of his body and hind feet on the other. He always believed that his night horse stood there to protect him from running cattle.[9]

If the boss of an outfit had a good heart and considered a green hand capable of learning, he might mount him on a wise old horse for teacher. A Texas boss put a tenderfoot hired in Kansas on Old Trusty for night work. The tenderfoot staked him, saddled but unbridled, as other cowboys in camp staked their night horses, near his pallet. One night he heard the cattle break and jumped up to find Old Trusty as close to him as the stake rope would allow. He had never been in a stampede. He did not take time to bridle the horse, just untied the rope and jumped into the saddle. Old Trusty took him alongside the lead runners and veered them into a mill — a circle — which soon wound up. After the run was over, Old Trusty stopped, heaved a long breath, and began grabbing mouthfuls of grass. He deserved his name and seemed now well satisfied with the job he had done.[10]

"As smart as a cutting horse," one of the old sayings of the range goes, and many a tall tale about cutting horses that could read brands, classify cattle as to age or sex, and would cut them accordingly, without bridle or guidance by man, has come down. A good cutting horse does learn quickly to recognize what his master, riding in a herd, is looking for, and as soon as his master indicates an animal, he begins working it out. I suppose that on some ranches there are just as good cutting horses now as ever existed, but I am writing about Spanish horses.

Many Spanish cutting horses were used for other work, and nearly any top cow horse would after a little practice be efficient at cutting. Some of the best ones looked sleepy when off duty. Often had the "Dante Alighieri face," ascribed by O. Henry to the pony ridden by "the Last of the Troubadours." These horses had to hold energy in reserve in order to endure and in order not to excite the herd. Reserve and restraint are a part of cow sense. When Old Sleepy, resting on three legs, head down and lower lip drooping, as he waited there in a thicket, heard brush pop, horn click or hoof thud, he became a changed being. His heart would go to thumping against his rider's legs, and if that rider could stay with him he would tear a hole through the brush getting to the wild runners.

"Catch me Pelicano," Manuel Hinojosa, the cow boss, would say. The herd was ready to be worked. Pelicano was a widish brown with many white hairs in his tail. He always looked satisfied with himself, but more in the manner of a burgher drinking beer than of a grandee on parade. As Manuel rode him into the herd he was all energy, and one could see that he was holding himself in as easily as he was holding a cow and calf together while he helped cut them out. Most people who do anything well beyond the mechanical enjoy doing it; it is the same with horses. A cowman of the old ways down in the brush told me that one time right after a rain he saw by tracks that a roping and cutting horse he had turned out to recover from lameness had run a cow and knocked her down. He had merely wanted to do what he enjoyed doing.

There is just one word besides bottom to apply to Spanish cow ponies. That is *gamy*. One not fourteen hands high, weighing maybe 800 pounds, carrying a man and saddle weighing up close to 200 pounds, would run up alongside an aged outlaw steer weighing 1200 pounds. After his rider cast the loop and it went true, but not a moment before, he squatted to take the jerk on the saddle horn. He took it. If the animal was thrown, he kept the rope tight while the rider sped to tie it down. He never saved himself from thorns, and in the brush country most of his kind had bunged-up knees. He hardly knew the taste of corn or oats, but he could mow the grass when he got a chance and assimilate it as soon as it was swallowed. Often he had a setfast on his back. No matter how he burned for a drink of water, he would go to the last ditch in the opposite direction. He was gamy.

When A. Phimister Proctor was commissioned in 1939 to make a bronze statue of a group of authentic mustangs,* the only Spanish horses in Texas available for models, so far as I and other men concerned knew, were owned by Tom T. East on his San Antonio Viejo ranch in the brushy border country. He had around 250 head of dun and grullo horses, all line-backed. They were descendants from a dun mustang stallion caught when about ten years old on the Rancho Randado. In 1920 Tom East

---

* The Seven Mustangs, presented to the people of Texas by Mr. and Mrs. Ralph D. Ogden of Austin, were unveiled on the campus of the University of Texas in 1948.

got a grullo stallion, son of the dun, and began breeding him to a few mares that were *puro Español*. In the course of years he found that no matter what the color of a stallion bred to dun mares, ninety per cent of the colts were dun. He tried raising Arabian horses also. "They have the bottom," he said. "You can run one all day, but they don't have cow sense."

The Randado used to raise about the best Spanish horses in Texas. It was a horse ranch, established late in the 18th century. During years of range expansion following the Civil War, Randado horses were celebrated thousands of miles away. They were incredibly tough. On the big works in the Randado country, before it was fenced, vaqueros rode a circle of over one hundred miles bringing in the caballadas without changing mounts. From dawn till dark, day following day, they rode mostly in a gallop, staked their mounts at night, and were never afoot.

It was fitting that A. Phimister Proctor's mustangs, plunging forever in bronze, should, while representing all Spanish horses, have been modeled upon coyote duns out of the Rancho Randado. Of that ranch nothing is left now but a decayed house, a watering tank made long ago by carrying dirt for the dam on cow hides pulled from the saddle horn — and a name. Tom East of the San Antonio Viejo is dead, and other blood is mixing into the last stud of duns and grullos in all the Spanish country of the Southwest.

XVI

ONLY THEIR DUST

THE REFRAIN of an old ballad of the Mexican frontier keeps running in my consciousness. It was made up about a man whose sweetheart had been seized, not unwillingly, by another and taken away horseback. The bereft lover followed to the top of a mountain:

> I went up the Pico Etéreo,
> I went up the Pico Etéreo,
> To see if I could catch sight of her in the distance,
> To see if I could catch sight of her in the distance.
> Only the dust I saw,
> Only the dust I saw
> Of the man who was taking her away.

The climax of the range industry — not economically, which is now, but dramatically — was in the great overland drives, during the quarter century following the Civil War, of Longhorn cattle from Texas to Kansas, New Mexico, Arizona, Colorado, even California, to Nebraska, the Dakotas, Wyoming, Montana, on into Canada. Wherever these cattle spread, Texas cow ponies of Spanish blood were ridden to manage them.

During the time of the Longhorn drives, probably a million range horses were trailed out of Texas. They went east of the Mississippi to pull plows and wagons for cotton farmers, and they went plainsward to break the sod for homesteaders. Among them were many captive mustangs, but the majority, many wild mares, many cow horses past their prime, many *potros* hardly halter-broke, were out of branded caballadas; nearly all were of the mustang breed. Yet so far as print goes, for every paragraph that relates to the driving of these range horses, a hundred pages relate to the trailing of Longhorn cattle. Andy Adams, who drove only horses over the trail, wrote the best account yet published on a trail herd of cattle, supplemented that with other narratives, and scarcely mentioned horse driving. The cowboy rode to glory but *horseboy* never became a name.

Driving horses was easier than driving cattle — when all went well. After a herd had been driven some distance out of their range, they could be turned loose at night, headed in the traveling direction, with little danger of their running or drifting away. That is, they could be turned loose safely if they were not thirsty and if good grass were at hand. They would graze off and on all night and the next morning be found not more than two or three miles away. To close-herd horses like cattle meant trouble.

But a hungry horse is going to try to find grass, and a thirsty horse is going to try to find water. One drouthy year, my old friend Ed McWhorter started up the trail from Live Oak County. His horse herd found hardly a sprig of grazing until they reached the San Saba River. "Several nights," Ed McWhorter said, "we simply fought those horses, beating them over the heads, to hold them back. We had to treat them like crazy cattle."

Drives to the east from California came earlier than the main drives from Texas, were more picturesque and in larger herds. The total number of animals driven out, however, was comparatively small, and the deserts diminished them severely. The drivers were principally New Mexicans from Santa Fe and freebooting Mountain Men. In 1830, after the Santa Fe trade with the United States was well established, a New Mexican caravan rode annually to California with packs of woolen goods — mostly serapes and blankets — to trade for horses and mules and Chinese silk. Upon leaving California these traders had a habit of picking up horse stock for which they had not traded.

At the end of 1847 their last expedition, made up of one woman and over 200 men, most of them peons, some armed only with bows and arrows and others with old swords, arrived on the West Coast with about 150 mule packs. After spending four months bartering from San Diego to Monterey, they headed east with 4628 horses, mules and burros that had been passed by brand inspectors. Twenty armed Californians followed them to see that they did not make away with stolen animals. A rider with Kit Carson who overtook the caravan on the desert estimated the herd at a thousand head and noted how bleached horse skeletons of other years marked the trail.[1]

This drive seems to have been the largest that the New Mexicans made. The discovery of gold reversed the flow of livestock, for some years at least. Miles Goodyear left California in March, 1848, with 231 head of horse stock, drove them to Missouri, failed to find a profitable market, and the next year drove them back to California and made money.[2]

Raids by the Mountain Men were more notorious than important.[3] Jim Beckwourth said of an alleged haul of 1800 "stray horses" from California rancheros that "the morals" of the Mountain Men "justified" their enterprise. Pegleg Smith, whose bellicosity and figures always increased under the influence of Taos lightning, at which time he would unstrap his wooden leg and use it as a shillalah, boasted that he had gone into "the Spanish country" and made away with "only about 3000 head" of horses. In 1841 Rufus B. Sage encountered the leavings of a herd that twenty-two Mountain Men had captured in California and defended against sixty pursuing Mexican cavalrymen, only to surrender to the desert. They had about half of the 2000 or 3000 horses they had started with. Joe Walker made an historic drive, but for all his knowledge of geography — he discovered the Yosemite Valley, and Walker Pass is named for him — could not circumvent desert thirst.

Shortly after the outbreak of the Mexican War, Bill Williams, aided by twenty-five or thirty other Mountain Men, all on fire with patriotism, rounded up 1500 horses and mules in southern California and set out with them for Santa Fe. A posse of 200 rancheros followed, and the patriots pushed ahead with such speed that 1000 animals dropped out on the desert from thirst and fatigue. Old Bill called a halt at a long waterhole where the rancheros halted also. "Well, boys," he said, "we have lost most of our caballada, but we have 500 left. We'll stop right here and recruit them. If them Mexicans want to take their animals, let them try." The Mexicans did not seem as anxious to fight as they had been to follow. For three days each of the opposing camps waited for the other to act. On the night of the third day the Mountain Men took every horse and mule their pursuers had. In high feather again, they moved on. According to one version of the story, they lost the entire caballada in a surprise attack by Indians and reached Santa Fe half afoot. According to another version, they saved 300 head, got as far east as Bent's Fort on the Arkansas with them, and there traded them off for a barrel of whiskey.

No Mexican or bravadoing trapper ever trailed a caballada into grimmer desolation than a Dane named Daniel Bruhn. He had been a soldier and was an artist and a cultivated gentleman. In the desert he solaced himself by picturing in letters, to be mailed months later, the stark life of a horse driver.[4]

[318]

In March, 1871, without a dollar, on a foreign frontier, he hired himself to join "a bandit crew such as it would be difficult to find the like of in Europe," equipped himself with Mexican sombrero, Garibaldi shirt, calfskin trousers, enormous iron spurs, knife and six-shooter, and began the "neck-breaking labor" of collecting 3000 horses running wild on the Kings River–San Joaquin plains. The outfit was made up of forty-one men. Their cruelties to the animals sickened Bruhn, but he stood up to his eighteen hours in the saddle. The herd was bound for Texas. Why Texas, which at the time had a surplus of horses, is not explained. On the way across the Sierra Nevada, an average of twenty-five of the "oldest horses" perished daily. Many weak horses rolled down into canyons and were left dead or dying. Riding horses as well as those in the herd were left behind, but gentle-natured Bruhn tailed one of his up and led it and in time saw it restored by grass and water. Six hundred animals died in the mountains. On the desert to the east two hundred more died.

In October, after about six months of living with wild horses and rough men, Bruhn was discharged, near Unionville in Nevada. He understood that the horses were to be wintered in the region and might not get to a market for a year or two. He went on to other occupations, until he settled down in Denmark as head of the Royal Academy of Fine Arts.

Any herd of over 500 horses was unmanageable. Rough ground and sparse water and grass made one that large impracticable. Even of cattle 3000 head made a herd too unwieldy for prosperous grazing, watering and driving over good country. The only range men ever to have experience with herds of 10,000 and up have been of the Hollywood variety. The horse herds driven from Texas averaged not over 300 or 400 head each.

Horses would never all lie down together on a bedground and sleep like cattle. Many slept on their feet and hardly ever lay down except to roll. In a herd of hundreds, some would be grazing nearly all night. Uncle Neville Dobie, who was the horseman of my tribe, claimed that most horses napped regularly three times during the night: about nine o'clock, about eleven, and then not long before daylight, this last hour being the time for the soundest sleep. If a cowboy on night herd did not watch, he would find his night horse wasting away from lack of regular sleep.

Men who had trailed horse herds as well as cattle herds considered stampeded horses the more difficult to bring under control. At a meeting of the Trail Drivers of Texas in San Antonio in 1926, Dan Murrah, now of the world unknown, gave me this incident. "We had about 400 horses in our herd. I always rode in the lead, and in the Indian Territory we were trailing down a wooded slope to a creek when I noticed the remains of a freshly abandoned camp, near some big trees. I guess it had been made by hunters, for I saw a big bear's paw on the ground. My horse shied, and I rode on. That country was full of bears and any horse is afraid of a bear. Not a minute after I passed the bear's paw, the herd behind me began screaming and bawling and tearing back up the hill. The ground shook with their running. I never heard such screaming among horses in all my life. Every horse had his mouth open and tongue out. All hell could not have stopped them. Some of the horses fell or were knocked into deep gullies, and the others plunged right on over them as if they had been a bridge. After we got the stampede checked, we found horses in the gullies with broken backs. We shot them out of mercy and had to make a circuit of several miles to cross the creek on which the stampede started."

One year Uncle Jim Dobie bought a big string of horses from the Laureles Ranch on the coast, shipped them to San Antonio, and sold them in the pens to a horse trader. They were delivered by Jeff McLemore, who used to ride over the country munching peanuts from a morral at his saddle horn. He knew horses. The buyer said something to him that he did not like and he kept silent. That is, he refrained from advising the buyer on the best way to drive wild horses out of town. The buyer led his herd right up San Pedro Avenue. The traffic stampeded them. Their manes were so long that when they ran they tossed their heads between the ground and the highest reach of their necks. They were as wild as mustangs. After they left San Pedro Avenue they ran to the Leon Springs country, and many never were seen by the buyer again.

After great numbers of cattle had been trailed northward and before horses had entirely lost their relative value, some of the south Texas ranges held far more horses than cattle. Only the naïve would go to official records for an estimate of how many there were. The ranchers did not know and for taxable purposes naturally gave themselves the benefit of all doubts. My father, Richard Dobie, and his brothers Jim and Neville bought out the Railey brand of horses in Live Oak County for $2800, range delivery. After months of gathering, they counted approximately 2800 head — more than twice the number the Raileys thought they had. All were trailed northward.

The breed did not disappear from the land — disappear almost as completely as Mayan civilization — through being driven away, but through castration. For a long time ranch breeders wanted Spanish mares on which to cross Thoroughbred, Morgan, Tennessee Walking, Quarter and other highbred stallions. The time came when no Spanish mares were left. Spanish horses were bred out of existence just as Spanish Longhorns were.

There are still a few wild horses in Nevada, Wyoming and other Western states. Only a trace of Spanish blood is left in most of them. When caught they are canned into dog food. While domesticated Spanish horses were being "bred up," the mustangs proper were killed off to save grass and to prevent tolling gentler animals into wildness. In 1873, for instance, Coleman, Fulton and Mathis started fencing in 121,000 acres of prairie land against the Gulf of Mexico. This was before the advent of barbed wire; the fence was plank. While the great pasture was being enclosed the owners sent men out with Winchesters to annihilate the mustangs.[5] In 1881, S. A. Bull took 2500 head of horse stock to Moore County on the Staked Plains, still unfenced. He and other horse ranchers organized to shoot the mustangs that were outlawing their stock.[6] A few years later, ranchers in Wyoming were paying a bounty of $25 for each mustang stallion killed and at the same time only $2 for a wolf scalp. Wolfers made a business of killing mustangs.[7]

Frontiersmen, always "wrathy to kill," shot mustangs for pleasure, just as they shot buffaloes, jack rabbits, herons and every other form of animal life within range. Living upon the prairies in the 1830's, Josiah Gregg observed that "most persons appear unable to restrain this wanton inclination to take life when a mustang approaches within rifle-shot. Many a stately steed thus falls a victim to the cruelty of man."

Among the last true mustangs on the **L F D** range, along the Texas–New Mexico line, was a paint stallion, with heavy dark mane and tail, that led a band of broomtailed mares. After a pair of chuck wagon mules, which had been coming in regularly for a feed of grain, joined this band of mustangs, the **L F D** manager hired two expert rifle shots to kill them. One of the experts made his living by giving exhibitions of fancy shooting to advertise a brand of ammunition. He knew little about horses, gentle or wild. Cowboys placed him and his aid in buffalo wallows and then chased the mustangs by them. The first one to fall from a bullet, shot while he was running full speed, was the paint stallion. Five other mustangs were killed on this run. In subsequent runs, all the others were shot.[8]

The slaughter in California began long before fences were thought of — for the very reason that desert-buttressed mountains naturally restricted the coastal range. In 1805, 7500 surplus horses were killed in the valley about San Jose; a year or so later, 7200 were destroyed around Santa Barbara; in 1810 great numbers near Monterey. During drouths, laws were promulgated limiting the number of mares any rancher might maintain, and between 1815 and 1825 wholesale slaughters were carried out up and down the coast from Los Angeles. Preceding the destruction, far-extended rodeos brought wild and domesticated horses alike into large corrals, whence owners took the animals they chose to keep. The others were destroyed in two ways. Numbers were rushed over bluffs onto rocks or into the Pacific Ocean to drown. Again, the animals were let out of pens, one by one, through narrow gates and lanced to death as they emerged. Horse hides were in so little demand, bringing maybe four bits against two dollars for a cow hide, that the slain were seldom skinned.[9]

East of the Spanish settlements, the great mustang manadas of the San Joaquin Valley ran without serious molestation until the gringos wanted their grass. There travelers saw band join band in flight until "frequently the plain would be covered with thousands and thousands flying in a living flood towards the hills. Huge masses of dust hung upon their rear and marked their track across the plain; even after they had passed entirely beyond the reach of vision, the vast clouds of dust which they were throwing into the air could be seen moving over the highlands." [10]

What is now the most highly motorized area in the world — that part of California centering around Los Angeles — was once the most intensely horsed. "The men appeared to be always on horseback," Dana wrote in *Two Years before the Mast*. They often ate in the saddle. What work they did was done on horseback. Their chief sports — racing, bull-tailing, roping grizzlies and elk, rodeo feats — depended on horses. Their bets on horse races were often in units of cattle and horses rather than in dollars. The art of the land lay in weaving horsehair and plaiting rawhide. If a man sat to play cards, his horse, saddled and ready for mounting, stood at hand. As soon as a child was born, it was carried horseback to be baptized. Boys literally grew up on horses. Any traveler who needed a fresh mount was free to rope and ride any horse he could catch, though he was expected to release it when the ride was completed to return to its range. Men abroad carried reatas as Mexicans in the jungles of Mexico carry machetes, or as townsmen carry fountain pens. Runaway sailors and trappers from over the mountains were given horses — not the best, however. Not a stable existed in the whole land, and few horses were ever fed. Horses were a part of nature, a part of men themselves. They were the most positive determinants of the California way of life.

The mustangs made other horses wild only because the other horses wanted to run wild. A stockman-farmer of recent times owned a brown "horse mule" — a male — that in his middle age, when about twelve years old, came to be called Reliability. No mule could have been gentler or more tractable. He never kicked, never broke away. He would stand hitched anywhere; he pulled the plow straight across the field, kept steady in the collar when harnessed to a wagon. He seemed to take both the good and the ill of his world with equable cheerfulness.

Then one fall Reliability and a half-dozen other mules were turned into a well-watered, brushy, eight-hundred-acre pasture. Some cattle also ran in this pasture; they were seldom worked and were pretty snaky. In the spring the owner sent two men to bring the mules home. They came back with all but Reliability. After combing the pasture for him, they had sighted him tearing through a thicket in company with a two-year-old pale-red heifer, wilder than a deer. They had spent hours and had utterly spent their horses trying to cut Reliability off from his companion and head him into the little bunch of mules.

In a few days the owner sent two other men, good ropers, back to catch Reliability. One roped him and he broke the rope. He had found freedom, along with Platonic love, and now he had no idea of returning to plow-mule tameness. Finally he was snared and forcibly led home, but he was never again contented with workaday domesticity. For one brief season he had lived wild and free, positively and delightfully; from that time on his memory was fixed. The only tractable slaves are those who have never known and never dreamed of freedom.

The instinct to turn mustang is always showing up in domestic species. One winter while I was spending a few weeks on a ranch in the Davis Mountains, a flock of wild turkeys roosted most of the nights in live oak trees just back of the ranch house. There were a few domestic turkeys at the ranch, and every morning a certain hen among them would go through the ordeal of trying to decide whether to follow the wild turkeys off or stay at home. She would accompany the wild ones a hundred yards or so, halting frequently until she was behind them. Then she would take a few steps homeward, again run towards the wild ones, turn once more towards her indifferent mates, only to reverse her course towards the equally indifferent wild ones, and thus for minutes trot back and forth, seesawing, torn between the instincts for running free and remaining tame according to habit. She never did get beyond sight of the ranch house.

It takes energy to break away — and after energy has failed, enough desire often remains to keep spirit alive. Almost the last Spanish horses I saw, where they had once been so vital and plentiful, were worn-out cow horses sold for a song to be shipped east and resold to share-croppers for two songs. "Never marry yourself to a horse," the practical ranchman said, and in effect he hitched Pegasus, grown stiff-kneed, to a plow.

The Papago Indian reservation — Papagueria, as it is called — encloses two and a half million acres of desert and mountain in southern Arizona against the international boundary line. Before the line was fenced, Papago stock used to drift far down the Altar Valley in Sonora. There were many wild horses, and no better or wilder horsemen ever rode than some of the Papagos.

Noted among them were two brothers named Siliaco and Sandiego. Their story came to me in Tucson, in April, 1951, from their tribesman Juan Xavier. He is a magnificent man in stature, in silence and in reserve, a great mystery in his eyes and in the contour of his face. After E. E. Cummings, poet and painter, came to know him while spending a season in Tucson, he painted a picture for him as a parting present. Juan Xavier wanted to respond with something personal also, something out of himself. He decided to give him a story of his land and people. His wife, formerly Gwyneth Harrington, whom he married while he was aiding her in anthropological work, wrote down the story as he told it for the friendship gift. With oral additions, he let me have a copy to read. He could not allow me to use it, however, without consent from the friend to whom he had presented it. A letter he and his wife wrote finally overtook Mr. Cummings in Rome. Now with his permission as well as that of Juan Xavier, I tell it.

Siliaco and Sandiego lived in the village of Tecolote (which means Owl) near the Sonora line. Sometimes they went down into the mountains and camped by a little lake where many men in the night had heard the wild horses coming in from the desert to drink and had heard strange noises among them. These brothers grew tall, slim and strong, but about the time they came to full manhood, their minds turned in a curious way.

They came to believe that they themselves were horses. Sandiego was married, but he and his brother deserted the village, separating themselves from all other people. They threw away their clothes and ran naked with the wild horses. Now and then people from a distance caught sight of them. A stallion would be seen leading his manada to a waterhole, mares and colts strung out behind him, behind them some wild burros, and then, last of all, Siliaco and Sandiego. They would be running, galloping, trotting like horses, throwing up their heads to sniff the wind, looking about for danger, and then bending over and drinking on all fours like horses. They could not live on grass. They must

[326]

have eaten mesquite beans, cholla buds and the fruit from cholla and other cactus in season, but this diet would not sustain them the year round. Nobody really knew how they lived, but it was believed that the mares gave them milk.

Certainly the wild mares and stallions were not afraid of them, though at sight or smell of any other human beings they fled. Perhaps the wild horses understood by the smell of the naked boys that they had the natures, even the minds, of horses. Sometimes one brother would be with one band of horses and the other with another band, and then again they would come together, shifting about as the wild horses shifted.

The Papagos are a swift running people; their young men are trained to foot-racing. Siliaco and Sandiego grew lither and swifter and more enduring than any others. They kept up with the wild horses wherever they ran.

Once Siliaco was caught and kept in a tamed condition for a little while. This is the way they tell it. Papago riders had gone down into Sonora to help in the Mexican roundups and to bring back any of their own cattle that had drifted to those ranges. While they were down there, a Mexican vaquero riding alone on the desert saw a palo verde tree covered heavily with wild gourd vines. The vines were so dense that he rode nearer to observe them, and as he approached the tree he saw something stir in the shade.

What animal could this be? he thought. Then a naked man with long hair jumped out and went running off at an astonishing speed. The vaquero thought it must be one of the Papagos who lived with the horses. He felt the wish to catch him, and there on the open desert he spurred after him. After a long chase he got within roping distance. He swung his loop and threw it. As the rope tightened around the wild man's middle, he behaved like a wild horse or steer that is roped. He plunged and twisted and tried to free himself, but was jerked down and had to submit.

The vaquero saw that the man was Siliaco. He began gentling him down with quiet talk, and after Siliaco became quiet he told him to come with him to camp for food and tobacco. Siliaco seemed to return in mind to human ways. He said he would come. He got up on the horse behind the vaquero, and thus they rode to camp.

Vaqueros there, both Mexican and Papago, saw them approaching. One Mexican yelled out, "Who is riding there naked behind you?"

The vaquero yelled back, "It is Siliaco."

All had heard about him, this Indian who ran with the wild horses. They gathered about him to see and wonder, but they were quiet and acted gently towards his disturbed mind. They gave him cigarettes and good beans and tortillas, fresh-cooked meat and hot sugared coffee. They gave him shirt and pantaloons to cover his body. As night came on, he sat with the other men around the fire, quiet and warm and fed and clothed, and listened to the talk and singing. His mind seemed again to be that of a man and not of a wild horse.

He stayed there in camp until the roundup was finished. Then he went with his captor and some other vaqueros to the Mexican village of El Plomo. The people in the village treated him kindly and with respect. One night, somebody saw him walking away. Eyes were always on him, for, after all, the people knew that he was not like other men. A man followed him, keeping out of sight, to see what he would do. After Siliaco had walked a good distance into the desert, he stopped and stood for a long while, looking at the stars. He seemed to be listening. Maybe he heard something in the wind like the sound of hoofs. Presently he jerked off his clothes, threw them aside, and ran on into the desert and the darkness. He never came back. Later he was seen again with the wild horses. Then after a time had passed he was not seen. The only evidence of what might have become of him

[328]

were the bones of a man found by a hunter in the mountains of Sonora.

Sandiego had no children when he ran away. Perhaps it was remembrance of his wife that brought him back. Anyway, he came back to the village of Tecolote and to the house and woman he had left. His mind cleared and his ways were steady. He was respected by the people, not for any special power, but because as a normal man he went on leading a good life. He had two sons. One joined the Mormon church and the other became a good cattleman. In his old age they saw that he was well dressed and well fed and were good to him in all ways.

He never spoke of his life with the wild horses, but he would never ride a horse or work one to wagon or plow. He always walked wherever he was going, though he would get into another man's wagon if a ride were offered him. He could travel in a sort of trotting walk all day, sometimes breaking into a run. His swiftness and endurance as a runner lasted into old age. He was proud of this power. If sometimes, lying hidden in stillness far out alone, he watched wild horses trotting like foxes down to water from the mesa, or grazing in alertness, never for a moment easy with the security felt by creatures subject to man, or running until even their dust disappeared, he never followed. He laid out a race course near his village and ran over it with other racers, and he ran over the mountains to his own solitudes until he died at the age of eighty. That was about the time also that the last of the wild horses disappeared from Papagueria.

Well, the wild ones — the coyote duns, the smokies, the blues, the blue roans, the snip-nosed pintos, the flea-bitten grays and the black-skinned whites, the shining blacks and the rusty browns, the red roans, the toasted sorrels and the stockinged bays, the splotched appaloosas and the cream-maned palominos, and all the others in shadings of color as various as the hues that show and fade on the clouds at sunset — they are all gone now, gone as completely as the free grass they vivified. Only through "visionary gleam" can any man ever again run with them, for only in the symbolism of poetry does ghost draw lover in hope-continued pursuit.

Yet a creature need not be seen to give its spirit to a land, to make its existence a part of the earth. The healed-over scratch of a bear's claw on a cottonwood trunk may make a valley between mountains memorable; the ruins of a rock chimney may evoke a pioneer woman who alone battled drouth and barbarism to rear four clean, strong sons. Certain place names over the West keep calling back what is gone: Mustang Bayou, Mustang Prairie, Mustang Island, Pinto Canyon, Horse Pen Bayou, Yegua Creek and Horsehead Crossing in Texas; Wild Horse Draw and Wild Horse Lake in western Kansas; Wild Horse Mountain, Red Horse Creek and Horse Pen Creek in Oklahoma; Wild Horse Butte and Wild Horse Hill in Nebraska; Pony Hills and Wild Horse Creek — one of scores by that name over the land — in South Dakota; Wild Horse Mesa, Mustang Mountains, Wild Horse Canyon, in Arizona, and White Horse Spring, where a never-roped mare drank alone with a succession of white colts; Caballo Mountains in New Mexico and Potrillo Mountain, too, where some *mesteñero* roped a colt; Cañon de las Yeguas in California and Mare Island, in old days Isla de la Yegua, now a place of U. S. Navy shipyards, where a solitary wild mare ran with a herd of elk; Wild Horse town and White Horse Plains in Colorado; Spotted Horse Creek in Wyoming; Wild Horse Diggings in Montana; Broomtail Flat in Oregon; Horse Plains in Idaho; White Horse Plains in Alberta. The wild horses have left a kind of song.

Gazing in solitude over foothills, desert, prairie or brushed plain, one may through the transporting power of imagination see wild horses tossing their heads where no track of their kind has been printed for many decades. But it will not be gentle horses ranging there, no matter how spirited, that raise the picture of the vanished. The gentle ones never emanate that something which was the essence of the wild ones, just as no girl after she has lost her innocence ever looks the same in her eyes.

I see them running, running, running
From the Spanish caballadas to be free,
From the mustanger's rope and rifle, to keep free,
Over seas of pristine grass, like fire-dancers on a mountain,
Like lightning playing against the unapproachable horizon.

I see them standing, standing, standing,
Sentinels of alertness in eye and nostril,
Every toss of maned neck a Grecian grace,
Every high snort bugling out the pride of the free.

I see them vanishing, vanishing, vanished,
The seas of grass shriveled to pens of barb-wired property,
The wind-racers and wind-drinkers bred into property also.

But winds still blow free and grass still greens,
And the core of that something which men live on believing
Is always freedom.

So sometimes yet, in the realities of silence and solitude,
For a few people unhampered a while by things,
The mustangs walk out with dawn, stand high, then
Sweep away, wild with sheer life, and free, free, free —
Free of all confines of time and flesh.

NOTES

1 · THE PROGENITOR OF THE MUSTANG

[1] For a succinct treatment of the prehistoric horse, "the little Eohippus," followed by Mesohippus and on to Pliohippus, see *The Ascent of Equus*, by Chester Stock and Hildegarde Howard, Los Angeles County Museum Science Series No. 8, Los Angeles, 1944. G. G. Simpson's *Horses*, N. Y., 1951, has everything on the subject.

[2] Tozzer, Basil, *The Horse in History*, London, 1908, 107, 149, 178. Wentworth, Lady, *Thoroughbred Racing Stock and Its Ancestors*, London, 1938, 167, 179–205 *passim*.

[3] Full treatment of island raising of horses is by John J. Johnson, "The Introduction of the Horse into the Western Hemisphere," *The Hispanic Historical Review*, XXIII (Nov., 1943), 587–610.

[4] Aiton, Arthur Scott, *Antonio de Mendoza, First Viceroy of New Spain*, Durham, North Carolina, 1927, 109. Bancroft, H. H., *History of Mexico*, San Francisco, 1887, III, 616.

[5] The subject of transportation is carefully reviewed, with full documentation, by John J. Johnson, as cited in Note 3 preceding 597–598.

[6] Cavendishe, William, Duke of Newcastle, *A New Method . . . to Dress Horses*, London, 1667, 49–51, 85.

[7] Johnson, John James, "The Spanish Horse in Peru before 1550," pages 19–37 in *Greater America: Essays in Honor of Herbert Eugene Bolton*, University of California Press, Berkeley and Los Angeles, 1945, 34. Wilhelm, Paul, Duke of Wuerttemberg, *Journey to North America, 1822–1824*, in *South Dakota Historical Collections*, XIX (1938), 378–379. See also Artemio de Valle-Arizpe, *Cuadros de México*, Mexico, D. F., 1943, 112–115.

[8] *George Rogers Clark Papers, 1771–1781*, Collections of the Illinois State Historical Library, Springfield, 1912, VIII, 75–76, 77–78, 88–89, 303–304.

[9] For a panegyric (climactic in verbosity) on Andalusian horses, see Pedro Fernandez de Andrada, *De la Naturaleza del Cavallo*, Seville, Spain, 1580, leaves 49–52. Many books go into the ancestry of the Spanish horse. H. F. Osborn, *Origin and History of the Horse*, New York, 1905, and F. B. Loomis, *The Evolution of the Horse*, Boston, 1926, are adequate.

[10] Tweedie, Major-General W., *The Arabian Horse, His Country and People*, Edinburgh and London, 1894, 220.

[11] Chard, Thornton, translator and editor of "The Criollo Horse of South America," by Emilio Solanet, *Journal of Heredity*, XXI (Nov., 1930), 468–471. Berenger, Richard, *The History and Art of Horsemanship*, London, 1771, I, 125–127. Hayes, Captain M. Horace, *Points of the Horse* (1903), London, 1922, 414. Guerrero, Carlos, "El Caballo Criollo," *Anales de la Asociación Criadores de Criollo*, Buenos Aires, Nov., 1938, 25.

[12] Jaquet, Jean, quoted by Lady Wentworth, *Thoroughbred Racing Stock and Its Ancestors*, London, 1938, 240. Solanet, Emilio, as cited in Note 11, 458.

[13] Solanet, as in Note 11, 466.

[14] Graham, R. B. Cunninghame, *Hernando de Soto*, London, 1912, 257–266.

[15] Brown, William Robinson, *The Horse of the Desert*, n.p., 1936, 76, quoted from Daumas.

[16] Blunt, Wilfrid Scawen, "The Origin of the Arabian Horse," *The New Review*, London, XV (July, 1896), 46–61; "The Genealogy of the Thoroughbred Horse," *The Nineteenth Century and After*, London, LIX (Jan., 1906), 58–71; also his chapter on Arabian Horses in *Bedouin Tribes of the Euphrates*, by Lady Anne Blunt, London, 1879, II, 243–276. Wentworth, Lady, *The Authentic Arabian Horse and His Descendants*, London, 1945, 83–85, 162–163, 183, 262–263. Professor Ridgeway's theories on a Libyan ancestor of the Arabian have been pretty much demolished. The whole matter of the wild Arabian horse is discussed by R. Lydekker in *The Horse and Its Relatives*, London, 1912, Chap. V.

[1] Valle-Arizpe, Artemio de, *Cuadros de México*, Mexico, D. F., 1943, 66, 68.

[2] *Diccionario Enciclopédico Hispano-Americano*, in treatment of the Spanish horse.

[3] Bolton, Herbert E., *Athanase de Mézières and the Louisiana-Texas Frontier, 1768–1780*, Cleveland, Ohio, 1914, II, 255–256.

[4] Azara, Félix de, *Viajes por la América Meridional* (1809), Madrid, Spain, 1923, I, 291–293. Lienrich, Heinrich, *A Pioneer at Sutter's Fort* (translated by Marguerite E. Wilbur), Los Angeles, California, 1941, 81.

[5] Aiton, Arthur Scott, *Antonio de Mendoza, First Viceroy of New Spain*, Durham, North Carolina, 1927, 48, 109, 172–173. Bancroft, H. H., *History of Mexico*, San Francisco, 1883–1888, II, 135 ff.

[6] Denhardt, Robert Moorman, "Spanish Horses and the New World," *The Historian*, University of New Mexico, Albuquerque, I (1938), 5–23; reprint in pamphlet form, 15–21.

[7] The Espejo Narrative in Herbert E. Bolton's *Spanish Exploration in the Southwest*, New York, 1916, 170, 172, 179, 185.

[8] Alexander, Hartley B., "The Horse in American Indian Culture," in *So Live the Works of Men* (anniversary volume honoring Edgar Lee Hewett), edited by Donald D. Brand and Fred E. Harvey, University of New Mexico Press, Albuquerque, 1939, 67. Castañeda, who tells the incident, does not give this interpretation.

[9] Bolton, Herbert E., *Coronado*, New York, 1949, 196, 206–207.

[10] Quoted, with permission from publisher and with improvements on translation, from Ignaz Pfefferkorn's *Sonora: A Description of the Province* (Germany, 1795–1796), translated and annotated by Theodore E. Treutlein, University of New Mexico Press, Albuquerque, 1949, 145, 147.

[11] Darwin, Charles, *The Voyage of the Beagle*, London edition of 1890, 66, 69. Falkner, Thomas, *A Description of Patagonia and the Adjoining Parts of South America* (1774), edited by Arthur E. S. Neumann, Chicago, 1935, 69.

[12] The pioneer scholar in the field was Clark Wissler, "The Influence of the Horse in the Development of Plains Culture," *American*

Anthropologist, Vol. 16 (New Series), January–March, 1914, 1–25; reprinted in pamphlet form, 25 pages. Clark Wissler makes basic assumptions and argues some points from negative evidence.

His work was followed a quarter century later by two studies by Francis Haines in the *American Anthropologist:* "Where Did the Plains Indians Get Their Horses?" Vol. 40 (1938), 112–117, and "The Northward Spread of Horses among the Plains Indians," 429–437. Dr. Haines supplemented the latter article with "Nez Percé and Shoshoni Influence on Northwest History," in *Greater America: Essays in Honor of Herbert Eugene Bolton*, University of California Press, Berkeley and Los Angeles, 1945, 379–384.

More illuminating than any preceding studies and better evidenced, are two by D. E. Worcester: "The Spread of the Spanish Horses in the Southwest," *New Mexico Historical Review*, XIX (July, 1944), 225–232; "Spanish Horses Among the Plains Tribes," *Pacific Historical Review*, XIV (Dec., 1945), 409–417.

Evidently little known as yet to scholars of the United States, but much more comprehensive and thoughtful, and more fully annotated than any other study on the subject, is F. G. Roe's "From Dogs to Horses among the Western Indian Tribes," in *Transactions* of the Royal Society of Canada, Ottawa, 1939, Third Series, Section II, Vol. XXXIII, 209–275 — an epic piece of scholarship. F. G. Roe knows what horses, dogs and human beings (Indians especially) are, as well as printed sources.

Excellent also is "The Horse in American Indian Culture," by Hartley B. Alexander, as cited in Note 8, preceding.

The Horse of the Americas, by Robert Moorman Denhardt, University of Oklahoma Press, Norman, 1947, sketches the field. More specific and annotated is Denhardt's "Spanish Horses and the New World," cited in Note 6.

Thornton Chard's "Did First Spanish Horses Leave Progeny?" in *American Anthropologist*, January–March, Vol. 42 (1940), is a scholarly treatment of the Spanish horses landed in Florida and Georgia in the 16th century. Conclusively, they left no progeny.

Walker D. Wyman, *The Wild Horses of the West*, Caldwell, Idaho, 1945, reviews the evidence in Chapter III ("The Indian Gets the Horse"). A map on the end papers of the book gives the years in which Indians of various regions were first seen with horses.

[13] Bishop, Morris, *The Odyssey of Cabeza de Vaca*, New York, 1933, 33–53.

[14] Sources for information on De Soto's expedition and accompanying horses are the narratives of Biedma, who, as the King's factor, wrote a succinct report; a much more detailed narrative by Ranjel, De Soto's unadmiring secretary; a relation in Portuguese by one of the adventurers known only as the Gentleman of Elvas; and, finally, the very long, often fabricated but richly detailed and richly human chronicle by Garcilaso de la Vega, called the Inca, who was not with the expedition but who preserved the memories of one of its most remarkable members.

The first three narratives mentioned have been variously published, but nowhere more neatly than in the two volumes entitled *Narratives of the Career of Hernando de Soto*, edited by Edward Gaylord Bourne, New York, 1922. *The Florida of the Inca*, by Garcilaso de la Vega, translated and edited by John and Jeannette Varner, was published in its entirety in the English language for the first time by the University of Texas Press, Austin, 1951. I have drawn extensively from it.

Final Report of the United States De Soto Expedition Commission, House Doc. No. 71, 76th Congress, 1st Session, Washington, D. C., 1939, contains a chapter on "Domestic Animals Brought to North America by De Soto" that summarizes and compares numbers of horses as given by the various chroniclers.

[15] Aiton, as cited in starred footnote on page 24, gives Muster Roll figures. Castañeda, *The Journey of Coronado*, translated by Winship, New York, 1904, mentions the mare, 114; Jaramillo, *ibid.*, 239, says "horse."

[16] Facts on Coronado's horses are scattered through the narratives by Castañeda and others, translated and edited by George Parker Winship, *The Journey of Coronado*, New York, 1904, and through Herbert E. Bolton's *Coronado* (which makes use of additional materials), New York, 1949. Bolton evidently utilized all the material available on horses. The half-baked index to his book does not list horses.

[17] Villagrá, Gaspar Pérez de, *History of New Mexico*, translated by Gilberto Espinosa, Los Angeles, California, 1933, 99.

[18] Hammond, George P., *Don Juan de Oñate and the Founding of New Mexico*, Albuquerque, 1927, 87. Villagrá as cited above.

[19] Bolton, as cited in Note 7 *ante*, 199–280. Benavides, Fray Alonso de, *Memorial*, 1630, translated by Mrs. Edward E. Ayer, Chicago, 1916, 56.

[20] The facts for this and the preceding paragraph are taken largely from Worcester and Wissler, cited in Note 12. Characterization of the Indians of northern Mexico is by Vito Alessio Robles, *Coahuila y Texas en la Época Colonial*, Mexico, D. F., 1938, 171–172.

[21] Thomas, A. B., *The Plains Indians and New Mexico, 1751–1758*, University of New Mexico Press, Albuquerque, 1940, 188–189. Worcester as cited in Note 12, 227.

[22] Thomas, Alfred Bernaby, *Teodoro de Croix*, University of Oklahoma Press, Norman, 1941, 55–57.

[23] Worcester, as cited, 228.

[24] *Joutel's Journal of La Salle's Last Voyage, 1684–1687*, Albany, New York, 1906, 113–114, 123–124, 126–127, 131, 139–152, 164.

[25] Kellogg, Louise Phelps, editor, *Early Narratives of the Northwest, 1634–1699*, New York, 1917, 315–320.

[26] Bolton, as cited in Note 7 *ante*, 375.

[27] The Du Tisné reports are incorporated in P. Margry, editor, *Mémoires et documents pour servir à l'histoire des origines françaises des pays d'outre-mer*, in six volumes, Paris, 1879, and are cited by page by both Worcester and Haines, Note 12. For Stephen H. Long's report, see *Account of an Expedition from Pittsburgh to the Rocky Mountains Performed in the Years 1819 and '20*, compiled by Edwin James, Philadelphia, 1823, I, 445–446.

[28] The tradition that Frank Shively of the Crow Agency in Montana gave me, March 16, 1940, is entirely different from that given to some green hand with the Montana Writers' Project, a copy of the report of which I have. The 1831 estimate on Crow horses is from *Glimpses of the Past*, Missouri Historical Society, St. Louis, 1942, 59. The number, 10,000, was corroborated by Maximilian, Prince of Wied, in 1833. See Thwaites, *Early Western Travels*, Cleveland, Ohio, 1904–1907, XXII, 351–352.

[29] Le Page du Pratz, *The History of Louisiana*, London, 1763, I, 109–110, 121–125.

[30] Vérendrye journals and comments in *South Dakota Historical Collections*, State Historical Society of South Dakota, Pierre, VII (1914), 204, 340, 346, 351.

[31] Nobody has worked so minutely with the tangle of dates and geography as F. G. Roe, cited in Note 12. See pages 232–257 of his treatise. An unannotated article by Paul Albert in *The Western Horseman*, VI (March–April, 1941), 28 ff., gives information, which I have seen elsewhere, on the Burnt Woods.

[32] Coues, Elliott, editor, *The Manuscript Journals of Alexander Henry and David Thompson*, New York, 1897, II, 626.

[33] For details and citations, see Roe, cited in Note 12, 256.

III · INDIAN HORSES AND HORSEMANSHIP

[1] Clark Wissler as cited in Note 12, Chap. II, remains the basic study of this subject. More thorough and wider in research than this essay is one yet (1952) unpublished, "The Influence of the Horse upon the 'Buffalo' Indians of the Plains," by Frank Gilbert Roe of Cadboro Bay, Victoria, British Columbia, who has generously allowed me to read it — an extension of his "From Dogs to Horses among the Western Indian Tribes," as cited in Note 12, Chap. II. Succinct summaries of the effect of the horse on Indian life are to be found in Stanley Vestal's *New Sources of Indian History, 1850–1891*, University of Oklahoma Press, Norman, 1934, 192–193, and James Mooney's *Calendar History of the Kiowa Indians, Seventeenth Annual Report of the Bureau of American Ethnology*, Washington, 1898, Part I, 161.

[2] Wharton, Clarence, *Satanta: The Great Chief of the Kiowas*, Dallas, Texas, 1935, 102–108. Richardson, Rupert N., *The Comanche Barrier*, Glendale, California, 1933, 301. Variance in description by eyewitnesses of Indian riding at Medicine Lodge is a commentary on the elusiveness of truth.

[3] Dixon, Billy, *Life and Adventures* (partly written by Olive K. Dixon and somewhat emended by me), Guthrie, Oklahoma, 1914, 203–205.

[4] Grinnell, George Bird, *The Cheyenne Indians: Their History and Ways of Life*, Yale University Press, New Haven, Conn., 1923, II, 17. James, General Thomas, *Three Years among the Indians and Mexicans*, St. Louis, 1906 (reprint of 1846 edition), 217–218. Barrett, S. M., *Geronimo's Story of His Life*, New York, 1906, 122–123, 169.

[5] Harris, Edward, *Up the Missouri with Audubon*, edited by John Francis McDermott, University of Oklahoma Press, Norman, 1951, 35–36, 99–100, 149.

[6] *Original Journals of the Lewis and Clark Expedition*, edited by Reuben Gold Thwaites, New York, 1905, V, 289–290.

[7] Marcy, Randolph B., *Exploration of the Red River of Louisiana*, Washington, D. C., 1854, 95. *The West of Alfred Jacob Miller*, edited by Marvin C. Ross, University of Oklahoma Press, Norman, 1951, plates 90, 96, 137.

[8] Wilson, Gilbert L., *The Horse and Dog in Hidatsa Culture*, Anthropological Papers of the American Museum of Natural History, New York, 1924, Vol. XV, Part II, 127–195. This is a very revealing study of Hidatsa horses and their relationship to the people.

[9] Henry, Alexander, *Travels and Adventures* (in the 1770's), edited by Milo Milton Quaife, Chicago, 1921, 280, 300.

[10] Ross, Alexander, *The Fur Hunters of the Far West* (London, 1855), reprint of Vol. I by the Lakeside Press, Chicago, 1924, 252. (I have rearranged his sentences.)

[11] Pond, Peter, *Journal of, 1740–45*, in *Collections* of the State Historical Society of Wisconsin, XVIII, 353.

[12] This detail and the one in the preceding paragraph concerning the blowing of leaves up a horse's nostrils are from an unpublished manuscript by George Bird Grinnell, "The Indian's War Pony," in the Southwest Museum, Los Angeles, California. A deal of the material, however, was incorporated in Grinnell's noble work cited in Note 4 *ante*, II, 139. "Painted Ponies," by Shayka Bear-Step, in *Western Horseman*, Colorado Springs, Colorado, XVI (December, 1951), 10–11, 26–28, interprets and illustrates symbols painted on horses.

[13] Coues, Elliott, *Manuscript Journals of Alexander Henry and David Thompson*, New York, 1897, I, 47. *Original Journals of the Lewis and Clark Expedition*, edited by Thwaites, as cited in Note 6, III, 48; IV, 322, 342. Leigh, William R., *The Western Pony*, New York, 1932, 87.

[14] Marcy, as cited in Note 7 preceding, 96–97; Miller, as cited in same note, 62.

[15] The Lewis and Clark observations have been culled from Thwaites, as cited in Note 6, I, 176, 219, 244, 258–259; II, 347–348, 372; III, 31–32, 47–48, 60; IV, 73–74, 322–323, 342, 363; V, 29–36, 58–59, 100, 289–290; VII, 141.

[16] M'Gillivray, Duncan, *Journal . . . at Fort George on the Saskatchewan, 1794-1795*, Toronto, 1929, 28-29.

[17] Francis Haines, scholar, is the main authority on the Nez Percé Indians and their horses. See his *Red Eagles of the North*, Portland, Oregon, 1939, 24, 124-130, 196; also articles in the *Western Horseman*, October, 1936, January to June, 1937. "Famed Nez Percé Horse," in *River of No Return*, by Robert G. Bailey, Lewiston, Idaho, 1947, 325-334.

In addition to the Lewis and Clark *Journals*, the following primary sources afford evidence on the Nez Percé horses: Washington Irving, *The Adventures of Captain Bonneville*, 1837, Chapter XII; Thomas J. Farnham, *Travels in the Great Western Prairies* (1843) in Thwaites, *Early Western Travels*, XXVIII, 343-344; Joel Palmer, *Journal of Travels over the Rocky Mountains* (1847) in Thwaites, XXX, 238; Gabriel Franchère, *Narrative of a Voyage to the Northwest Coast of America* (1814), in Thwaites, VI, 340-341; John Keast Lord, *The Naturalist in Vancouver Island and British Columbia*, London, 1866, II, 86-88, 105-106.

[18] Coues, as cited in Note 13 preceding, I, 377.

[19] Coues, Elliott, editor, *The Expeditions of Zebulon Montgomery Pike*, New York, 1895, II, 533, 542.

[20] Murray, Charles Augustus, *Travels in North America, 1834-1836*, New York, 1839, I, 243-245.

[21] *American Turf Register and Sporting Magazine*, Baltimore, 1833, 501-503.

[22] George Catlin's pictures illustrate various editions of his *Letters and Notes on . . . North American Indians . . . 1832-1839*. Alfred Jacob Miller, belatedly discovered, is magnificently represented in Bernard De Voto's *Across the Wide Missouri*, Boston, 1947, and in *The West of Alfred Jacob Miller*, as cited in Note 7. Scores of sketches and finished pictures by Rudolph Friederich Kurz are reproduced in his *Journal (1846-1852)*, Bureau of American Ethnology, Washington, D. C., 1937.

[23] Wilhelm, Paul, Duke of Wuerttemberg, *Journey to North America, 1822-1824*, in *South Dakota Historical Collections*, State Historical Society of South Dakota, Pierre, XIX (1938), 378-379.

[24] Dodge, Richard Irving, *The Plains of the Great West and Their Inhabitants* (published in England under title of *The Hunting Grounds of the Great West*), New York, 1877, 424-426.

[25] Dodge, R. I., *Our Wild Indians*, Hartford, Conn., 1883, 341–342.

[26] Joes, Robert Leslie, "The Old French-Canadian Horse: Its History in Canada and the United States," *The Canadian Historical Review*, XXVIII (June, 1947), 125–155. Greenlay, G. L., "The Buffalo Runners," *The Western Horseman*, V (May–June, 1940), 11 ff.

IV · THE COMANCHE MOON

[1] Bolton, Herbert E., *Athanase de Mézières and the Louisiana-Texas Frontier, 1768–1780*, Cleveland, Ohio, 1914, I, 218–219.

[2] Anza's diary, quoted in *Pichardo's Treatise on the Limits of Louisiana and Texas*, edited by Charles Wilson Hackett, University of Texas Press, Austin, 1934, II, 259. Coues, Elliott, editor, *The Expeditions of Zebulon Montgomery Pike*, New York, 1895, II, 537. Thomas, A. B., *The Plains Indians and New Mexico, 1751–1778*, University of New Mexico Press, Albuquerque, 1940, 44, 169–189; see *Comanches* in Index.

[3] Tixier, Victor, *Travels* [1839–1840] *on the Osage Prairies* (originally printed in 1844), edited by John Francis McDermott, University of Oklahoma Press, Norman, 1940, 268.

[4] As cited in Note 1 above, II, 175.

[5] Hackett, as cited in Note 2 above, I, 247; III, 411, and *passim*.

[6] For comprehension of the extent of tribal trading in Spanish horses and of Spanish jealousy of the French, there is no better source than Hackett's monumental *Pichardo*, cited in Note 2 *ante*. Each of the three volumes is carefully indexed and, by consulting *Horses*, an inquirer may go far in the subject; Vol. III, 348–411, tells most of the story. The Bexar Archives, in the University of Texas Library, are replete with information on the subject. See also Mattie Austin Hatcher, *The Opening of Texas to Foreign Settlement, 1801–1821*, University of Texas Bulletin, 1927, 53–54, 115, 141–142, 174, 303–305; *The Austin Papers*, edited by Eugene C. Barker, Vol. II, Part I, 507–510.

[7] Bolton, as cited in Note 1, I, 76–77, 104, 269–270, 334; II, 32–46.

[8] Pagés, Monsieur de, *Travels round the World in 1767 . . . 1771*, London, 1791, I, 88–89.

[9] Menchaca, Antonio, *Memoirs*, published by the Yanaguana Society, San Antonio, Texas, 1937, 14, 19–20.

[10] Richardson, Rupert N., *The Comanche Barrier*, Glendale, California, 1933, 186 (sources cited).

[11] Richardson, as cited in note preceding, 193–210. U. S. Military maps of the Comanche trails are reproduced, 194–195.

[12] Williams, O. W., "Baja el Sol," undated leaflet, printed at Fort Stockton, Texas.

[13] Ruxton, George F., *Adventures in Mexico and the Rocky Mountains*, London, 1847, 83, 101–102.

[14] Webb, James Josiah, *Adventures in the Santa Fe Trade 1844–1847*, edited by Ralph P. Bieber, Glendale, California, 1931, 230–232. Bartlett, John R., *Personal Narrative*, New York, 1856, II, 467–468.

[15] Gregg, Josiah, *Commerce of the Prairies*, New York, 1844, II, 54, 314. Richardson, as cited in Note 10 preceding, 19, 87, 287.

[16] Emory, Lieut. Col. W. H., *Notes of a Military Reconnaissance from . . . Missouri to San Diego*, Ex. Doc. No. 41, 30th Congress, 1st Session, Washington, D. C., 1848, 586. Griffin, John S., *A Doctor Comes to California* (diary), California Historical Society, San Francisco, 1943, 27.

[17] James, General Thomas, *Three Years Among the Indians and Mexicans* (1846), St. Louis, 1916, 202, 225. Sibley, Dr. John, "Report from Natchitoches in 1807," *Indian Notes and Monographs*, Museum of the American Indian, Heye Foundation, New York, 1922, 41, 77–78. *Niles Register*, XLVII (Oct. 4, 1834), quoted by Grant Foreman in *Pioneer Days in the Early Southwest*, Cleveland, Ohio, 1926, 137n. Catlin, George, *Letters and Notes on the Manners, Customs and Condition of the North American Indians*, London, 1841, II, 62. Marcy, R. B., *Exploration of the Red River of Louisiana, 1852*, Washington, D. C., 1854, 95–97. Labadi report in *Report of the Secretary of Interior*, 1867, Part II, 214–215.

[18] James, as cited in preceding note, 229–235. Catlin, as cited, II, 62. Roemer, Ferdinand, *Texas*, translated by Oswald Mueller, San Antonio, Texas, 1935, 268–270.

V · INDIAN HORSE-STEALING AND MUSTANGING

[1] Phinney, Mary Allen, *Allen-Isham Genealogy: Jirah Isham Allen, Montana Pioneer*, etc., Rutland, Vermont, about 1929, 148–150.

[2] Stuart, Granville, *Forty Years on the Frontier*, Cleveland, Ohio, 1925, I, 134.

[3] Grinnell, as cited in Note 4, Chap. III *ante*, I, 32.

[4] These accounts of Apache cunning are taken from J. Ross Browne, *Adventures in the Apache Country*, New York, 1869, 272–273.

[5] Stuart, Granville, as cited in Note 2, I, 135.

[6] Grinnell, George Bird, *The Fighting Cheyennes*, New York, 1915, 10–13, 33–39, 65.

[7] Peter Skene Ogden, "Journal," *Quarterly* of the Oregon Historical Society, XI (1910), 367.

[8] Foreman, Grant, *Indians and Pioneers*, Yale University Press, New Haven, Conn., 1930, 150 n. Lewis and Clark noted recurrently some abandoned horse.

[9] Ogden, as cited in Note 7 preceding, 357.

[10] Fowler, Jacob, *The Journal of Jacob Fowler*, edited by Elliott Coues, New York, 1898, 50–92.

[11] *The Life and Adventures of James P. Beckwourth*, "written from his own dictation" by T. D. Bonner (New York, 1856), edited by Bernard De Voto, New York, 1931, 234–256. Robert H. Lowie estimates the number of Crow horses at between 9000 and 10,000: *The Crow Indians*, New York, 1935, xiv.

[12] Thwaites, editor, *Original Journals of the Lewis and Clark Expedition*, New York, 1905, III, 32. Coues, Elliott, *The Manuscript Journals of Alexander Henry and David Thompson*, New York, 1897, II, 708. Ferris, W. A., *Life in the Rocky Mountains*, Denver, Colorado, 1940, 251. Mallery, Garrick, "Picture Writing of the American Indians," in *Tenth Annual Report of the Bureau of Ethnology* (1888–1889), Washington, D. C., 1893, 656–658.

[13] Grinnell, as cited in Note 4, Chapter III *ante*, I, 291–295; II, 3. Michaux, André, *Travels into Kentucky, 1793–1796* (London, 1805), in Thwaites, *Early Western Travels*, III, 245.

[14] Irving, Washington, *A Tour on the Prairies*, Chapters XIX, XX, XXV. Ellsworth, Henry Leavitt, *Washington Irving on the Prairie* (journal of 1832 edited by Stanley T. Williams and Barbara D. Simison), New York, 1937, 84–85, 109–111. Tixier, Victor, *Travels on the Osage Prairies* (1839–1840), edited by John Francis McDermott, University of Oklahoma Press, Norman, 1940, 244–246. Catlin, George, *Letters and Notes on . . . North American Indians*, London, 1841, I, 23, 142–143.

[15] Holley, Mary Austin, *Texas* (1836), Austin, Texas, 1935, 96–98.

[16] Grinnell and Tixier as cited in Notes 13 and 14. Catlin as in Note 14, II, 57–60. Edwin James, *Account of S. H. Long's Expedition, 1819–1820* (London, 1823), in Thwaites, *Early Western Travels*, XVI, 272–273.

[17] Coues, as in Note 12 preceding, II, 708. Grinnell as in Note 13. Ellsworth, as in Note 14, 135.

[18] James, General Thomas, *Three Years among the Indians and Mexicans*, St. Louis, 1916, 213–215.

For other accounts of roundups by Indians see James Pike, *The Scout and Ranger* (1865), edited by C. L. Cannon, Princeton University Press, Princeton, New Jersey, 1932, 96–97; Tixier as cited in Note 14.

[19] Catlin, as cited in Note 16. Möllhausen, Baldwin, *Diary of a Journey from the Mississippi to the Coasts of the Pacific* (1853), London, 1858, I, 187.

[20] Catlin, Grinnell, Tixier as cited *ante*.

[21] Irving, John Treat, *Indian Sketches Taken During a U. S. Expedition to Make Treaties with the Pawnee and Other Tribes in 1833*, New York, 1888, 190–191.

[22] Murray, Charles Augustus, *Travels in North America, 1834–1836*, New York, 1839, I, 279–280.

[23] Long Lance, Chief Buffalo Child, *Long Lance*, New York, 1928, 202–204. Dawson, George B., *The Indian Blanket Act* (pamphlet), Oakland, California, 1950.

[24] Catlin, as cited in Note 14, II, 89–91.

[25] Scott, Hugh Lenox, *Some Memoirs of a Soldier*, New York, 1928, 38–39. Letter and manuscript on *The Land of the Dacotahs*, from Wallis Huidekoper, a highly civilized range man of Big Timber, Montana. Crawford, Lewis F., *Ranching Days in Dakota*, Baltimore, Maryland, 1950, 23.

VI · MESTEÑAS

[1] For history of the Mesta, see Klein, Julius, *The Mesta*, Harvard University Press, Cambridge, Mass., 1920, particularly pages 8–15, 55, 276.

[2] Tixier, Victor, *Travels on the Osage Prairies*, edited by John Francis McDermott, Norman, Okla., 1940, 244–246.

³ Quoted by Artemio de Valle-Arizpe in a meaty chapter, "El Caballo en América," in *Cuadros de México*, Mexico, D. F., 1943, 47.

⁴ Hackett, Charles Wilson, *Pichardo's Treatise on the Limits of Louisiana and Texas*, University of Texas Press, Austin, 1941, III, 459. Morfi, Fray Juan Augustín de, *Viaje de Indios y Diario del Nuevo México* (1777), edited by Vito Alessio Robles, Mexico, D. F., 1935, 343.

⁵ Dusenberry, William, "Constitutions of Early and Modern Stock Growers' Associations," *Southwestern Historical Quarterly*, Austin, Texas, LIII (Jan., 1950), 255–275.

⁶ Explanation of the *mesteña-mostrenca* laws, together with frontier protests against them and official protests against violations, is found in the Laredo Archives, stored in the Webb County Court House at Laredo, Texas, under dates of March 11, 1783, June 10, 1788, Dec. 15, 1791, Nov. 22, 1836, Nov. 28, 1836, together with certain undated documents. No calendar has been made of these valuable archives. To Mr. Seb. S. Wilcox, official Reporter of the 49th Judicial District of Texas and unofficial custodian of the archives, I am indebted for information contained therein.

⁷ The Bexar (San Antonio de Bexar) Archives in the Library of the University of Texas are replete with references to the Mustang Fund. See, for instance, October 1–November 14, 1807; July 22 and Aug. 29, 1808.

⁸ *Gammel's Laws of Texas*, I, 78 (law of Coahuila and Texas, 1827); III, 986–987 (re-enactment by Texas legislature of law of 1827); III, 1476–1477, IV, 261–262, 1016 (modifications of law pertaining to territory between San Antonio River and Rio Grande). Bates, Ed. F., *History and Reminiscences of Denton County*, Denton, Texas, 1918, 93–94.

⁹ Hackett, Charles W., *Historical Documents relating to New Mexico*, etc., Washington, D. C., 1923, I, 361–363.

¹⁰ "Letter of Father Massanet and Itineraries of the De León Expeditions of 1689 and 1690," in Herbert E. Bolton's *Spanish Exploration in the Southwest*, New York, 1916, 353–423 (specifically, 360, 367, 369, 383, 393, 396–397, 408).

¹¹ "The Expedition of Don Domingo de Terán de los Ríos into Texas," translated by Mattie Austin Hatcher, *Preliminary Studies of the Texas Catholic Historical Society*, Austin, II (Jan., 1932), 12, 15.

¹² Testimony of the Frenchmen St. Denis and Jalot, 1715, in *Docu-*

mentos para la historia eclesiástica y civil de la Provincia de Texas,
Tomo XXVII, Libro I, 123–124 (338–339 of renumbered pages),
Archives of University of Texas Library.

[13] Bexar Archives for June, 1807. Robles, Vito Alessio, *Coahuila y
Texas en la Época Colonial,* Mexico, D. F., 1938, 607–608, 612.

[14] For founding of San Antonio, see Hoffmann, Fritz Leo, *Diary of
the Alarcón Expedition,* Los Angeles, California, 1935, 43. For stampede, Bexar Archives (Library of University of Texas), Aug. 11,
1806.

[15] Darwin, Charles, *The Voyage of the Beagle,* London edition of
1890, 104.

[16] Castañeda, Carlos E., *Our Catholic Heritage in Texas,* Austin,
1938, III, 130–196 *passim.* G. C. Robinson cites the judge's report in
Mustangs and Cow Horses, edited by Dobie, Boatright and Ransom,
Texas Folklore Society, Austin, 1940, 4.

[17] Morfi, as cited in Note 4 preceding, 303, 334–345, 369.

[18] The two most interesting reporters were Luis Berlandier and
Rafael Chovel, naturalists. Their journals are published in *Diario de
Viage de la Comisión de Limites . . . ,* Mexico, 1850. The diary kept
by José María Sánchez was translated by Carlos E. Castañeda, *Southwestern Historical Quarterly,* XXIX (1926), 249–288.

[19] Grant, U. S., *Personal Memoirs,* New York, 1885, I, 86–87.

[20] McClintock, William A., "Journal of a Trip through Texas and
Northern Mexico in 1846–1847," *Southwestern Historical Quarterly,*
XXXIV (1931), 232–233. See also description (1834) by Benjamin
Lundy, *The Life, Travels and Opinions of,* Philadelphia, 1847, 99.

[21] Dwyer, Thomas A., "Horse and Mule-Raising in Western
Texas," in *A Brief Description of Western Texas,* etc., San Antonio,
Texas, 1872, 43–44.

[22] Duval, John C., *Early Times in Texas* (1867), Austin, Texas,
1892, 27; *The Young Explorers,* Austin, 1892, 112–113; *The Adventures of Big-Foot Wallace,* Macon, Georgia, 1870, 293–294.

[23] Bartlett, John Russell, *Personal Narrative of Explorations and
Incidents,* New York, 1854, II, 522–524.

[24] Falkner, Thomas, *A Description of Patagonia and the Adjoining
Parts of South America* (1774), edited by Arthur E. S. Neumann,
Chicago, 1935, 39. Azara, Félix de, as quoted by R. B. Cunninghame
Graham, *The Horses of the Conquest,* London, 1930, 115, and in
"Del Caballo," *Anales de la Asociación Criadores de Caballo* (from

manuscript in Archivos de Indias), Buenos Aires, Dec., 1930, 47. *Argentine Republic: Agricultural and Pastoral Census of the Nation*, Buenos Aires, 1909, III, 67.

[25] Cox, Ross, *Adventures on the Columbia River* (1849), reprint by California State Library, San Francisco, 1914, II, 44; *The Fur Hunters of the Far West* (1855), reprint in Lakeside Classics series, Chicago, 1924, I, 194.

[26] Carson, James H., *Life in California*, Stockton, California, 1852, 59–60. Davis, William Heath, *Seventy-five Years in California*, San Francisco, 1929, 36–37. Johnson, Overton, and Winter, William H., *Route across the Rocky Mountains*, Princeton University Press reprint, 1932 (of 1846 edition), 115–118.

[27] Thorp, Jack, as told to Neil McCullough Clark, *Pardner of the Wind*, Caldwell, Idaho, 1945, 74. Dobie, J. Frank, *A Vaquero of the Brush Country*, Dallas, Texas, 1929, 238.

[28] "Sesom" (Moses, J. W.), "Mustanging in Texas," San Antonio *Daily Express*, July 29, 1888.

VII · WILD AND FREE

[1] Solms-Braunfels, Karl, Prince of, *Texas 1844–1845*, translated from the German, Houston, Texas, 1936, 27–28.

[2] Gregg, Josiah, *Commerce of the Prairies* (1844) in Thwaites, *Early Western Travels*, Cleveland, Ohio, 1905, XX, 262.

[3] This description is taken mainly from O. W. Williams, *Historic Review of Animal Life in Pecos County*, Fort Stockton, Texas, n.d. (reprinted from a series of articles by O. W. Williams in the Fort Stockton *Pioneer*, 1908), 13–15. George Catlin's description of mustangs in what is now western Oklahoma is the most precise in some respects that I have found — *Letters and Notes on the . . . North American Indians*, London, 1841, II, 57–60. I have fortified the Williams description somewhat with Catlin's.

[4] Long, Stephen H., *Account of an Expedition . . . to the Rocky Mountains* (1819–1820), Philadelphia, 1823, I, 485. See also Wells, William E., *The Desert's Hidden Wealth*, Los Angeles, California, (or Hill City, Kansas), 1934, 93–95.

[5] Wyeth, John B., *Oregon, or a Short History of a Long Journey* (1833), edited by Thwaites in *Early Western Travels*, XXI, 87.

Elias R. Wightman, Stephen F. Austin's surveyor, in Helm, Mary S., *Scraps of Early Texas History*, Austin, 1884, 193–194.

[6] Coues, Elliott, *The Manuscript Journals of Alexander Henry and David Thompson*, New York, 1897, II, 708. Luis Berlandier and Rafael Chovel, diarists, in *Diario de Viage de la Comisión de Límites . . .*, Mexico, 1850, entry dated Feb. 24, 1828.

[7] Hudson, W. H., "Horse and Man," in *The Naturalist in La Plata*, New York, 1892, 357. Leonard, Zenas, *Narrative* (1839), Cleveland, Ohio, 1904, 237–238.

[8] Brown, William Robinson, *The Horse of the Desert*, n.p. 1936, 39 (quoted from Charles Du Huys, *The Percheron Horse*, 1868).

[9] On tamer methods, see Collins, Dennis, *The Indians' Last Fight or the Dull Knife Raid*, Girard, Kansas, n.d., 46. Zenas Leonard accompanied California vaqueros on a wild-horse hunt. See *Narrative of the Adventures of Zenas Leonard* (1839), the Lakeside Press, Chicago, 1934, 193–194.

[10] Hodge, Frederick W., *Handbook of American Indians*, Washington, D. C., 1907–1910. See entry under "Horses," Vol. I.

[11] Head, Captain F. B., *Rough Notes Taken during Some Rapid Journeys across the Pampas*, Boston, 1827, 78, 138.

[12] "Autobiography" of Gideon Lincecum in *Publications* of the Mississippi Historical Society, VIII (1904), 487.

[13] Rollinson, J. K., *Pony Trails in Wyoming*, Caldwell, Idaho, 1941, 367–368.

[14] Hudson, as cited in Note 7, 357–358.

[15] *Mustangs and Cow Horses*, edited by Dobie, Boatright and Ransom, published by the Texas Folklore Society, Austin, Texas, 1940, 325–338.

[16] Long, as cited in Note 4 preceding, II, 95. For instance of mustang-buffalo associations, see Pike, Zebulon M., entry for October 29, 1806, in *Expeditions*.

[17] Roberts, Cecil, *Adrift in America*, London, 1891, 183–186.

[18] Salensky, W., *Prjevalsky's Horse*, translated by Hayes and Bradley, London, 1907, 58. Azara, Félix de, "Del Caballo" (from unpublished documents in Archivos de Indias), *Anales de la Asociación Criadores de Criollo*, Buenos Aires, Dec., 1930, 45. Darwin, Charles, *The Voyage of the Beagle* (1832–1836), London edition of 1890, 159. Ellsworth, Henry Leavitt, *Washington Irving on the Prairie*, edited by Stanley T. Williams and Barbara D. Simison, New York,

n.d., 130–132. Pike, Zebulon M., *An Account of Expeditions*, etc., journal entry for October 29, 1806. Pancoast, Charles Edward, *A Quaker Forty-Niner*, University of Pennsylvania Press, Philadelphia, 1930, 221. Long (or James) as cited in Note 4, II, 123. Abert, J. W., *Gúadal P'a* (journal of 1845), edited by H. Bailey Carroll, Panhandle-Plains Historical Society, Canyon, Texas, 1941, 44. Carson, Thomas, *Ranching, Sport and Travel*, New York, n.d., 130–132. Beverly, Bob, "Horse Intelligence," *The Cattleman*, Fort Worth, Texas, XXXVII (Sept., 1950), 44.

[19] I saw this bird's skin, also the flower, dried, in the home of Dr. Robert Thomas Moore, ornithologist, Pasadena, California, February 19, 1949, and from him got the facts. For example of elk horn-shedding, see Barker, Elliott S., *When the Dogs Barked 'Treed,'* University of New Mexico Press, Albuquerque, 1946, 50; also, Price, Major Sir Rose Lambert, *A Summer on the Rockies*, London, 1898, 91–92.

[20] See Hudson on "The Dying Huanaco," as cited in Note 7. He quotes Darwin as well as other observers.

[21] Adams, H. E., in *The Western Horseman*, VI (Nov.–Dec., 1941), 26.

[22] Waring, Guy, *My Pioneer Past*, Boston, 1936, 58.

[23] Azara, Félix de, *Viajes por la América Meridional* (1809), Madrid, Spain, 1923, I, 291–293.

[24] Madray, Mrs. I. C., *A History of Bee County*, Beeville, Texas, 1939, 37.

[25] Records, Ralph H., "Wildlife on the T–5 and Spade Ranches," *Chronicles of Oklahoma*, XXI (Sept., 1943), 297. Audubon, Maria R., *Audubon and His Journals*, New York, 1900, II, 83. Leigh, William R., *The Western Pony*, New York, 1933, 33. Pocock, Roger, *Horses*, London, 1917, 68–69.

[26] Ross, Alexander, *The Fur Hunters of the Far West* (London, 1855), reprint of Vol. I, Lakeside Press, Chicago, 1924, 52–54.

[27] Vosburgh, John R., *Texas Lion Hunter*, San Antonio, 1949, 81–84.

[1] McReynolds, Robert, *Thirty Years on the Frontier*, Colorado Springs, Colorado, 1906, 70–71.

[2] Besides some observations of my own on range horses and gatherings from talk by old-timers of the open range, I owe details of stallion fights to John Young, whose reminiscences are recorded in my book *A Vaquero of the Brush Country;* to Robert McReynolds, as cited in Note 1, 63–71; to *Buffalo Jones' Forty Years of Adventure* (compiled by Col. Henry Inman), Topeka, Kansas, 1899, 169–176; to Frank Collinson, in *Mustangs and Cow Horses*, edited by Dobie, Boatright and Ransom, Austin, 1940, 72; and to various other sources cited in this chapter.

[3] Grinnell, George Bird, unpublished manuscript on "The Indian's War Pony," in Southwest Museum, Los Angeles, California.

[4] Beverly, Bob, "Horse Intelligence," in *The Cattleman*, Fort Worth, Texas, XXXVII (Sept., 1950), 44. Bankson, Russell A. (from Great Falls, Montana), "Expect to Capture 5000 Wild Horses," New York *Times*, Sunday, June 23, 1929.

[5] Carson, Thomas, *Ranching, Sport and Travel*, New York, n.d., 128. McReynolds, as cited in Note 1, 69–70.

[6] Grinnell, as cited in Note 3.

[7] Taken with some revisions from Frank Collinson as cited in Note 2, 81–83, and from his letter to me dated June 25, 1940. Acknowledgment is gratefully made to Mrs. Frank Collinson, of El Paso, Texas, for permission to make use of her husband's writings.

[8] Collinson as cited in Note 2, 79–80.

[9] Butcher, S. D., *Pioneer History of Custer County*, Broken Bow, Nebraska, 1901, 218–221.

[10] This account was given me by Don Alberto Guajardo of Piedras Negras, Coahuila, Mexico. For sketch of him, see page 207.

[11] Salensky, W., *Prjevalsky's Horse*, translated by Hayes and Bradley, London, 1907, 58.

[12] This mustanger was George Salmon, of the brush country. His judgment is corroborated in Lauderdale, R. J., and Doak, John, *Life on the Range and on the Trail*, San Antonio, 1936, 31; Steele, Rufus, *Mustangs of the Mesas*, Hollywood, California, 1941, 64, 84, 113.

[13] According to gauchos, wild stallions on the Falkland Islands compelled mares to abandon new colts. (Darwin, *Voyage of the Beagle*, London edition of 1890, 182.) The killing of colts was rare, despite Harry Pullings in "A Horse! A Horse! My Kingdom for a Horse," *The Cattleman*, Fort Worth, Texas, Vol. XIX, No. 7 (Dec., 1932), 25.

[14] Records, Ralph H., "Wildlife on the T-5 and Spade Ranches," *Chronicles of Oklahoma*, XXI (Sept., 1943), 281–282.

[15] Saunders, Robert, in *Daily Oklahoman*, July 17, 1921, and manuscript written by W. H. Clift, in Archives of Library of the University of Oklahoma. Davis, L. L., *Blankets on the Sand*, Wichita Falls, Texas, 1948, 20–21.

[16] McCarthy, John, editor, *Some Experiences of Boss Neff in Texas and Oklahoma Panhandle*, Amarillo, Texas, 1941, 7–8, 17. Kreuger, M., *Pioneering in Texas*, San Antonio, 1930, 71–74.

[17] Bliss, Zenas R., *Reminiscences*, manuscript in Archives of University of Texas Library, I, 19–22.

[18] Thorp, Jack (N. Howard), *Pardner of the Wind*, as told to Neil M. Clark, Caldwell, Idaho, 1945, 76.

[19] This is a generalization hard to prove. Range men simply asserted the fact. Observation of semidomesticated manadas on controlled ranges establishes it. See Ángel Cabrera, *Caballos de América*, Buenos Aires, 1945, 276–277.

[20] McDermott, John Francis, editor, *The Western Journals of Washington Irving*, University of Oklahoma Press, Norman, 1944, 136. Murray, W. H. H., "Horse Breeding in Texas," *Wallace's Monthly*, VIII (Sept., 1881), 569–572. Collinson, as cited in Note 2 preceding, 69.

[21] George W. Saunders, who was born in Gonzales County, Texas, in 1854 and died at San Antonio, where he had long lived, in 1933, was a remarkable man. He organized the trail drivers of Texas, and persuaded enough of them to write reminiscences to fill two volumes, which he got published. In 1927 he described to me the great horse roundup.

[22] Bancroft, Hubert Howe, *California Pastoral, 1769–1848* (Vol. XXXIV in *Works* of Bancroft), San Francisco, 1888, 448.

[1] In *Tales of the Mustang*, a book of 89 pages published in an edition of 300 copies by The Book Club of Texas, Dallas, 1936, I put all I knew at the time about the White Steed of the Prairies. Before that I had put parts of the tradition into several magazine articles: "Tales of the Mustang," *Country Gentleman*, October, 1926; "The Pacing White Mustang," *American Mercury*, December, 1927; "When the Mustangs Ranged the Plains," *New York Herald Tribune Magazine*, August 9, 1931. A chapter on "Mustangs," in my book *On the Open Range*, Dallas, 1931, contains the Little Gretchen story of the White Mustang. By 1940 I had accumulated other stories and facts, and under title of "The Deathless Pacing White Stallion" I published these additions in *Mustangs and Cow Horses*, edited by J. Frank Dobie, Mody C. Boatright and Harry H. Ransom, Texas Folklore Society, Austin, 1940 — a book that went out of print a year or so after it was issued. *Western Horseman*, March and April issues, 1949, published a retelling of the main episodes of the tradition. A contraction of this appeared in *Zane Grey's Western Magazine*, Vol. 5 (Dec., 1951), 103–113.

In the decade since 1940 I have accumulated only minor additions to the legend. Now, adding them, I have brought together all my findings.

[2] *The United States Magazine and Democratic Review*, New York, XII (1843), 367–368.

[3] "The Plains," by François des Montaignes, in *The Western Journal and Civilian*, St. Louis, X (1853), 443.

[4] I used to look for these stories but quit looking long ago. The last one I noted was "Beyond the Outposts," by Peter Henry Moreland, in *Western Story Magazine*, Feb. 14, 1925.

[5] Told me by L. S. Rountree, Austin, Texas, in 1929. This story was published in "The Deathless Pacing White Mustang," in *Mustangs and Cow Horses*.

[6] From "Mustangs and Mustanging in Southwest Texas," by G. C. Robinson, in *Mustangs and Cow Horses*, 11–12. Clabe Robinson had the best memory in Live Oak County, where I was reared. I encouraged him to write this article and sent it to the *Dallas Morning*

News, which published it Sept. 9, 1928, paying him $25. He died in utter poverty a few years later.

[7] It must have been about 1939 when Mr. Morgan, then living in Wichita Falls, Texas, gave me the history. I published it in *Mustangs and Cow Horses.*

[8] I had seen a brief article by Curly Hatcher in *Frontier Times,* Bandera, Texas, May, 1927, 35. The present narrative is combined from that and a letter answering some of my inquiries.

[9] "Fifty-eight Years in Texas," by C. M. Grady, in *Frontier Times,* Bandera, Texas, June, 1934, 379 ff.

[10] Kupper, Winifred T., *Sheep and a Sheepman of the Southwest,* M.A. thesis, University of Texas, 1938, 209. Coues, Elliott, editor, *The Manuscript Journals of Alexander Henry and David Thompson,* New York, 1897, 288.

[11] The story, somewhat bastardized folklore, is from a collection entitled "Frontier Yarns," in *Putnam's Magazine,* New York, VIII (1856), 503–507.

[12] Pfefferkorn, Ignaz, *Sonora: A Description of the Province* (published in Germany 1794–1795), translated and annotated by Theodore E. Treutlein, University of New Mexico Press, Albuquerque, 1949, 95–96.

[13] Maury, Dabney H., *Recollections of a Virginian,* New York, 1894, 268.

[14] "The Peruvian Horse," *The Western Horseman,* VI (Nov.–Dec., 1941), 5 ff.

[15] Webber, Charles W., *Wild Scenes and Wild Hunters,* Philadelphia, 1852, 470.

[16] L. Gough, Amarillo, Texas, in a letter dated Feb. 10, 1930, to Boone McClure, in Archives of the Panhandle-Plains Historical Society, Canyon, Texas. Orally, Judge L. Gough gave me the same fact.

[17] David, Robert B., *Finn Burnett, Frontiersman,* Glendale, California, 1937, 76.

[18] Ferris, W. A., *Life in the Rocky Mountains,* Denver, Colorado, 1940, 331.

[19] Bourke, John G., *On the Border with Crook,* London, 1892, 379.

X · DEATH AND LIBERTY

[1] Gibson, George Rutledge, *Journal of a Soldier under Kearney and Doniphan*, edited by Ralph P. Bieber, Glendale, California, 1935, 151. For subsequent fame of the black stallion, see Webb, W. E., *Buffalo Land*, Topeka, Kansas, 1873, 210–212.

[2] Smith, S. Compton, *Chile Con Carne*, New York, 1857, 123–149.

[3] Lee, Nelson, *Three Years among the Comanches*, Albany, New York, 1859, 32–33.

[4] This tale was given me by Dr. J. O. Dyer of Galveston, author of the fanciful tale of Little Gretchen and the Pacing White Mustang. He claimed to have gotten it from early settlers.

[5] Joe Storm, a former student of mine who was killed in World War II, gave me this story. Under title of "Sons of the Devil" it was published in *Puro Mexicano* (Publications No. XII of the Texas Folklore Society), Austin, 1935, 190–193. I retold it in *Tales of the Mustang* (1936).

[6] Topence, Alexander, *Reminiscences*, Ogden, Utah, 1923, 124–125.

[7] The story is told by Rufus Steele, who garnered from mustangers a remarkable amount of mustang lore, in *Mustangs of the Mesas*, Hollywood, California, 1941, 199–208. The book was published by his wife after his death (1935) and is too meagerly known. Permission to use this story in my own telling has been secured from Mrs. Rufus Steele, now living at Berkeley, P. O. Box 442, California.

[8] While I was teaching English at Oklahoma A. and M. College, 1923–1925, I read two, maybe three, feature articles about Starface in the *Daily Oklahoman*. They were old-timer accounts from Kenton, in Starface's old territory, and were written in a natural manner by a man who did not try to be slick and did not try to patronize either human beings or horses. I met a man also who claimed to have chased Starface, but my story is based on the feature articles.

It was first published in the *Country Gentleman*, October, 1926, superbly illustrated by Paul Bransom, who presented me with the original illustration. I have looked at it with admiration a thousand times. In 1936 I put the story into *Tales of the Mustang*.

[9] Steele, as cited in Note 7, 91, 94–97.

[10] Henderson, J. D., "The Mustang Pony as I Knew Him," *The Cattleman*, Forth Worth, Texas, Vol. XXXI, No. 4 (Sept., 1944), 58.

[11] W. K. Shipman told me this story in 1940. He was then living out from San Antonio, seventy-six years old, a very honest-minded man. The account was printed in *Mustangs and Cow Horses*.

[12] Latta, F. F., *Uncle Jeff's Story*, Tulare, California, 1929, 42–43.

[13] Lang, Lincoln A., *Ranching With Roosevelt*, Philadelphia, 1926, 296–299.

XI · CAPTIVE MUSTANGS: ORDINARY AND EXTRAORDINARY

[1] Holley, Mary Austin, *Texas* (Baltimore, 1833), Dallas, 1935, 153. Smithwick, Noah, *The Evolution of a State: Recollections of Old Texas Days*, Austin, Texas, 1900, 18–19, 43. Kuykendall, J. H., "Reminiscences of Early Texans," *Quarterly* of the Texas State Historical Association, VI, (1903), 237 n. Sowell, A. J., *Early Settlers and Indian Fighters of Southwest Texas*, Austin, 1900, 834.

[2] Austin, Stephen F., "Journal on His First Trip to Texas, 1821," *Quarterly* of the Texas State Historical Association, VII (1903–1904), 300. Holley, Mary Austin, as cited in note preceding, 96–98. Mrs. Holley's characterization is repeated by Edward Stiff, *The Texan Emigrant*, Cincinnati, 1840, 40.

[3] [Fiske], *A Visit to Texas*, New York, 1834, 58–76, 189, 254.

[4] Flack, Captain, *The Texan Ranger or Real Life in the Backwoods*, London, 1866, 300–304.

[5] Gregg, Josiah, *Commerce of the Prairies* (1844), in *Early Western Travels* edited by Thwaites, XIX, 312–314; XX, 92–93, 260–261.

[6] Gray, William Fairfax, *Diary*, Houston, Texas, 1919, 113. Morrell, Z. N., *Flowers and Fruits in the Wilderness*, Dallas, Texas, 1886, 126–127. *Frontier Times*, Bandera, Texas, November, 1925, 5. Emory, William H., *Report of the United States and Mexican Boundary Survey*, Washington, D. C., 1857, I, 56–57.

[7] Stiff, as cited in Note 2, 114.

[8] The account here given is taken from James H. Carson, *Life in California*, Stockton, California, 1852, 60–62; Wallace Smith, *Garden of the Sun*, Los Angeles, California, 1939, 166; John Adam Hussey,

"Sacramento – the Grey Charger of the Tulares," *The Western Horseman*, II (Nov.–Dec., 1937), 18 ff.

⁹ L. Gough, Amarillo, Texas, Feb. 10, 1930, to Boone McClure of the Panhandle-Plains Historical Society, Canyon, Texas.

¹⁰ Information from Miss Ruth Dodson, Mathis, Texas.

¹¹ Reprinted by permission of E. P. Dutton and Company, New York, from *The Book of a Naturalist*, New York, 1919, 119–122.

¹² I first told of Alacrán, in somewhat abbreviated form, in an article on "The Spanish Cow Pony," *Saturday Evening Post*, November 24, 1934. With more details the story was published in *The Western Horseman*, Colorado Springs, Colorado, September–October, 1948.

XII · MUSTANGER WAYS

¹ An animated description of an Indian chase in the Sierra Baguales (Mustang Mountains) of Patagonia is found in *A Yankee in Patagonia*, by Katherine and Robert Barrett, Cambridge, England, 1931, 84–86.

² See James H. Carson, *Life in California*, Stockton, California, 1852, 62–63, for a spirited account.

³ Robinson, G. C., "Mustangs and Mustanging in Southwest Texas," in *Mustangs and Cow Horses*, Texas Folklore Society, Austin, 1940, 10.

⁴ Moses, J. W., "A Mustanger of 1850," in *Mustangs and Cow Horses*, as cited in note preceding, 43.

⁵ Beverley, Robert, *The History and Present State of Virginia* (London, 1705), edited by Louis B. Wright, University of North Carolina Press, Chapel Hill, 1947, 312.

⁶ Durst, Leon H., *Durstana Centennial* (mimeographed pamphlet, dated from Junction, Texas, 1950, 42); letter from Bruno L. Durst, Houston, Texas, Sept. 14, 1950.

⁷ *Kansas Historical Quarterly*, IX (August, 1940), 313.

⁸ "Report from Natchitoches in 1807," by Dr. John Sibley, *Indian Notes and Monographs*, Heye Foundation, New York, 1922, 48.

⁹ Pike, James, *The Scout and Ranger* (Cincinnati, 1865), Princeton University Press, Princeton, New Jersey, 1932, 123.

¹⁰ Neelley, Mrs. C. L., "Known as Pioneers," *Semi-Weekly Farm News*, Dallas, Texas, April 29, 1938.

[11] Thorp, Jack, as told to Neil McCullough Clark, *Pardner of the Wind*, Caldwell, Idaho, 1945, 74–75.

[12] *Glimpses of the Past*, Missouri Historical Society, St. Louis, II (1934–1935), 40–41.

[13] Thwaites, Reuben Gold, editor, *Travels and Explorations of the Jesuit Missionaries in New France, 1610–1791*, Cleveland, Ohio, 1900, LXIX, 219, 221.

[14] Kreuger, M., *Pioneer Life in Texas, an Autobiography*, San Antonio, Texas, 1930, 71–74.

[15] The trick is detailed by Arthur Morecamp (pseud. for Thomas Pilgrim, who died in 1882) in *Live Boys; or, Charley and Nasho in Texas*, Boston, 1878, 79–87. This is the earliest published narrative — an arranged chronicle rather than fiction — so far as I know, dealing with trail driving from Texas.

[16] For fuller treatment of this character, see "Mustang Gray: Fact, Tradition and Song," by J. Frank Dobie, in *Tone the Bell Easy*, yearbook published by Texas Folklore Society, Austin, 1932.

[17] *Prose and Poetry of the Live Stock Industry of the United States*, prepared by authority of the National Live Stock Association, Kansas City, Missouri, 1904, 1905, 714.

[18] A good description of a coastal chase after colts is in *The Texan Ranger or Real Life in the Backwoods*, by Captain Flack, London, 1866, 300–304.

[19] Williams, O. W., *Historic Review of Animal Life in Pecos County* (Texas), Fort Stockton, Texas, n.d., 13–15. (Private reprint of essays in the Fort Stockton *Pioneer*, 1908).

[20] The account here is taken from his reminiscences published in *Mustangs and Cow Horses*, cited in Note 3, 77–79.

[21] Cook, John R., *The Border and the Buffalo*, Topeka, Kansas, 1907, 253–255.

[22] Pfefferkorn, Ignaz, *Sonora: A Description of the Province* (first published in Germany 1794–1795), translated and annotated by Theodore E. Treutlein, University of New Mexico Press, Albuquerque, 1949, 97–98; also 45, 95.

[23] *El Museo Mexicano*, article signed "E. E.," Mexico, D. F., 1843, II, 39–40.

[24] Pike in 1807 described mustang *corridas* as he saw or heard about them in the Nacogdoches country of eastern Texas. — Coues, Elliott, *The Expeditions of Zebulon Montgomery Pike*, New York, 1895, II,

783. The first newspaper published in Texas, printed for about two months, August-September, 1819, at Nacogdoches, ran a rewrite, without credit, of Pike's description. See *Southwestern Historical Quarterly*, XXXVI (July, 1932), 43–44.

[25] *El Museo Mexicano*, as cited in Note 23 *ante*.

[26] Moses, J. W., in *Mustangs and Cow Horses*, as cited in Note 3 *ante*, 39–42. Ford, John S., *Memoirs*, manuscript in Archives of University of Texas Library, III, 531.

[27] Reminiscences of an "Old Settler," in *A Memorial and Biographical History of Navarro, Henderson, Anderson, Limestone, Freestone and Leon Counties* (Texas), Chicago, 1893, 106–109.

[28] Collinson, Frank, in *Mustangs and Cow Horses*, as cited in Note 3, 74.

[29] Steele, Rufus, *Mustangs of the Mesas*, Hollywood, California, 1941, 68–70.

[30] Carson, Thomas, *Ranching, Sport and Travel*, New York, n.d., 126–128. Ward, H. G., *Mexico in 1827*, London, 1828, I, 552–553 (from "Account of the Province of Texas," by General Wavel).

[31] Collins, Dennis, *The Indians' Last Fight or the Dull Knife Raid*, Girard, Kansas, n.d., 43–46.

[32] Madray, Mrs. I. C., *A History of Bee County*, Beeville, Texas, 1939, 5 (quoting Patrick Burke, an old mustanger).

[33] Leonard, Zenas, *Narrative* (1839), edited by Milo Quaife, the Lakeside Press, Chicago, 1934, 194.

[34] Documents relating to Philip Nolan in Archives, University of Texas Library. Minor Papers, Archives of Louisiana State University. Daniel Clark, Jr. and William Dunbar letters (photostated) in Library of Congress. Andrew Ellicott, *Journal*, Philadelphia, 1814, 29. *Texas Historical Quarterly*, VII, 1904, 308–317. Thesis on Philip Nolan, 1932, by Maurine T. Wilson, University of Texas Library. Pike, as cited in Note 24, I, lii. Many of the Jefferson papers have not yet been catalogued. When the great project of publishing them by Princeton University is accomplished, perhaps something of the natural history sought by Jefferson will be revealed.

XIII · AS THE MUSTANGERS TOLD IT

[1] I made notes during the talk and shortly thereafter filled them out. In 1936, during the Texas Centennial, I included the sketch in an

article on Mustangers in a series written for the Fort Worth *Press* and other newspapers of the Scripps-Howard chain in Texas. The present sketch is derived from that, though I have added a detail or two from an article on Lemmons by Florence Fenley in *The Cattleman*, September, 1940, reprinted in *Mustangs and Cow Horses* the same year.

[2] This section of my book is based principally on the records of Moses and Dwyer, both published from original sources in *Mustangs and Cow Horses*, 1940. J. W. Moses wrote under the name of Sesom (Moses spelled backwards). The San Antonio *Daily Express* of April 1, April 8, April 15 and July 29 (Sundays) of 1888 published his reminiscences dealing with mustang horses and mustang cattle. Thomas A. Dwyer's observations and reminiscences, written with more perspective, entitled "Horse and Mule-Raising in Western Texas," came out in a pamphlet, *A Brief Description of Western Texas*, etc., San Antonio, 1872.

An excellent account of Indian interference with border mustanging is found in "Life of Jesse Sumpter, Oldest Citizen of Eagle Pass," manuscript in University of Texas Library archives. *The Life and Diary of Reading W. Black, a History of Early Uvalde*, by Ike Moore, Uvalde, Texas, 1934, contains, pages 66–72, diary entries of 1855 that bear on mustanging in the Nueces River country.

[3] This story has been rewritten from a factual narrative by Frank Collinson published in *Ranch Romances*, First November issue, 1936 — a sequel to Collinson's reminiscences on mustanging in Second March issue of *Ranch Romances*, 1936. From Collinson's original manuscripts, which had been severely cut by the magazine editors, and from additions supplied in letters from Collinson, I arranged his mustang lore into a long first-person narrative-article for *Mustangs and Cow Horses*, Texas Folklore Society, Austin, 1940, 69–95. Chapter VIII of the present book contains information on his career. He died in El Paso in 1943.

XIV · UNDER THE SADDLE

[1] Dodge, Col. Richard Irving, *Our Wild Indians: Thirty-Three Years' Personal Experience among the Red Men of the Great West*, Hartford, Connecticut, 1883, 586–587.

² Harlan, Jacob Wright, *California '46 to '88*, San Francisco, 1888, 166–170.

³ There are various accounts of the Frémont ride. The most precise in detail is by Walter Colton, *Three Years in California*, New York, 1850, 377–384. An excellent account from original sources is by Frederick S. Dellenbaugh, *Frémont and '49*, New York, 1914, 375–377.

⁴ *The Western Horseman*, VI (March–April, 1941), 18, gives an account of a *canelo* that in 1878 carried a two-hundred-pound man 148 miles in 23½ hours.

⁵ *The Unpublished Letters of Bayard Taylor*, San Marino, California, 1937, 23.

⁶ Aubry's rides have been sketched by numerous writers, most of them rewriting others without knowledge of facts. In 1928 the *Southwest Review* published an article of mine entitled "The Saga of the Saddle" in which I told the story, now revised. Professor Ralph P. Bieber of Washington University, at St. Louis, had generously led me to several original sources. Since then his twelve-volumed *Southwest Historical Series*, richly edited, has appeared. Volume VII, *Exploring Southwestern Trails* (Glendale, California, 1938), contains not only Aubry's *Diaries* of his trips to California but a full treatment of Aubry's life, including accounts of the rides over the Santa Fe Trail.

The only significant addition I can add to this scholar's documentation is Aubry's own succinct account of the climactic ride. It was written out by him for R. B. Marcy of the U. S. Army. In 1888, just before he died, Marcy was running a series of articles on big-game hunting for *Outing*. In the April issue, the editor of *Outing*, pages 83–84, printed, with a few comments by Marcy, Aubry's "autobiographical statement." This statement, along with Marcy's first-hand comments, settles a few points.

⁷ A Study of the horses, with sources documented, is found in Thornton Chard's "Endurance Rides of the Early 60's," *Journal of Heredity*, XVII (January, 1926), 353–362.

⁸ Harris, Albert T., *The Blood of the Arab*, Chicago, 1941, 44–52. The Arabian Horse Club Registry of America, Chicago, has granted me permission to use the letters of Frank T. Hopkins, as quoted in the book by Harris.

⁹ Sometime after midnight, sitting on a curbstone on a street in

Austin, R. R. Smith, then of Jourdanton, Texas, now dead, told me this story. He was a lawyer and had talked to Gregorio Cortez in the penitentiary. I am not sure but think that Smith represented him. He had a remarkable memory and was a remarkable storyteller. That same night he told the story of Ellie Newman, the dreamer-rider. Both these stories are included in a chapter entitled "Riders of the Stars," in *The Flavor of Texas*, Dallas, 1936, a book of mine that has been out of print for 15 years. In a chapter entitled "Rides and Riders," in *On the Open Range*, Dallas, 1931, I included the story of W. B. Slaughter's ride, told near the beginning of the present chapter.

[10] Under title of "A Boy and His Horse," this story was published in *Esquire*, September, 1945. It is almost impossible for me to republish anything I have written without revising it, and the story has been revised for this book.

XV · THE COYOTE DUN AND OTHER COW HORSES

[1] Pocock, Roger, *Horses*, London, 1917, 32.

[2] Murray, Charles Augustus, *Travels in North America*, New York, 1839, I, 263.

[3] Tweedie, W., *The Arabian Horse, His Country and People*, Edinburgh and London, 1894, 257, 261. Wentworth, Lady, *The Authentic Arabian Horse*, London, 1945, 193.

[4] Literature on the subject is extensive. Very thorough is "The Inheritance of the Dun Coat-Colour," by James Wilson, *Scientific Proceedings*, Royal Dublin Society, Vol. 13 (1911–1913), 184–201.

[5] Wetmore, Helen Cody, *Last of the Great Scouts*, Duluth, Minnesota, 1899, 153, 177–178.

[6] Statement to me in 1932 by Henry Seale of Benchley, Texas, an exceedingly well-informed man on stock and tradition.

[7] Graham, R. B. Cunninghame, *The Horses of the Conquest*, London, 1930, 8–11.

[8] For elaboration of the theory see Craig, C. W. T., *Paraguayan Interlude*, New York, 1935, 48–49.

[9] Everett, Malissa C., "A Pioneer Woman," *West Texas Historical Association Year Book*, Abilene, Texas, III (1927), 68.

[10] *Hoofs and Horns*, Tucson, Arizona, May, 1940, 4.

[1] Hussey, John Adam, "The New Mexico–California Caravan of 1847–1848," *New Mexico Historical Review*, XVIII (January, 1943), 1–16. Brewerton, George Douglas, *Overland with Kit Carson*, edited by Stallo Vinton (a reprint of articles that Brewerton contributed to *Harper's New Monthly Magazine* in 1853), New York, 1930, Chapter II. Mofras, Duflot de, *Travels on the Pacific Coast* (1840–42), edited by Marguerite Eyer Wilbur, Santa Ana, California, 1937, I, 185.

[2] Hussey, as cited in note preceding, 14. Kelly, Charles, and Howe, Maurice L., *Miles Goodyear, First Citizen of Utah, Trapper, Trader and California Pioneer*, Salt Lake City, 1937, 96–109.

[3] Literature on the subject includes: Beckwourth, James P., *The Life and Adventures of* (1856), New York, 1931, 327–328. Bell, Horace, *Reminiscences of a Ranger or, Early Times in Southern California*, Los Angeles, 1881, 281–283. Bidwell, John, *Echoes of the Past about California* (1890), Lakeside Press, Chicago, 1928, 18–19. Brewerton, as cited in Note 1. Cleland, Robert Glass, *This Reckless Breed of Men*, New York, 1950, 264–275. Favour, Alpheus H., *Old Bill Williams, Mountain Man*, University of North Carolina Press, Chapel Hill, 1936, 85–99. This book cites many first-hand sources. Sage, Rufus B., *Rocky Mountain Life* (1857), Boston, 1858, 51.

[4] Westergaard, Waldemar, *Denmark and Slesvig (1848–1864) with a Collection of Illustrative Letters by Daniel Bruhn, including his Letters from California and Nevada (1864–1872)*, Nyt Nordisk Forlag, Arnold Busck, Copenhagen, 1946, 113–125.

Mr. Waldemar Westergaard, University of California, Los Angeles, author-editor of the volume, has graciously given me permission to make use of Bruhn's letters. The book is distributed by the University of California Press.

[5] [Unidentified] *Gazette*, April 11, 1874.

[6] Bull, S. A., interview with J. Evetts Haley, Feb. 27, 1927, in Archives, Panhandle-Plains Historical Society, Canyon, Texas.

[7] Brisbin, James F., "Hunting the Wild Horse," *Wallace's Monthly*, March, 1888, 39–41.

[8] Whitlock, V. ("Ol' Waddy"), "Days on the Range," Beaumont, Texas, *Journal*, March 14, 1939.

[9] Bancroft, H. H., *California*, San Francisco, 1885, II, 182–183, 669; *California Pastoral*, San Francisco, 1888, 345–347. Larkin, Thomas, *New Spain and the West*, Los Angeles, 1932, II, 108. Lugo, José del Carmen, *Vida de un Ranchero*, typescript in Huntington Library from manuscript in Bancroft Library, 58, 61–62. Vallejo, Guadalupe, "Ranch and Mission Days in Alta California," *Century Magazine*, XLI (1890), 189. Warner, J. J., *Historical Sketch of Los Angeles County, California*, Los Angeles, 1876, 9.

[10] Johnson, Overton, and Winter, William H., *Route across the Rocky Mountains* (originally published in 1846), Princeton University Press, Princeton, New Jersey, 1932, 115–118.

INDEX

INDEX

This is an analytical index. It omits many proper names reference to which would not lead to knowledge. The two main entries, Mustangs and Spanish horses, overlap each other, but I see no way to get around this overlapping. Notes are not indexed.

[367]

Buckskin Joe, Buffalo Bill's horse, 300–301

Buenos Aires, 99, 121, 125*n*.

Buffalo Bill, 285, 300–301

Buffalo horse, 47, 48, 52

Buffalo Jones, 287

Buffaloes, 102, 122, 240, 262–263

Bullfrogs, 102

Burros: 40, 113, 114*n*., 125*n*., 136–137, 192, 218, 225, 232, 317; wild, 102, 138, 227

Button, notorious mustang, 201–203

Buzzards, 310

CALDWELL, MATHEW, 223*n*.

California horses and horsemen, 41, 56, 62, 106, 113–115, 197–199, 272–273, 277–279, 285–286, 316–319, 322–324

Canadian horses, 61

Canadian River, 44, 109*n*., 169, 200, 300

Carson, Kit, 56, 198, 317

Carson, Thomas, 131

Catlin, George, 46*n*., 58–59, 72, 82, 84*n*., 88–89

Cattle. *See* Longhorn cattle.

Cavalry horses, 61

Cavendish, William, Duke of Newcastle, 4, 11

Cayuse, name for range horse, 41

Chapman, John, 116

Chard, Thornton, 7, 61*n*., 297*n*.

Chihuahua, 37, 67, 68, 70, 125, 216, 218, 272

Chili, in horse nostrils, 175

Chimborazo Mountain, Ecuador, and hummingbird, 119–120

Cimarrón, 94

Cimarron River, 95, 109*n*., 170, 183–186 *passim*, 195*n*.

Clark, George Rogers, 5–6

Clark, Neil M., 216

Clogs, 232

Coahuila, 37, 68, 97, 207

Cobo, Fray Bernabé, 95

Cole, Ame, buffalo hunter, 253–255, 269

Collinson, Frank, 132–134, 225, 245–251

Colorado River, Texas, 38, 95*n*., 151

Columbia River, 54, 81, 106

Columbus, 4

Comanche, tamed mustang stallion, 135–137

"Comanche moon," 68

Comancheros, 71

Comanches. *See under* Indian tribes.

Corder, Ben, 224–225

Coronado, Julian, range boss, 135–137

Coronado expedition and horses, 12, 22, 24, 26, 28, 30

Coronado's Muster Roll, 24*n*.

Corpus Christi, Texas, 103, 105, 149

Corrumpa River, Oklahoma, 183

Corsica, cattle of, 298

Cortés, conquistador, 13, 14, 21, 24, 97*n*.

Cortez, Gregorio, 287–289

Cottonwood bark as horse provender, 48–49, 53

Cow horses, 296–314, 316

Cowboy: graduation into cowman, 307; origin of, 15, 107

Cowboys and horses, 14, 20, 51, 84*n*.

Cox, Ross, 106

"Coyote yell," 281

Coyotes, 102

Crabbet Stud, 10, 11

Creasing. *See under* Mustangers.

Cristiano, horse of the pampas, 204–206

Crook, General George, 54*n*., 169

Cross Timbers, 72, 145

Cruz, Santa Ana, mustanger, 152–153

Cummings, E. E., poet, 326

Custer, John, 303

Cutting horses, 312–313

DALE, E. E., 163

Dana, Richard Henry, 323

Darwin, Charles, 11, 27, 46*n*., 51, 119, 140*n*., 299

Davenport, Homer, *My Quest of the Arabian Horse*, 14–15

Davis Mountains, 216

De Mézières, 63

De Pagés, 65

De Soto, Hernando, with horses in Florida, 12, 28–34

Deer, 101, 102, 297

Denhardt, Robert Moorman, 12*n*.

Diaz, Bernal del Castillo, 13, 21

Dix, Captain John J., 243–244

Dixon, Billy, 45

Dobie, Jim (J. M.), 320–321

Dobie, Neville, 319–320, 321

Dobie, Richard (R. J.), 321

Dodge, Richard I., 59, 60, 272